IDEAL COMMONWEALTHS

PLUTARCH'S LYCURGUS

MORE'S UTOPIA

BACON'S NEW ATLANTIS

CAMPANELLA'S CITY OF THE SUN

AND A FRAGMENT OF
HALL'S MUNDUS ALTER ET IDEM

WITH AN INTRODUCTION BY HENRY MORLEY
LL.D., PROFESSOR OF ENGLISH LITERATURE AT
UNIVERSITY COLLEGE, LONDON

INTRODUCTION.

Plato in his "Republic" argues that it is the aim of Individual Man as of the State to be wise, brave and temperate. In a State, he says, there are three orders, the Guardians, the Auxiliaries, the Producers. Wisdom should be the special virtue of the Guardians; Courage of the Auxiliaries; and Temperance of all. These three virtues belong respectively to the Individual Man, Wisdom to his Rational part; Courage to his Spirited; and Temperance to his Appetitive: while in the State as in the Man it is Injustice that disturbs their harmony.

Because the character of Man appears in the State unchanged, but in a larger form, Plato represented Socrates as studying the ideal man himself through an Ideal Commonwealth.

In another of his dialogues, "Critias," of which we have only the beginning, Socrates wishes that he could see how such a commonwealth would work, if it were set moving. Critias undertakes to tell him. For he has received tradition of events that happened more than nine thousand years ago, when the Athenians themselves were such ideal citizens. Critias has received this tradition, he says, from a ninety-year-old grandfather, whose father, Dropides, was the friend of Solon. Solon, lawgiver and poet, had heard it from the priests of the goddess Neïth or Athene at Sais, and had begun to shape it into a heroic poem.

This was the tradition:—Nine thousand years before the time of Solon, the goddess Athene, who was worshipped also in Sais, had given to her Athenians a healthy climate, a fertile soil, and temperate people strong in wisdom and courage. Their Republic was like that which Socrates imagined, and it had to bear the shock of a great invasion by the people of the vast island Atlantis. This island, larger than all Libya and Asia put together, was once in the sea westward beyond the Atlantic waves,—thus America was dreamed of long before it was discovered. Atlantis had ten kings, descended from ten sons of Poseidon (Neptune), who was the god magnificently worshipped by its people. Vast power and dominion, that extended through all Libya as far as

Egypt, and over a part of Europe, caused the Atlantid kings to grow ambitious and unjust. Then they entered the Mediterranean and fell upon Athens with enormous force. But in the little band of citizens, temperate, brave, and wise, there were forces of Reason able to resist and overcome brute strength. Now, however, gone are the Atlantids, gone are the old virtues of Athens. Earthquakes and deluges laid waste the world. The whole great island of Atlantis, with its people and its wealth, sank to the bottom of the ocean. The ideal warriors of Athens, in one day and night, were swallowed by an earthquake, and were to be seen no more.

Plato, a philosopher with the soul of a poet, died in the year 347 before Christ. Plutarch was writing at the close of the first century after Christ, and in his parallel Lives of Greeks and Romans, the most famous of his many writings, he took occasion to paint an Ideal Commonwealth as the conception of Lycurgus, the half mythical or all mythical Solon of Sparta. To Plutarch's Life of Lycurgus, as well as to Plato, Thomas More and others have been indebted for some part of the shaping of their philosophic dreams.

The discovery of the New World at the end of the fifteenth century followed hard upon the diffusion of the new invention of printing, and came at a time when the fall of Constantinople by scattering Greek scholars, who became teachers in Italy, France and elsewhere, spread the study of Greek, and caused Plato to live again. Little had been heard of him through the Arabs, who cared little for his poetic method. But with the revival of learning he had become a force in Europe, a strong aid to the Reformers.

Sir Thomas More's Utopia was written in the years 1515-16, when its author's age was about thirty-seven. He was a young man of twenty when Columbus first touched the continent named after the Florentine Amerigo Vespucci, who made his voyages to it in the years 1499-1503. More wrote his Utopia when imaginations of men were stirred by the sudden enlargement of their conceptions of the world, and Amerigo Vespucci's account of his voyages, first printed in 1507, was fresh in every scholar's mind. He imagined a traveller, Raphael Hythloday—whose name is from Greek words that mean "Knowing in Trifles"—who had sailed with Vespucci on his three last voyages, but had not returned from the last voyage until, after separation from his comrades, he had wandered into some farther discovery of his own. Thus he had found, somewhere in those parts, the island of Utopia. Its name is from Greek words meaning Nowhere. More had gone on an embassy to Brussels with Cuthbert Tunstal when he wrote his philosophical satire upon European, and more particularly English, statecraft, in the form of an Ideal Commonwealth described by Hythloday as he had found it in Utopia. It was printed at Louvain in the latter part of the year 1516, under the editorship of Erasmus, and that enlightened young secretary to the municipality of Antwerp, Peter Giles, or Ægidius, who is introduced into the story. "Utopia" was not printed in England in the reign of Henry VIII., and could not be, for its satire was too direct to be misunderstood, even when it mocked English policy with ironical praise for doing exactly what it failed to do. More was a wit and a philosopher, but at the same time so practical and earnest that Erasmus tells of a burgomaster at Antwerp who fastened upon the parable of Utopia with such goodwill that he learnt it by heart. And in 1517 Erasmus advised a correspondent to send for Utopia, if he had not yet read it, and if he wished to see the true source of all political evils.

Francis Bacon's "New Atlantis," first written in Latin, was published in 1629, three years after its author's death. Bacon placed his Ideal Commonwealth in those seas where a great Austral continent was even then supposed to be, but had not been discovered. As the old Atlantis implied a foreboding of the American continent, so the New Atlantis implied foreboding of the Australian. Bacon in his philosophy sought through experimental science the dominion of men over things, "for Nature is only governed by obeying her." In his Ideal World of the New Atlantis, Science is made the civilizer who binds man to man, and is his leader to the love of God.

Thomas Campanella was Bacon's contemporary, a man only seven years younger; and an Italian who suffered for his ardour in the cause of science. He was born in Calabria in 1568, and died in 1639. He entered the Dominican order when a boy, but had a free and eager appetite for knowledge. He urged, like Bacon, that Nature should be studied through her own works, not through books; he attacked, like Bacon, the dead faith in Aristotle, that instead of following his energetic spirit of research, lapsed into blind idolatry. Campanella strenuously urged that men should reform all sciences by following Nature and the books of God. He had been stirring in this way for ten years, when there arose in Calabria a conspiracy against the Spanish rule. Campanella, who was an Italian patriot was seized and sent to Naples. The Spanish inquisition joined in attack on him. He was accused of books he had not written and of opinions he did not hold; he was seven times put to the question and suffered, with firmness of mind, the most cruel tortures. The Pope interceded in vain for him with the King of Spain. He suffered imprisonment for twenty-seven years, during which time he wrote much, and one piece of his prison work was his ideal of "The City of the Sun."

Released at last from his prison, Campanella went to Rome, where he was defended by Pope Urban VIII. against continued violence of attack. But he was compelled at last to leave Rome, and made his escape as a servant in the livery of the French ambassador. In Paris, Richelieu became Campanella's friend; the King of France gave him a pension of three thousand livres; the Sorbonne vouched for the orthodoxy of his writings. He died in Paris, at the age of seventy-one, in the Convent of the Dominicans.

Of Campanella's "Civitas Solis," which has not hitherto been translated into English, the translation here given, with one or two omissions of detail which can well be spared, has been made for me by my old pupil and friend, Mr. Thomas W. Halliday.

In the works (published in 1776) of the witty Dr. William King, who played much with the subject of cookery, is a fragment found among his remaining papers, and given by his editors as an original piece in the manner of Rabelais. It seems never to have been observed that this is only a translation of that part of Joseph Hall's "Mundus Alter es Idem," which deals with the kitchen side of life. The fragment will be found at the end of this volume, preceded by a short description of the other parts of Hall's World which is other than ours, and yet the same.

March 1885.

PLUTARCH'S LIFE OF LYCURGUS.

Life of Lycurgus.

Of Lycurgus the lawgiver we have nothing to relate that is certain and uncontroverted. For there are different accounts of his birth, his travels, his death, and especially of the laws and form of government which he established. But least of all are the times agreed upon in which this great man lived. For some say he flourished at the same time with Iphitus, and joined with him in settling the cessation of arms during the Olympic games. Among these is Aristotle the philosopher, who alleges for proof an Olympic quoit, on which was preserved the inscription of Lycurgus's name. But others who, with Eratosthenes and Apollodorus, compute the time by the succession of the Spartan kings, place him much earlier than the first Olympiad. Timæus, however, supposes that, as there were two Lycurguses in Sparta at different times, the actions of both are ascribed to one, on account of his particular renown; and that the more ancient of them lived not long after Homer: nay, some say he had seen him. Xenophon too confirms the opinion of his antiquity, when he makes him contemporary with the Heraclidæ. It is true, the latest of the Lacedæmonian kings were of the lineage of the Heraclidæ; but Xenophon there seems to speak of the first and more immediate descendants of Hercules. As the history of those times is thus involved, in relating the circumstances of Lycurgus's life, we shall endeavour to select such as are least controverted, and follow authors of the greatest credit.

Simonides the poet, tells us, that Prytanis, not Eunomus, was father to Lycurgus. But most writers give us the genealogy of Lycurgus and Eunomus in a different manner; for, according to them, Sous was the son of Patrocles, and grandson of Aristodemus, Eurytion the son of Sous, Prytanis of Eurytion, and Eunomus of Prytanis; to this Eunomus was born Polydectes, by a former wife, and by a second, named Dianassa, Lycurgus. Eutychidas, however, says Lycurgus was the sixth from Patrocles, and the eleventh from Hercules. The most distinguished of his ancestors was Sous, under whom the Lacedæmonians made the Helotes their slaves, and gained an extensive tract of land from the Arcadians. Of this Sous it is related, that, being besieged by the Clitorians in a difficult post where there was no water, he agreed to give up all his conquests, provided that himself and all his army should drink of the neighbouring spring. When these conditions were sworn to, he assembled his forces, and offered his kingdom to the man that would forbear drinking; not one of them, however, would deny himself, but they all drank. Then Sous went down to the spring himself, and having only sprinkled his face in sight of the enemy, he marched off, and still held the country, because all had not drank. Yet, though he was highly honoured for this, the family had not their name from him, but from his son, were called Eurytionidæ; and this, because Eurytion seems to be the first who relaxed the strictness of kingly government, inclining to the interest of the people, and ingratiating himself with them. Upon this relaxation their encroachments increased, and the succeeding kings, either becoming odious, treating them with greater rigour, or else giving way through weakness or in hopes of favour, for a long time anarchy and confusion prevailed in Sparta; by which one of its kings, the father of Lycurgus, lost his life. For while he was endeavouring to part some persons who were concerned in a fray, he received a wound by a kitchen knife, of which he died, leaving the kingdom to his eldest son Polydectes.

But he too dying soon after, the general voice gave it for Lycurgus to ascend the throne; and he actually did so, till it appeared that his brother's widow was pregnant. As soon as he perceived this, he declared that the kingdom belonged to her issue, provided it were male, and he kept the administration in his hands only as his guardian. This he did with the title of Prodicos, which the Lacedæmonians give to the guardians of infant kings. Soon after, the queen made him a private overture, that she would destroy her child, upon condition that he would marry her when king of Sparta. Though he detested her wickedness, he said nothing against the proposal, but pretending to approve it, charged her not to take any drugs to procure an abortion, lest she should endanger her own health or life; for he would take care that the child, as soon as born, should be destroyed. Thus he artfully drew on the woman to her full time, and, when he heard she was in labour, he sent persons to attend and watch her delivery, with orders, if it were a girl, to give it to the women, but if a boy, to bring it to him, in whatever business he might be engaged. It happened that he was at supper with the magistrates when she was delivered of a boy, and his servants, who were present, carried the child to him. When he received it, he is reported to have said to the company, "Spartans, see here your new-born king." He then laid him down upon the chair of state, and named him Charilaus, because of the joy and admiration of his magnanimity and justice testified by all present. Thus the reign of Lycurgus lasted only eight months. But the citizens had a great veneration for him on other accounts, and there were more that paid him their attentions, and were ready to execute his commands, out of regard to his virtues, than those that obeyed him as a guardian to the king, and director of the administration. There were not, however, wanting those that envied him, and opposed his advancement, as too high for so young a man; particularly the relations and friends of the queen-mother, who seemed to have been treated with contempt. Her brother Leonidas, one day boldly attacked him with virulent language, and scrupled not to tell him that he was well assured he would soon be king; thus preparing suspicions, and matter of accusation against Lycurgus, in case any accident should befall the king. Insinuations of the same kind were likewise spread by the queen-mother. Moved with this ill-treatment, and fearing some dark design, he determined to get clear of all suspicion, by travelling into other countries, till his nephew should be grown up, and have a son to succeed him in the kingdom.

He set sail, therefore, and landed in Crete. There having observed the forms of government, and conversed with the most illustrious personages, he was struck with admiration of some of their laws, and resolved at his return to make use of them in Sparta. Some others he rejected. Among the friends he gained in Crete was Thales, with whom he had interest enough to persuade him to go and settle at Sparta. Thales was famed for his wisdom and political abilities: he was withal a lyric poet, who under colour of exercising his art, performed as great things as the most excellent lawgivers. For his odes were so many persuasives to obedience and unanimity, as by means of melody and numbers they had great grace and power, they softened insensibly the manners of the audience, drew them off from the animosities which then prevailed, and united them in zeal for excellence and virtue. So that, in some measure, he prepared the way for Lycurgus towards the instruction of the Spartans. From Crete Lycurgus passed to Asia, desirous, as is said, to compare the Ionian expense and luxury with the Cretan frugality and hard diet, so as to judge what effect each had on their several manners and governments; just as physicians compare bodies that are weak and sickly with the healthy and robust. There also, probably, he met with Homer's poems, which were preserved by the posterity of Cleophylus. Observing that many moral sentences and much political knowledge were intermixed with his stories, which had an irresistible charm, he collected them into one body, and transcribed them with pleasure, in order to take them home with him. For his glorious poetry was not yet fully known in Greece; only some particular pieces were in a few hands, as they happened to be dispersed. Lycurgus was the first that made them generally known. The Egyptians likewise suppose that he visited them; and as of all their institutions he was most pleased with their distinguishing the military men from the rest of the people, he took the same method at Sparta, and, by separating from these the mechanics and artificers, he rendered the constitution more noble and more of a piece. This assertion of the Egyptians is confirmed by some of the Greek writers. But we know of no one, except Aristocrates, son of Hipparchus, and a Spartan, who has affirmed that he went to Libya and Spain, and in his Indian excursions conversed with the Gymnosophists.

The Lacedæmonians found the want of Lycurgus when absent, and sent many embassies to entreat him to return. For they perceived that their kings had barely the title and outward appendages of royalty, but in nothing else differed from the multitude; whereas Lycurgus had abilities from nature to guide the measures of government, and powers of persuasion, that drew the hearts of men to him. The kings, however, where consulted about his return, and they hoped that in his presence they should experience less insolence amongst the people. Returning then to a city thus disposed, he immediately applied himself to alter the whole frame of the constitution; sensible that a partial change, and the introducing of some new laws, would be of no sort of advantage; but, as in the case of a body diseased and full of bad humours, whose temperament is to be corrected and new formed by medicines, it was necessary to begin a new regimen. With these sentiments he went to Delphi, and when he had offered and consulted the god, he returned with that celebrated oracle, in which the priestess called him "Beloved of the gods, and rather a god than a man." As to his request that he might enact good laws, she told him, Apollo had heard his request, and promised that the constitution he should establish would be the most excellent in the world. Thus encouraged, he applied to the nobility, and desired them to put their hands to the work; addressing himself privately at first to his friends, and afterwards by degrees, trying the disposition of others, and preparing them to concur in the business. When matters were ripe, he ordered thirty of the principal citizens to appear armed in the market-place by break of day, to strike terror into such as might desire to oppose him. Hermippus has given us the names of twenty of the most eminent of them; but he that had the greatest share in the whole enterprise, and gave Lycurgus the best assistance in the establishing of his laws, was called Arithmiades. Upon the first alarm, king Charilaus, apprehending it to be a design against his person, took refuge in the Chalcioicos. But he was soon satisfied, and accepted of their oath. Nay, so far from being obstinate, he joined in the undertaking. Indeed, he was so remarkable for the gentleness of his disposition, that Archelaus, his partner in the throne, is reported to have said to some that were praising the young king, "Yes, Charilaus is a good man to be sure, who cannot find in his heart to punish the bad." Among the many new institutions of Lycurgus, the first and most important was that of a senate; which sharing, as Plato says, in the power of the kings, too imperious and unrestrained before, and having equal authority with them, was the means of keeping them within the bounds of moderation, and highly contributed to the preservation of the state. For before it had been veering and unsettled, sometimes inclining to arbitrary power, and sometimes towards a pure democracy; but this establishment of a senate, an intermediate body, like ballast, kept it in a just equilibrium, and put it in a safe posture: the twenty-eight senators adhering to the kings, whenever they saw the people too encroaching, and, on the other hand, supporting the people, when the kings attempted to make themselves absolute. This, according to Aristotle, was the number of senators fixed upon, because two of the thirty associates of Lycurgus deserted the business through fear. But Sphærus tells us there were only twenty-eight at first entrusted with the design. Something, perhaps, there is in its being a perfect number, formed of seven multiplied by four, and withal the first number, after six, that is equal to all its parts. But I rather think, just so many senators were created, that, together with the two kings, the whole body might consist of thirty members.

He had this institution so much at heart, that he obtained from Delphi an oracle in its behalf, called *rhetra*, or the decree. This was couched in very ancient and uncommon terms, which interpreted, ran thus: "When you have built a temple to the Syllanian Jupiter, and the Syllanian Minerva, divided the people into tribes and classes, and established a senate of thirty persons, including the two kings, you shall occasionally summon the people to an assembly between Babyce and Cnacion, and they shall have the determining voice." Babyce and Cnacion are now called Oenus. But Aristotle thinks, by Cnacion is meant the river, and by Babyce the bridge. Between these they held their assemblies, having neither halls, nor any kind of building for that purpose. These things he thought of no advantage to their councils, but rather a disservice; as they distracted the attention, and turned it upon trifles, on observing the statues and pictures, the splendid roofs, and every other theatrical ornament. The people thus assembled had no right to propose any subject of debate, and were only authorized to ratify or reject what might be proposed to them by the senate and the kings. But because, in process of time, the people, by additions or retrenchments, changed the terms, and perverted the sense of the decrees, the kings Polydorus and Theopompus inserted in the *rhetra* this clause: "If the people attempt to corrupt any law, the senate and chiefs shall retire:" that is, they shall dissolve the assembly, and annul the alterations. And they found means to persuade the Spartans that this too was ordered by Apollo; as we learn from these verses of Tyrtæus:

> Ye sons of Sparta, who at Phœbus' shrine
> Your humble vows prefer, attentive hear
> The god's decision. O'er your beauteous lands
> Two guardian kings, a senate, and the voice
> Of the concurring people, lasting laws
> Shall with joint power establish.

Though the government was thus tempered by Lycurgus, yet soon after it degenerated into an oligarchy, whose power was exercised with such wantonness and violence, that it wanted indeed a bridle, as Plato expresses it. This curb they found in the authority of the Ephori, about a hundred and thirty years after Lycurgus. Elatus was the first invested with this dignity, in the reign of Theopompus; who, when his wife upbraided him, that he would leave the regal power to his children less than he received it, replied, "Nay but greater, because more lasting." And, in fact, the prerogative, so stripped of all extravagant pretensions, no longer occasioned either envy or danger to its possessors. By these means they escaped the miseries which befell the Messenian and Argive kings, who would not in the least relax the severity of their power in favour of the people. Indeed, from nothing more does the wisdom and foresight of Lycurgus appear, than from the disorderly governments, and the bad understanding that subsisted between the kings and people of Messena and Argos, neighbouring states, and related in blood to Sparta. For, as at first they were in all respects equal to her, and possessed of a better country, and yet preserved no lasting happiness, but, through the insolence of the kings and disobedience of the people, were harassed with perpetual troubles, they made it very evident that it was really a felicity more than human, a blessing from heaven to the Spartans, to have a legislator who knew so well how to frame and temper their government. But this was an event of a later date.

A second and bolder political enterprise of Lycurgus was a new division of the lands. For he found a prodigious inequality, the city overcharged with many indigent persons, who had no land, and the wealth centred in the hands of a few. Determined, therefore, to root out the evils of insolence, envy, avarice, and luxury, and those distempers of a state still more inveterate and fatal, I mean poverty and riches, he persuaded them to cancel all former divisions of land, and to make new ones, in such a manner that they might be perfectly equal in their possessions and way of living. Hence, if they were ambitious of distinction they might seek it in virtue, as no other difference was left between them but that which arises from the dishonour of base actions and the praise of good ones. His proposal was put in practice. He made nine thousand lots for the territory of Sparta, which he distributed among so many citizens, and thirty thousand for the inhabitants of the rest of Laconia. But some say he made only six thousand shares for the city, and that Polydorus added three thousand afterwards; others, that Polydorus doubled the number appointed by Lycurgus, which were only four thousand five hundred. Each lot was capable of producing (one year with another) seventy bushels of grain for each man, and twelve for each woman, besides a quantity of wine and oil in proportion.

Such a provision they thought sufficient for health and a good habit of body, and they wanted nothing more. A story goes of our legislator, that some time after returning from a journey through the fields just reaped, and seeing the shocks standing parallel and equal, he smiled, and said to some that were by, "How like is Laconia to an estate newly divided among many brothers!"

After this, he attempted to divide also the movables, in order to take away all appearance of inequality; but he soon perceived that they could not bear to have their goods directly taken from them, and therefore took another method, counterworking their avarice by a stratagem. First he stopped the currency of the gold and silver coin, and ordered that they should make use of iron money only, then to a great quantity and weight of this he assigned but a small value; so that to lay up ten *minæ*, a whole room was required, and to remove it, nothing less than a yoke of oxen. When this became current, many kinds of injustice ceased in Lacedæmon. Who would steal or take a bribe, who would defraud or rob, when he could not conceal the booty; when he could neither be dignified by the possession of it, nor if cut in pieces be served by its use? For we are told that when hot, they quenched it in vinegar, to make it brittle and unmalleable, and consequently unfit for any other service. In the next place, he excluded unprofitable and superfluous arts: indeed, if he had not done this, most of them would have fallen of themselves, when the new money took place, as the manufactures could not be disposed of. Their iron coin would not pass in the rest of Greece, but was ridiculed and despised; so that the Spartans had no means of purchasing any foreign or curious wares; nor did any merchant-ship unlade in their harbours. There were not even to be found in all their country either sophists, wandering fortune-tellers, keepers of infamous houses, or dealers in gold and silver trinkets, because there was no money. Thus luxury, losing by degrees the means that cherished and supported it, died away of itself: even they who had great possessions, had no advantage from them, since they could not be displayed in public, but must lie useless, in unregarded repositories. Hence it was, that excellent workmanship was shown in their useful and necessary furniture, as beds, chairs, and tables; and the Lacedæmonian cup called *cothon*, as Critias informs us, was highly valued, particularly in campaigns: for the water, which must then of necessity be drank, though it would often otherwise offend the sight, had its muddiness concealed by the colour of the cup, and the thick part stopping at the shelving brim, it came clearer to the lips. Of these improvements the lawgiver was the cause; for the workmen having no more employment in matters of mere curiosity, showed the excellence of their art in necessary things.

Desirous to complete the conquest of luxury, and exterminate the love of riches, he introduced a third institution, which was wisely enough and ingeniously contrived. This was the use of public tables, where all were to eat in common of the same meat, and such kinds of it as were appointed by law. At the same time they were forbidden to eat at home, upon expensive couches and tables, to call in the assistance of butchers and cooks, or to fatten like voracious animals in private. For so not only their manners would be corrupted, but their bodies disordered; abandoned to all manner of sensuality and dissoluteness, they would require long sleep, warm baths, and the same indulgence as in perpetual sickness. To effect this was certainly very great; but it was greater still, to secure riches from rapine and from envy, as Theophrastus expresses it, or rather by their eating in common, and by the frugality of their table, to take from riches their very being. For what use or enjoyment of them, what peculiar display of magnificence could there be, where the poor man went to the same refreshment with the rich? Hence the observation, that it was only at Sparta where Plutus (according to the proverb) was kept blind, and like an image, destitute of life or motion. It must further be observed, that they had not the privilege to eat at home, and so to come without appetite to the public repast: they made a point of it to observe any one that did not eat and drink with them, and to reproach him as an intemperate and effeminate person that was sick of the common diet.

The rich, therefore (we are told), were more offended with this regulation than with any other, and, rising in a body, they loudly expressed their indignation: nay, they proceeded so far as to assault Lycurgus with stones, so that he was forced to fly from the assembly and take refuge in a temple. Unhappily, however, before he reached it, a young man named Alcander, hasty in his resentments, though not otherwise ill-tempered, came up with him, and, upon his turning round, struck out one of his eyes with a stick. Lycurgus then stopped short, and, without giving way to passion, showed the people his eye beat out, and his face streaming with blood. They were so struck with shame and sorrow at the sight, that they surrendered Alcander to him, and conducted him home with the utmost expressions of regret. Lycurgus thanked them for their care of his person, and dismissed them all except Alcander. He took him into his house, but showed no ill treatment either by word or action; only ordering him to wait upon him, instead of his usual servants and attendants. The youth, who was of an ingenuous disposition, without murmuring, did as he was commanded. Living in this manner with Lycurgus, and having an opportunity to observe the mildness and goodness of his heart, his strict temperance and indefatigable industry, he told his friends that Lycurgus was not that proud and severe man he might have been taken for, but, above all others, gentle and engaging in his behaviour. This, then, was the chastisement, and this punishment he suffered, of a wild and headstrong young man to become a very modest and prudent citizen. In memory of his misfortune, Lycurgus built a temple to Minerva Optiletis, so called by him from a term which the Dorians use for the eye. Yet Dioscorides, who wrote a treatise concerning the Lacedæmonian government, and others, relate that his eye was hurt, but not put out, and that he built the temple in gratitude to the goddess for his cure. However, the Spartans never carried staves to their assemblies afterwards.

The public repasts were called by the Cretans Andria; but the Lacedæmonians styled them Phiditia, either from their tendency to friendship and mutual benevolence, *phiditia* being used instead of *philitia*; or else from their teaching frugality and parsimony, which the word *pheido* signifies. But it is not all impossible that the first letter might by some means or other be added, and so *phiditia* take place of *editia*, which barely signifies eating. There were fifteen persons to a table, or a few more or less. Each of them was obliged to bring in monthly a bushel of meal, eight gallons of wine, five pounds of cheese, two pounds and a half of figs, and a little money to buy flesh and fish. If any of them happened to offer a sacrifice of first fruits, or to kill venison, he sent a part of it to the public table: for after a sacrifice or hunting, he was at liberty to sup at home: but the rest were to appear at the usual place. For a long time this eating in common was observed with great exactness: so that when king Agis returned from a successful expedition against the Athenians, and from a desire to sup with his wife, requested to have his portion at home, the Polemarchs refused to send it: nay, when, through resentment, he neglected, the day following, to offer the sacrifice usual on occasion of victory, they set a fine upon him. Children also were introduced at these public tables, as so many schools of sobriety. There they heard discourses concerning government, and were instructed in the most liberal breeding. There they were allowed to jest without scurrility, and were not to take it ill when the raillery was returned. For it was reckoned worthy of a Lacedæmonian to bear a jest: but if any one's patience failed, he had only to desire them to be quiet, and they left off immediately. When they first entered, the oldest man present pointed to the door, and said, "Not a word spoken in this company goes out there." The admitting of any man to a particular table was under the following regulation. Each member of that small society took a little ball of soft bread in his hand. This he was to drop, without saying a word, into a vessel called *caddos*, which the waiter carried upon his head. In case he approved of the candidate, he did it without altering the figure, if not, he first pressed it flat in his hand; for a flatted ball was considered as a negative. And if but one such was found, the person was not admitted, as they thought it proper that the whole company should be satisfied with each other. He who thus rejected, was said to have no luck in the *caddos*. The dish that was in the highest esteem amongst them was the black broth. The old men were so fond of it that they ranged themselves on one side and eat it, leaving the meat to the young people. It is related of a king of Pontus, that he purchased a Lacedæmonian cook, for the sake of this broth. But when he came to taste it he strongly expressed his dislike; and the cook made answer, "Sir, to make this broth relish, it is necessary first to bathe in the Eurotas." After they had drank moderately, they went home without lights. Indeed, they were forbidden to walk with a light either on this or any other occasion, that they might accustom themselves to march in the darkest night boldly and resolutely. Such was the order of their public repasts.

Lycurgus left none of his laws in writing; it was ordered in one of the *Rhetræ* that none should be written. For what he thought most conducive to the virtue and happiness of a city, was principles interwoven with the manners and breeding of the people. These would remain immovable, as founded in inclination, and be the strongest and most lasting tie; and the habits which education produced in the youth, would answer in each the purpose of a lawgiver. As for smaller matters, contracts about property, and whatever occasionally varied, it was better not to reduce these to a written form and unalterable method, but to suffer them to change with the times, and to admit of additions or retrenchments at the pleasure of persons so well educated. For he resolved the whole business of legislation into the bringing up of youth. And this, as we have observed, was the reason why one of his ordinances forbad them to have any written laws.

Another ordinance levelled against magnificence and expense, directed that the ceilings of houses should be wrought with no tool but the axe and the doors with nothing but the saw. For, as Epaminondas is reported to have said afterwards, of his table, "Treason lurks not under such a dinner," so Lycurgus perceived before him, that such a house admits of no luxury and needless splendour. Indeed, no man could be so absurd as to bring into a dwelling so homely and simple, bedsteads with silver feet, purple coverlets, golden cups, and a train of expense that follows these: but all would necessarily have the bed suitable to the room, the coverlet of the bed and the rest of their utensils and furniture to that. From this plain sort of dwellings, proceeded the question of Leotychidas the elder to his host, when he supped at Corinth, and saw the ceiling of the room very splendid and curiously wrought, "Whether trees grew square in his country."

A third ordinance of Lycurgus was, that they should not often make war against the same enemy, lest, by being frequently put upon defending themselves, they too should become able warriors in their turn. And this they most blamed king Agesilaus for afterwards, that by frequent and continued incursions into Boeotia, he taught the Thebans to make head against the Lacedæmonians. This made Antalcidas say, when he saw him wounded, "The Thebans pay you well for making them good soldiers who neither were willing nor able to fight you before." These ordinances he called *Rhetræ*, as if they had been oracles and decrees of the Deity himself.

As for the education of youth, which he looked upon as the greatest and most glorious work of a lawgiver, he began with it at the very source, taking into consideration their conception and birth, by regulating the marriages. For he did not (as Aristotle says) desist from his attempt to bring the women under sober rules. They had, indeed, assumed great liberty and power on account of the frequent expeditions of their husbands, during which they were left sole mistresses at home, and so gained an undue deference and improper titles; but notwithstanding this he took all possible care of them. He ordered the virgins to exercise themselves in running, wrestling, and throwing quoits and darts; that their bodies being strong and vigorous, the children afterwards produced from them might be the same; and that, thus fortified by exercise, they might the better support the pangs of child-birth, and be delivered with safety. In order to take away the excessive tenderness and delicacy of the sex, the consequence of a recluse life, he accustomed the virgins occasionally to be seen naked as well as the young men, and to dance and sing in their presence on certain festivals. There they sometimes indulged in a little raillery upon those that had misbehaved themselves, and sometimes they sung encomiums on such as deserved them, thus exciting in the young men a useful emulation and love of glory. For he who was praised for his bravery and celebrated among the virgins, went away perfectly happy: while their satirical glances thrown out in sport, were no less cutting than serious admonitions; especially as the kings and senate went with the other citizens to see all that passed. As for the virgins appearing naked, there was nothing disgraceful in it, because everything was conducted with modesty, and without one indecent word or action. Nay, it caused a simplicity of manners and an emulation for the best habit of body; their ideas too were naturally enlarged, while they were not excluded from their share of bravery and honour. Hence they were furnished with sentiments and language, such as Gorgo the wife of Leonidas is said to have made use of. When a woman of another country said to her, "You of Lacedæmon are the only women in the world that rule the men;" she answered, "We are the only women that bring forth men."

These public dances and other exercises of the young maidens naked, in sight of the young men, were, moreover, incentives to marriage: and, to use Plato's expression, drew them almost as necessarily by the attractions of love, as a geometrical conclusion follows from the premises. To encourage it still more, some marks of infamy were set upon those that continued bachelors. For they were not permitted to see these exercises of the naked virgins; and the magistrates commanded them to march naked round the market-place in the winter, and to sing a song composed against themselves, which expressed how justly they were punished for their disobedience to the laws. They were also deprived of that honour and respect which the younger people paid to the old; so that nobody found fault with what was said to Dercyllidas, though an eminent commander. It seems, when he came one day into company, a young man, instead of rising up and giving place, told him, "You have no child to give place to me, when I am old."

In their marriages, the bridegroom carried off the bride by violence; and she was never chosen in a tender age, but when she had arrived at full maturity. Then the woman that had the direction of the wedding, cut the bride's hair close to the skin, dressed her in man's clothes, laid her upon a mattrass, and left her in the dark. The bridegroom, neither oppressed with wine nor enervated with luxury, but perfectly sober, as having always supped at the common table, went in privately, untied her girdle, and carried her to another bed. Having stayed there a short time, he modestly retired to his usual apartment, to sleep with the other young men; and observed the same conduct afterwards, spending the day with his companions, and reposing himself with them in the night, nor even visiting his bride but with great caution and apprehensions of being discovered by the rest of the family; the bride at the same time exerted all her art to contrive convenient opportunities for their private meetings. And this they did not for a short time only, but some of them even had children before they had an interview with their wives in the daytime. This kind of commerce not only exercised their temperance and chastity, but kept their bodies fruitful, and the first ardour of their love fresh and unabated; for as they were not satiated like those that are always with their wives, there still was place for unextinguished desire. When he had thus established a proper regard to modesty and decorum with respect to marriage, he was equally studious to drive from that state the vain and womanish passion of jealousy; by making it quite as reputable to have children in common with persons of merit, as to avoid all offensive freedom in their own behaviour to their wives. He laughed at those who revenge with wars and bloodshed the communication of a married woman's favours; and allowed, that if a man in years should have a young wife, he might introduce to her some handsome and honest young man, whom he most approved of, and when she had a child of this generous race, bring it up as his own. On the other hand, he allowed, that if a man of character should entertain a passion for a married woman on account of her modesty and the beauty of her children, he might treat with her husband for admission to her company, that so planting in a beauty-bearing soil, he might produce excellent children, the congenial offspring of excellent parents. For, in the first place, Lycurgus considered children, not so much the property of their parents as of the state; and therefore he would not have them begot by ordinary persons, but by the best men in it. In the next place, he observed the vanity and absurdity of other nations, where people study to have their horses and dogs of the finest breed they can procure either by interest or money; and yet keep their wives shut up, that they may have children by none but themselves, though they may happen to be doting, decrepit, or infirm. As if children, when sprung from a bad stock, and consequently good for nothing, were no detriment to those whom they belong to, and who have the trouble of bringing them up, nor any advantage, when well descended and of a generous disposition. These regulations tending to secure a healthy offspring, and consequently beneficial to the state, were so far from encouraging that licentiousness of the women which prevailed afterwards, that adultery was not known amongst them. A saying, upon this subject of Geradas, an ancient Spartan, is thus related. A stranger had asked him, "What punishment their law appointed for adulterers?" He answered, "My friend, there are no adulterers in our country." The other replied, "But what if there should be one?" "Why then," says Geradas, "he must forfeit a bull so large that he might drink of the Eurotas from the top of Mount Taygetus." When the stranger expressed his surprise at this, and said, "How can such a bull be found?" Geradas answered with a smile, "How can an adulterer be found in Sparta?" This is the account we have of their marriages.

It was not left to the father to rear what children he pleased, but he was obliged to carry the child to a place called Lesche, to be examined by the most ancient men of the tribe, who were assembled there. If it was strong and well-proportioned, they gave orders for its education, and assigned it one of the nine thousand shares of land; but if it was weakly and deformed, they ordered it to be thrown into the place called Apothetæ, which is a deep cavern near the mountain Taygetus; concluding that its life could be no advantage either to itself or to the public, since nature had not given it at first any strength or goodness of constitution. For the same reason the women did not wash their new-born infants with water, but with wine, thus making some trial of their habit of body; imagining that sickly and epileptic children sink and die under the experiment, while healthy became more vigorous and hardy. Great care and art was also exerted by the nurses; for, as they never swathed the infants, their limbs had a freer turn, and their countenances a more liberal air; besides, they used them to any sort of meat, to have no terrors in the dark, nor to be afraid of being alone, and to leave all ill humour and unmanly crying. Hence people of other countries purchased Lacedæmonian nurses for their children; and Alcibiades the Athenian is said to have been nursed by Amicla, a Spartan. But if he was fortunate in a nurse, he was not so in a preceptor: for Zopyrus, appointed to that office by Pericles, was, as Plato tells us, no better qualified than a common slave. The Spartan children were not in that manner, under tutors purchased or hired with money, nor were the parents at liberty to educate them as they pleased: but as soon as they were seven years old, Lycurgus ordered them to be enrolled in companies, where they were all kept under the same order and discipline, and had their exercises and recreations in common. He who showed the most conduct and courage amongst them, was made captain of the company. The rest kept their eyes upon him, obeyed his orders, and bore with patience the punishment he inflicted: so that their whole education was an exercise of obedience. The old men were present at their diversions, and often suggested some occasion of dispute or quarrel, that they might observe with exactness the spirit of each, and their firmness in battle.

As for learning, they had just what was absolutely necessary. All the rest of their education was calculated to make them subject to command, to endure labour, to fight and conquer. They added, therefore, to their discipline, as they advance in age;

cutting their hair very close, making them go barefoot, and play, for the most part, quite naked. At twelve years of age, their under garment was taken away, and but one upper one a year allowed them. Hence they were necessarily dirty in their persons, and not indulged the great favour of baths, and oils, except on some particular days of the year. They slept in companies, on beds made of the tops of reeds, which they gathered with their own hands, without knives, and brought from the banks of the Eurotas. In winter they were permitted to add a little thistle-down, as that seemed to have some warmth in it.

At this age, the most distinguished amongst them became the favourite companions of the elder; and the old men attended more constantly their places of exercise, observing their trials of strength and wit, not slightly and in a cursory manner, but as their fathers, guardians, and governors: so that there was neither time nor place where persons were wanting to instruct and chastise them. One of the best and ablest men of the city was, moreover, appointed inspector of the youth: and he gave the command of each company to the discreetest and most spirited of those called Irens. An Iren was one that had been two years out of the class of boys: a Melliren one of the oldest lads. This Iren, then, a youth twenty years old, gives orders to those under his command in their little battles, and has them to serve him at his house. He sends the oldest of them to fetch wood, and the younger to gather pot-herbs: these they steal where they can find them, either slily getting into gardens, or else craftily and warily creeping to the common tables. But if any one be caught, he is severely flogged for negligence or want of dexterity. They steal, too, whatever victuals they possibly can, ingeniously contriving to do it when persons are asleep, or keep but indifferent watch. If they are discovered, they are punished not only with whipping, but with hunger. Indeed, their supper is but slender at all times, that, to fence against want, they may be forced to exercise their courage and address. This is the first intention of their spare diet: a subordinate one is, to make them grow tall. For when the animal spirits are not too much oppressed by a great quantity of food, which stretches itself out in breadth and thickness, they mount upwards by their natural lightness, and the body easily and freely shoots up in height. This also contributes to make them handsome; for thin and slender habits yield more freely to nature, which then gives a fine proportion to the limbs; whilst the heavy and gross resist her by their weight. So women that take physic during their pregnancy, have slighter children indeed, but of a finer and more delicate turn, because the suppleness of the matter more readily obeys the plastic power. However, these are speculations which we shall leave to others.

The boys steal with so much caution, that one of them having conveyed a young fox under his garment, suffered the creature to tear out his bowels with his teeth and claws, choosing rather to die than to be detected. Nor does this appear incredible, if we consider what their young men can endure to this day; for we have seen many of them expire under the lash at the altar of Diana Orthia.

The Iren, reposing himself after supper, used to order one of the boys to sing a song; to another he put some question which required a judicious answer: for example, "Who was the best man in the city?" or "What he thought of such an action?" This accustomed them from their childhood to judge of the virtues, to enter into the affairs of their countrymen. For if one of them was asked, "Who is a good citizen, or who an infamous one," and hesitated in his answer, he was considered a boy of slow parts, and of a soul that would not aspire to honour. The answer was likewise to have a reason assigned for it, and proof conceived in few words. He whose account of the matter was wrong, by way of punishment had his thumb bit by the Iren. The old men and magistrates often attended these little trials, to see whether the Iren exercised his authority in a rational and proper manner. He was permitted, indeed, to inflict the penalties; but when the boys were gone, he was to be chastised himself, if he had punished them either with too much severity or remissness.

The adopters of favourites also shared both in the honour and disgrace of their boys: and one of them is said to have been mulcted by the magistrates, because the boy whom he had taken into his affections let some ungenerous word or cry escape him as he was fighting. This love was so honourable and in so much esteem, that the virgins too had their lovers amongst the most virtuous matrons. A competition of affection caused no misunderstanding, but rather a mutual friendship between those that had fixed their regards upon the same youth, and an united endeavour to make him as accomplished as possible.

The boys were also taught to use sharp repartee, seasoned with humour, and whatever they said was to be concise and pithy. For Lycurgus, as we have observed, fixed but a small value on a considerable quantity of his iron money; but, on the contrary, the worth of speech was to consist in its being comprised in a few plain words, pregnant with a great deal of sense: and he contrived that by long silence they might learn to be sententious and acute in their replies. As debauchery often causes weakness and sterility in the body, so the intemperance of the tongue makes conversation empty and insipid. King Agis, therefore, when a certain Athenian laughed at the Lacedæmonian short swords, and said, "The jugglers would swallow them with ease upon the stage," answered in his laconic way, "And yet we can reach our enemies' hearts with them." Indeed, to me there seems to be something in this concise manner of speaking which immediately reaches the object aimed at, and forcibly strikes the mind of the hearer. Lycurgus himself was short and sententious in his discourse, if we may judge by some of his answers which are recorded; that, for instance, concerning the constitution. When one advised him to establish a popular government in Lacedæmon, "Go," said he, "and first make a trial of it in thy own family." That again, concerning sacrifices to the Deity, when he was asked why he appointed them so trifling and of so little value, "That we might never be in want," said he, "of something to offer him." Once more, when they inquired of him, what sort of martial exercises he allowed of, he answered, "All, except those in which you stretch out your hands." Several such like replies of his are said to be taken from the letters which he wrote to his countrymen: as to their question, "How shall we best guard against the invasion of an enemy?"—"By continuing poor, and not desiring in your possessions to be one above another." And to the question, whether they should enclose Sparta with walls, "That city is well fortified, which has a wall of men instead of brick." Whether these and some other letters ascribed to him are genuine or not, is no easy matter to determine. However, that they hated long speeches, the following apophthegms are a farther proof. King Leonidas said to one who discoursed at an improper time about affairs of some concern, "My friend, you should not talk so much to the purpose, of what it is not to the purpose to talk of." Charilaus, the nephew of Lycurgus, being asked why his uncle had made so few laws, answered, "To men of few words, few laws are sufficient." Some people finding fault with Hecatæus the sophist, because, when admitted to one of the public repasts, he said nothing all the time, Archidamidas replied, "He that knows how to speak, knows also when to speak."

The manner of their repartees, which, as I said, were seasoned with humour, may be gathered from these instances. When a troublesome fellow was pestering Demaratus with impertinent questions, and this in particular several times repeated, "Who is the best man in Sparta?" He answered, "He that is least like you." To some who were commending the Eleans for managing the Olympic games with so much justice and propriety, Agis said, "What great matter is it, if the Eleans do justice once in five years?" When a stranger was professing his regard for Theopompus, and saying that his own countrymen called him Philolacon (a lover of the Lacedæmonians), the king answered him, "My good friend, it were much better, if they called you Philopolites" (a lover of your own countrymen). Plistonax, the son of Pausanias, replied to an orator of Athens, who said the Lacedæmonians had no learning. "True, for we are the only people of Greece that have learned no ill of you." To one who asked what number of men there was in Sparta, Archidamidas said, "Enough to keep bad men at a distance."

Even when they indulged a vein of pleasantry, one might perceive that they would not use one unnecessary word, nor let an expression escape them that had not some sense worth attending to. For one being asked to go and hear a person who imitated the nightingale to perfection, answered, "I have heard the nightingale herself." Another said, upon reading this epitaph,

Victims of Mars, at Selinus they fell,
Who quench'd the rage of tyranny—

"And they deserved to fall, for, instead of *quenching* it, they should have let it *burn out.*" A young man answered one that promised him some game-cocks that would stand their death, "Give me those that will be the death of others." Another seeing some people carried into the country in litters, said, "May I never sit in any place where I cannot rise before the aged!" This was the manner of their apophthegms: so that it has been justly enough observed that the term *lakonizein* (to act the Lacedæmonian) is to be referred rather to the exercises of the mind, than those of the body.

Nor were poetry and music less cultivated among them, than a concise dignity of expression. Their songs had a spirit, which could rouse the soul, and impel it in an enthusiastic manner to action. The language was plain and manly, the subject serious and moral. For they consisted chiefly of the praises of heroes that had died for Sparta, or else of expressions of detestation for such wretches as had declined the glorious opportunity, and rather chose to drag on life in misery and contempt. Nor did they forget to express an ambition for glory suitable to their respective ages. Of this it may not be amiss to give an instance. There were three choirs on their festivals, corresponding with the three ages of man. The old men began,

Once in battle bold we shone;

the young men answered,

Try us: our vigour is not gone;

and the boys concluded,

The palm remains for us alone.

Indeed, if we consider with some attention such of the Lacedæmonian poems as are still extant, and get into those airs which were played upon the flute when they marched to battle, we must agree that Terpander and Pindar have very fitly joined valour and music together. The former thus speaks of Lacedæmon,

There gleams the youth's bright falchion: there the muse
Lifts her sweet voice: there awful Justice opes
Her wide pavilion.

And Pindar sings,

There in grave council sits the sage;
There burns the youth's resistless rage
To hurl the quiv'ring lance;
The Muse with glory crowns their arms,
And Melody exerts her charms,
And Pleasure leads the dance.

Thus we are informed, not only of their warlike turn, but their skill in music. For as the Spartan poet says,

To swell the bold notes of the lyre,
Becomes the warrior's lofty fire.

And the king always offered sacrifice to the muses before a battle, putting his troops in mind, I suppose, of their early education and of the judgment that would be passed upon them; as well as that those divinities might teach them to despite danger, while they performed some exploit fit for them to celebrate.

On these occasions they relaxed the severity of their discipline, permitting their men to be curious in dressing their hair, and elegant in their arms and apparel, while they expressed their alacrity, like horses full of fire and neighing for the race. They let their hair, therefore, grow from their youth, but took more particular care, when they expected an action, to have it well combed and shining; remembering a saying of Lycurgus, that "a large head of hair made the handsome more graceful, and the ugly more terrible." The exercises, too, of the young men, during the campaigns, were more moderate, their diet not so hard, and their whole treatment more indulgent: so that they were the only people in the world with whom military discipline wore, in time of war, a gentler face than usual. When the army was drawn up, and the enemy near, the king sacrificed a goat, and commanded them all to set garlands upon their heads, and the musicians to play Castro's march, while himself began the pæan, which was the signal to advance. It was at once a solemn and dreadful sight to see them measuring their steps to the sound of music, and without the least disorder in their ranks or tumult of spirits, moving forward cheerfully and composedly, with harmony, to battle. Neither fear nor rashness was likely to approve men so disposed, possessed as they were of a firm presence of mind, with courage and confidence of success, as under the conduct of heaven. When the king advanced against the enemy, he had always with him some one that had been crowned in the public games of Greece. And they tell us, that a Lacedæmonian, when large sums were offered him on condition that he would not enter the Olympic lists, refused them, having with much difficulty thrown his antagonist, one put this question to him, "Spartan, what will you get by this victory?" He answered with a smile, "I shall have the honour to fight foremost in the ranks before my prince." When they had routed the enemy, they continued the pursuit till they were assured of the victory: after that they immediately desisted; deeming it neither generous nor worthy of a Grecian to destroy those who made no farther resistance. This was not only a proof of magnanimity, but of great service to their cause. For when their adversaries found that they killed such as stood it out, but spared the fugitives, they concluded it was better to fly than to meet their fate upon the spot.

Hippias the sophist tells us, that Lycurgus himself was a man of great personal valour, and an experienced commander. Philostephanus also ascribes to him the first division of cavalry into troops of fifty, who were drawn up in a square body. But Demetrius the Phalerean says, that he never had any military employment, and that there was the profoundest peace imaginable when he established the constitution of Sparta. His providing for a cessation of arms during the Olympic games is likewise a mark of the humane and peaceable man. Some, however, acquaint us, and among the rest Hermippus, that Lucurgus at first had no communication with Iphitus; but coming that way, and happening to be a spectator, he heard behind him a human voice (as he thought) which expressed some wonder and displeasure that he did not put his countrymen upon resorting to so great an assembly. He turned round immediately, to discover whence the voice came, and as there was no man to be seen, concluded it was from heaven. He joined Iphitus, therefore; and ordering, along with him, the ceremonies of the festival, rendered it more magnificent and lasting.

The discipline of the Lacedæmonians continued after they were arrived at years of maturity. For no man was at liberty to live as he pleased; the city being like one great camp, where all had their stated allowance, and knew their public charge, each man concluding that he was born, not for himself, but for his country. Hence, if they had no particular orders, they employed themselves in inspecting the boys, and teaching them something useful, or in learning of those that were older than themselves. One of the greatest privileges that Lycurgus procured his countrymen, was the enjoyment of leisure, the consequence of his forbidding them to exercise any mechanic trade. It was not worth their while to take great pains to raise a fortune, since riches there were of no account: and the Helotes, who tilled the ground, were answerable for the produce above-mentioned. To this purpose we have a story of a Lacedæmonian, who, happening to be at Athens while the court sat, was informed of a man who was fined for idleness; and when the poor fellow was returning home in great dejection, attended by his condoling friends, he desired the company to show him the person that was condemned for keeping up his dignity. So much beneath them they reckoned all attention to mechanics arts, and all desire of riches!

Lawsuits were banished from Lacedæmon with money. The Spartans knew neither riches nor poverty, but possessed an equal competency, and had a cheap and easy way of supplying their few wants. Hence, when they were not engaged in war, their time was taken up with dancing, feasting, hunting, or meeting to exercise, or converse. They went not to market under thirty years of age, all their necessary concerns being managed by their relations and adopters. Nor was it reckoned a credit to the old to be seen sauntering in the market-place; it was deemed more suitable for them to pass great part of the day in the schools of exercise, or places of conversation. Their discourse seldom turned upon money, or business, or trade, but upon the praise of the excellent, or the contempt of the worthless; and the last was expressed with that pleasantry and humour, which conveyed instruction and correction without seeming to intend it. Nor was Lycurgus himself immoderately severe in his manner; but, as Sosibius tells us, he dedicated a little statue to the god of laughter in each hall. He considered facetiousness as a seasoning of their hard exercise and diet, and therefore ordered it to take place on all proper occasions, in their common entertainments and parties of pleasure.

Upon the whole, he taught his citizens to think nothing more disagreeable than to live by (or for) themselves. Like bees, they acted with one impulse for the public good, and always assembled about their prince. They were possessed with a thirst of honour, an enthusiasm bordering upon insanity, and had not a wish but for their country. These sentiments are confirmed by some of their aphorisms. When Pædaretus lost his election for one of the "three hundred," he went away "rejoicing that there were three hundred better men than himself found in the city." Pisistratidas going with some others, ambassador to the king of Persia's lieutenants, was asked whether they came with a public commission, or on their own account, to which he answered, "If successful, for the public; if unsuccessful, for ourselves." Agrileonis, the mother of Brasidas, asking some Amphipolitans that waited upon her at her house, whether Brasidas died honourably and as became a Spartan? they greatly extolled his merit, and said there was not such a man left in Sparta; whereupon she replied, "Say not so, my friends; for Brasidas was indeed a man of honour, but Lacedæmon can boast of many better men than he."

The senate, as I said before, consisted at first of those that were assistants to Lycurgus in his great enterprise. Afterwards, to fill up any vacancy that might happen, he ordered the most worthy men to be selected, of those that were full threescore years old. This was the most respectable dispute in the world, and the contest was truly glorious; for it was not who should be swiftest among the swift, or strongest of the strong, but who was the wisest and best among the good and wise. He who had the preference was to bear this mark of superior excellence through life, this great authority, which put into his hands the lives and honour of the citizens, and every other important affair. The manner of the election was this: when the people were assembled, some persons appointed for the purpose were shut up in a room near the place; where they could neither see nor be seen, and only hear the shouts of the constituents: for by them they decided this and most other affairs. Each candidate walked silently through the assembly, one after another according to lot. Those that were shut up had writing tables, in which they set down in different columns the number and loudness of the shouts, without knowing who they were for; only they marked them as first, second, third, and so on, according to the number of the competitors. He that had the most and loudest acclamations, was declared duly elected. Then he was crowned with a garland, and went round to give thanks to the gods: a number of young men followed, striving which should extol him most, and the women celebrated his virtues in their songs, and blessed his worthy life and conduct. Each of his relations offered him a repast, and their address on the occasion was, "Sparta honours you with this collation." When he had finished the procession, he went to the common table, and lived as before. Only two portions were set before him, one of which he carried away: and as all the women related to him attended at the gates of the public hall, he called her for whom he had the greatest esteem, and presented her with the portion, saying at the same time, "That which I received as a mark of honour, I give to you." Then she was conducted home with great applause by the rest of the women.

Lycurgus likewise made good regulations with respect to burials. In the first place, to take away all superstition, he ordered the dead to be buried in the city, and even permitted their monuments to be erected near the temples; accustoming the youth to such sights from their infancy, that they might have no uneasiness from them, nor any horror for death, as if people were polluted with the touch of a dead body, or with treading upon a grave. In the next place, he suffered nothing to be buried with the corpse, except the red cloth and the olive leaves in which it was wrapped. Nor would he suffer the relations to inscribe any names upon the tombs, except of those men that fell in battle, or those women who died in some sacred office. He fixed eleven days for the time of mourning: on the twelfth they were to put an end to it, after offering sacrifice to Ceres. No part of life was left vacant and unimproved, but even with their necessary actions he interwove the praise of virtue and the contempt of vice: and he so filled the city with living examples, that it was next to impossible, for persons who had these from their infancy before their eyes, not to be drawn and formed to honour.

For the same reason he would not permit all that desired to go abroad and see other countries, lest they should contract foreign manners, gain traces of a life of little discipline, and of a different form of government. He forbid strangers too to resort to Sparta, who could not assign a good reason for their coming; not, as Thucydides says, out of fear they should imitate the constitution of that city, and make improvements in virtue, but lest they should teach his own people some evil. For along with foreigners come new subjects of discourse; new discourse produces new opinions; and from these there necessarily spring new passions and desires, which, like discords in music, would disturb the established government. He, therefore, thought it more expedient for the city to keep out of it corrupt customs and manners, than even to prevent the introduction of a pestilence.

Thus far, then, we can perceive no vestiges of a disregard to right and wrong, which is the fault some people find with the laws of Lycurgus, allowing them well enough calculated to produce valour, but not to promote justice. Perhaps it was the Cryptia, as they called it, or ambuscade, if that was really one of this lawgiver's institutions, as Aristotle says it was, which gave Plato so bad an impression both of Lycurgus and his laws. The governors of the youth ordered the shrewdest of them from time to time to disperse themselves in the country, provided only with daggers and some necessary provisions. In the daytime they hid themselves, and rested in the most private places they could find, but at night they sallied out into the roads, and killed all the Helotes they could meet with. Nay, sometimes by day, they fell upon them in the fields, and murdered the ablest and strongest of them. Thucydides relates in his history of the Peloponnesian war, that the Spartans selected such of them as were distinguished for their courage, to the number of two thousand or more, declared them free, crowned them with garlands, and conducted them to the temples of the gods; but soon after they all disappeared; and no one could, either then or since, give account in what manner they were destroyed. Aristotle particularly says, that the Ephori, as soon as they were invested in their office, declared war against the Helotes, that they might be massacred under pretence of law. In other respects they treated them with great inhumanity: sometimes they made them drink till they were intoxicated, and in that condition led them into the public halls, to show the young men what drunkenness was. They ordered them too to sing mean songs, and to dance ridiculous dances, but not to meddle with any that were genteel and graceful. Thus they tell us, that when the Thebans afterwards invaded Laconia, and took a great number of the Helotes prisoners, they ordered them to sing the odes of Terpander, Aleman, or Spendon the Lacedæmonian, but they excused themselves, alleging that it was forbidden by their masters. Those who say that a freeman in Sparta was most a freeman, and a slave most a slave, seem well to have considered the difference of states. But in my opinion, it was in after-times that these cruelties took place among the Lacedæmonians, chiefly after the great earthquake, when, as history informs us, the Helotes, joining the Messenians, attacked them, did infinite damage to the country, and brought the city to the greatest extremity. I can never ascribe to Lycurgus so abominable an act as that of the ambuscade. I would judge in this case by the mildness and justice which appeared in the rest of his conduct, to which also the gods gave their sanction.

When his principal institutions had taken root in the manners of the people, and the government was come to such maturity as to be able to support and preserve itself, then, as Plato says of the Deity, that he rejoiced when he had created the world, and given it its first motion; so Lycurgus was charmed with the beauty and greatness of his political establishment, when he saw it exemplified in fact, and move on in due order. He was next desirous to make it immortal, so far as human wisdom could effect it, and to deliver it down unchanged to the latest times. For this purpose he assembled all the people, and told them the provisions he had already made for the state were indeed sufficient for virtue and happiness, but the greatest and most important matter was still behind, which he could not disclose to them till he had consulted the oracle; that they must therefore inviolably observe his laws, without altering anything in them, till he returned from Delphi; and then he would acquaint them with the pleasure of Apollo. When they had all promised to do so, and desired him to set forward, he took an oath of the kings and senators, and afterwards of all the citizens, that they would abide by the present establishment till Lycurgus came back. He then took his journey to Delphi.

When he arrived there, he offered sacrifice to the gods, and consulted the oracle, whether his laws were sufficient to promote virtue, and secure the happiness of the state. Apollo answered, that the laws were excellent, and that the city which kept to the constitution he had established, would be the most glorious in the world. This oracle Lycurgus took down in writing, and sent it to Sparta. He then offered another sacrifice, and embraced his friends and his son, determined never to release his citizens from their oath, but voluntarily there to put a period to his life; while he was yet of an age when life was not a burden, when death was not desirable, and while he was not unhappy in any one circumstance. He, therefore, destroyed himself by abstaining from food, persuaded that the very death of lawgivers should have its use, and their exit, so far from being insignificant, have its share of virtue, and be considered as a great action. To him, indeed, whose performances were so illustrious, the conclusion of life was the crown of happiness, and his death was left guardian of those invaluable blessings he had procured his countrymen through life, as they had taken an oath not to depart from his establishment till his return. Nor was he deceived in his expectations. Sparta continued superior to the rest of Greece, both in its government at home and reputation abroad, so long as it retained the institution of Lycurgus: and this it did during the space of five hundred years, and the reign of fourteen successive kings, down to Agis the son of Archidamus. As for the appointment of the Ephori, it was so far from weakening the constitution, that it gave it additional vigour, and though it seemed to be established in favour of the people, it strengthened the aristocracy.

But in the reign of Agis money found its way into Sparta, and with money came its inseparable attendant—avarice. This was by means of Lysander; who, though himself incapable of being corrupted by money, filled his country with the love of it, and with luxury too. He brought both gold and silver from the wars, and thereby broke through the laws of Lycurgus. While these were in force, Sparta was not so much under the political regulations of a commonwealth, as the strict rules of a philosophic life; and as the poets feign of Hercules, that only with a club and lion's skin he travelled over the world, clearing it of lawless ruffians and cruel tyrants; so the Lacedæmonians with a piece of parchment and coarse coat kept Greece in a voluntary obedience, destroyed usurpation and tyranny in the states, put an end to wars, and laid seditions asleep, very often without either shield or lance, and only by sending one ambassador; to whose directions all parties concerned immediately submitted. Thus bees, when their prince appears, compose their quarrels and unite in one swarm. So much did justice and good government prevail in that state, that I am surprised at those who say the Lacedæmonians knew indeed how to obey, but not how to govern: and on this occasion quote the saying of king Theopompus, who, when one told him that Sparta was preserved by the good administration of its kings, replied, "Nay, rather by the obedience of their subjects." It is certain that people will not continue pliant to those who know not how to command; but it is the part of a good governor to teach obedience. He who knows how to lead well, is sure to be well followed: and as it is by the art of horsemanship that a horse is made gentle and tractable, so it is by the abilities of him that fills the throne that the people become ductile and submissive. Such was the conduct of the Lacedæmonians, that people did not only endure, but even desired to be their subjects. They asked not of them either ships, money or troops, but only a Spartan general. When they had received him, they treated him with the greatest honour and respect; so Gylippus was revered by the Sicilians, Brasidas by the Chalcidians, Lysander, Callicratidas, and Agesilaus by all the people of Asia. These, and such as these, wherever they came, were called moderators and reformers, both of the magistrates and people, and Sparta itself was considered as a school of discipline, where the beauty of life and political order were taught in the utmost perfection. Hence Stratonicus seems facetiously enough to have said, that he would order "the Athenians to have the conduct of mysteries and processions; the Eleans to preside in games, as their particular province; and the Lacedæmonians to be beaten, if the other did amiss." This was spoken in jest: but Antisthenes, one of the scholars of Socrates, said (more seriously) of the Thebans, when he saw them pluming themselves upon their success at Leuctra, "They were just like so many school-boys rejoicing that they had beaten their master."

It was not, however, the principal design of Lycurgus that his city should govern many others, but he considered its happiness like that of a private man, as flowing from virtue and self-consistency: he therefore so ordered and disposed it, that by the freedom and sobriety of its inhabitants, and their having a sufficiency within themselves, its continuance might be the more secure. Plato, Diogenes, Zeno, and other writers upon government, have taken Lycurgus for their model: and these have attained great praise, though they left only an idea of something excellent. Yet he who, not in idea and in words, but in fact produced a most inimitable form of government, and by showing a whole city of philosophers, confounded those who imagine that the so much talked of strictness of a philosophic life is impracticable; he, I say, stands in the rank of glory far beyond the founders of all the other Grecian states. Therefore Aristotle is of opinion, that the honours paid him in Lacedæmon were far beneath his merit. Yet those honours were very great; for he has a temple there, and they offer him a yearly sacrifice, as a god. It is also said, that when his remains were brought home, his tomb was struck with lightning: a seal of divinity which no other man, however eminent, has had, except Euripides, who died and was buried at Arethusa in Macedonia. This was matter of great satisfaction and triumph to the friends of Euripides, that the same thing should befall him after death, which had formerly happened to the most venerable of men, and the most favoured of heaven. Some say, Lycurgus died at Cirrha; but Apollothemis will have it, that he was brought to Elis and died there; and Timæus and Aristoxenus write, that he ended his days in Crete; nay, Aristoxenus adds, that the Cretans show his tomb at Pergamia, near the high road. We are told, he left an only son named Antiorus: and as he died without issue, the family was extinct. His friends and relations observed his anniversary, which subsisted for many ages, and the days on which they met for that purpose they called Lycurgidæ. Aristocrates, the son of Hipparchus, relates, that the friends of Lycurgus, with whom he sojourned, and at last died in Crete, burned his body, and, at his request, threw his ashes into the sea. Thus he guarded against the possibility of his remains being brought back to Sparta by the Lacedæmonians, lest they should then think themselves released from their oath, on the pretence that he was returned, and make innovations in the government. This is what we had to say of Lycurgus.

SIR THOMAS MORE'S UTOPIA.

UTOPIA.

BOOK I.

Henry the Eighth, the unconquered King of England, a prince adorned with all the virtues that become a great monarch, having some differences of no small consequence with Charles the most serene prince of Castile, sent me into Flanders, as his ambassador, for treating and composing matters between them. I was colleague and companion to that incomparable man Cuthbert Tonstal, whom the king with such universal applause lately made Master of the Rolls; but of whom I will say nothing; not because I fear that the testimony of a friend will be suspected, but rather because his learning and virtues are too great for me to do them justice, and so well known, that they need not my commendations unless I would, according to the proverb, "Show the sun with a lanthorn." Those that were appointed by the prince to treat with us met us at Bruges, according to agreement; they were all worthy men. The Margrave of Bruges was their head, and the chief man among them; but he that was esteemed the wisest, and that spoke for the rest, was George Temse, the Provost of Casselsee; both art and nature had concurred to make him eloquent: he was very learned in the law; and as he had a great capacity, so by a long practice in affairs he was very dextrous at unravelling them. After we had several times met without coming to an agreement, they went to Brussels for some days to know the prince's pleasure. And since our business would admit it, I went to Antwerp. While I was there, among many that visited me, there was one that was more acceptable to me than any other, Peter Giles, born at Antwerp, who is a man of great honour, and of a good rank in his town, though less than he deserves; for I do not know if there be anywhere to be found a more learned and a better bred young man: for as he is both a very worthy and a very knowing person, so he is so civil to all men, so particularly kind to his friends, and so full of candour and affection, that there is not perhaps above one or two anywhere to be found that is in all respects so perfect a friend. He is extraordinarily modest, there is no artifice in him; and yet no man has more of a prudent simplicity: his conversation was so pleasant and so innocently cheerful, that his company in a great measure lessened any longings to go back to my country, and to my wife and children, which an absence of four months had quickened very much. One day as I was returning home from Mass at St. Mary's, which is the chief church, and the most frequented of any in Antwerp, I saw him by accident talking with a stranger, who seemed past the flower of his age; his face was tanned, he had a long beard, and his cloak was hanging carelessly about him, so that by his looks and habit I concluded he was a seaman. As soon as Peter saw me, he came and saluted me; and as I was returning his civility, he took me aside, and pointing to him with whom he had been discoursing, he said, "Do you see that man? I was just thinking to bring him to you." I answered, "He should have been very welcome on your account." "And on his own too," replied he, "if you knew the man, for there is none alive that can give so copious an account of unknown nations and countries as he can do; which I know you very much desire." Then said I, "I did not guess amiss, for at first sight I took him for a seaman." "But you are much mistaken," said he, "for he has not sailed as a seaman, but as a traveller, or rather a philosopher. This Raphael, who from his family carries the name of Hythloday, is not ignorant of the Latin tongue, but is eminently learned in the Greek, having applied himself more particularly to that than to the former, because he had given himself much to philosophy, in which he knew that the Romans have left us nothing that is valuable, except what is to be found in Seneca and Cicero. He is a Portuguese by birth, and was so desirous of seeing the world, that he divided his estate among his brothers, run the same hazard as Americus Vesputius, and bore a share in three of his four voyages, that are now published; only he did not return with him in his last, but obtained leave of him almost by force, that he might be one of those twenty-four who were left at the farthest place at which they touched, in their last voyage to New Castile. The leaving him thus did not a little gratify one that was more fond of travelling than of returning home, to be buried in his own country; for he used often to say, that the way to heaven was the same from all places; and he that had no grave, had the heaven still over him. Yet this disposition of mind had cost him dear, if God had not been very gracious to him; for after he, with five Castilians, had travelled over many countries, at last, by strange good fortune, he got to Ceylon, and from thence to Calicut, where he very happily found some Portuguese ships; and, beyond all men's expectations, returned to his native country." When Peter had said this to me, I thanked him for his kindness, in intending to give me the acquaintance of a man whose conversation he knew would be so acceptable; and upon that Raphael and I embraced each other. After those civilities were past which are usual with strangers upon their first meeting, we all went to my house, and entering into the garden, sat down on a green bank, and entertained one another in discourse. He told us, that when Vesputius had sailed away, he and his companions that stayed behind in New Castile, by degrees insinuated themselves into the affections of the people of the country, meeting often with them, and treating them gently: and at last they not only lived among them without danger, but conversed familiarly with them; and got so far into the heart of a prince, whose name and country I have forgot, that he both furnished them plentifully with all things necessary, and also with the conveniences of travelling; both boats when they went by water, and waggons when they travelled over land: he sent with them a very faithful guide, who was to introduce and recommend them to such other princes as they had a mind to see: and after many days' journey, they came to towns, and cities, and to commonwealths, that were both happily governed and well peopled. Under the equator, and as far on both sides of it as the sun moves, there lay vast deserts that were parched with the perpetual heat of the sun; the soil was withered, all things looked dismally, and all places were either quite uninhabited, or abounded with wild beasts and serpents, and some few men, that were neither less wild nor less cruel than the beasts themselves. But as they went farther, a new scene opened, all things grew milder, the air less burning, the soil more verdant, and even the beasts were less wild: and at last there were nations, towns, and cities, that had not only mutual commerce among themselves, and with their neighbours, but traded both by sea and land, to very remote countries. There they found the conveniences of seeing many countries on all hands, for no ship went any voyage into which he and his companions were not very welcome. The first vessels that they saw were flat-bottomed, their sails were made of reeds and wicker woven close together, only some were of leather; but afterwards they found ships made with round keels, and canvas sails, and in all respects like our ships; and the seamen understood both astronomy and navigation. He got wonderfully into their favour, by showing them the use of the needle, of which till then they were utterly ignorant. They sailed before with great caution, and only in summer-time, but now they count all seasons alike, trusting wholly to the loadstone, in which they are perhaps more secure than safe; so that there is reason to fear that this discovery, which was thought would prove so much to their advantage, may by their imprudence become an occasion of much mischief to them. But it were too long to dwell on all that he told us he had observed in every place; it would be too great a digression from our present purpose: whatever is necessary to be told, concerning those wise and prudent institutions which he observed among civilized nations, may perhaps be related by us on a more proper occasion. We asked him many questions concerning all these things, to which he answered very willingly; only we made no inquiries after monsters, than which nothing is more common; for everywhere one may hear of ravenous dogs and wolves, and cruel men-eaters; but it is not so easy to find states that are well and wisely governed.

As he told us of many things that were amiss in those new-discovered countries, so he reckoned up not a few things from which patterns might be taken for correcting the errors of these nations among whom we live; of which an account may be given, as I have already promised, at some other time; for at present I intend only to relate those particulars that he told us of the manners and laws of the Utopians: but I will begin with the occasion that led us to speak of that commonwealth. After Raphael had discoursed with great judgment on the many errors that were both among us and these nations; had treated of the wise institutions both here and there, and had spoken as distinctly of the customs and government of every nation through which he had passed, as if he had spent his whole life in it; Peter being struck with admiration, said, "I wonder, Raphael, how it comes that you enter into no king's service, for I am sure there are none to whom you would not be very acceptable: for your learning and knowledge, both of men and things, is such, that you would not only entertain them very pleasantly, but be of great use to them, by the examples you could set before them, and the advices you could give them; and by this means you would both serve your own interest, and be of great use to all your friends."—"As for my friends," answered he, "I need not be much concerned, having already done for them all that was incumbent on me; for when I was not only in good health, but fresh and young, I distributed that among my kindred and friends which other people do not part with till they are old and sick; when they then unwillingly give that which they can enjoy no longer themselves. I think my friends ought to rest contented with this, and not to expect that for their sakes I should enslave myself to any king whatsoever."—"Soft and fair," said Peter, "I do not mean that you should be a slave to any king, but only that you should assist them, and be useful to them."—"The change of the word," said he, "does not alter the matter."—"But term it as you will," replied Peter, "I do not see any other way in which you can be so useful, both in private to your friends, and to the public, and by which you can make your own condition happier."—"Happier!" answered Raphael, "is that to be compassed in a way so abhorrent to my genius? Now I live as I will, to which I believe few courtiers can pretend. And there are so many that court the favour of great men, that there will be no great loss if they are not troubled either with me or with others of my temper." Upon this, said I, "I perceive, Raphael, that you neither desire wealth nor greatness; and indeed I value and admire such a man much more than I do any of the great men in the world. Yet I think you would do what would well become so generous and philosophical a soul as yours is, if you would apply your time and thoughts to public affairs, even though you may happen to find it a little uneasy to yourself: and this you can never do with so much advantage, as by being taken into the counsel of some great prince, and putting him on noble and worthy actions, which I know you would do if you were in such a post; for the springs both of good and evil flow from the prince, over a whole nation, as from a lasting fountain. So much learning as you have, even without practice in affairs, or so great a practice as you have had, without any other learning, would render you a very fit counsellor to any king whatsoever."—"You are doubly mistaken," said he, "Mr. More, both in your opinion of me, and in the judgment you make of things: for as I have not that capacity that you fancy I have; so, if I had it, the public would not be one jot the better, when I had sacrificed my quiet to it. For most princes apply themselves more to affairs of war than to the useful arts of peace; and in these I neither have any knowledge, nor do I much desire it: they are generally more set on acquiring new kingdoms, right or wrong, than on governing well those they possess. And among the ministers of princes, there are none that are not so wise as to need no assistance, or at least that do not think themselves so wise, that they imagine they need none; and if they court any, it is only those for whom the prince has much personal favour, whom by their fawnings and flatteries they endeavour to fix to their own interests: and indeed Nature has so made us, that we all love to be flattered, and to please ourselves with our own notions. The old crow loves his young, and the ape her cubs. Now if in such a Court, made up of persons who envy all others, and only admire themselves, a person should but propose anything that he had either read in history, or observed in his travels, the rest would think that the reputation of their wisdom would sink, and that their interest would be much depressed, if they could not run it down: and if all other things failed, then they would fly to this, that such or such things pleased our ancestors, and it were well for us if we could but match them. They would set up their rest on such an answer, as a sufficient confutation of all that could be said; as if it were a great misfortune, that any should be found wiser than his ancestors; but though they willingly let go all the good things that were among those of former ages, yet if better things are proposed they cover themselves obstinately with this excuse of reverence to past times. I have met with these proud, morose, and absurd judgments of things in many places, particularly once in England."—"Was you ever there?" said I.—"Yes, I was," answered he, "and stayed some months there, not long after the rebellion in the west was suppressed with a great slaughter of the poor people that were engaged in it.

"I was then much obliged to that reverend prelate, John Morton, Archbishop of Canterbury, Cardinal, and Chancellor of England: a man," said he, "Peter (for Mr. More knows well what he was), that was not less venerable for his wisdom and virtues, than for the high character he bore. He was of a middle stature, not broken with age; his looks begot reverence rather than fear; his conversation was easy, but serious and grave; he sometimes took pleasure to try the force of those that came as suitors to him upon business, by speaking sharply, though decently to them, and by that he discovered their spirit and presence of mind, with which he was much delighted, when it did not grow up to impudence, as bearing a great resemblance to his own temper; and he looked on such persons as the fittest men for affairs. He spoke both gracefully and weightily; he was eminently skilled in the law, had a vast understanding, and a prodigious memory; and those excellent talents with which Nature had furnished him, were improved by study and experience. When I was in England the king depended much on his counsels, and the government seemed to be chiefly supported by him; for from his youth he had been all along practised in affairs; and having passed through many traverses of fortune, he had with great cost acquired a vast stock of wisdom, which is not soon lost when it is purchased so dear. One day when I was dining with him there happened to be at table one of the English lawyers, who took occasion to run out in a high commendation of the severe execution of justice upon thieves, who, as he said, were then hanged so fast, that there were sometimes twenty on one gibbet; and upon that he said he could not wonder enough how it came to pass, that since so few escaped, there were yet so many thieves left who were still robbing in all places. Upon this, I who took the boldness to speak freely before the Cardinal, said, there was no reason to wonder at the matter, since this way of punishing thieves was neither just in itself nor good for the public; for as the severity was too great, so the remedy was not effectual; simple theft not being so great a crime that it ought to cost a man his life, no punishment how severe soever being able to restrain those from robbing who can find out no other way of livelihood. 'In this,' said I, 'not only you in England, but a great part of the world imitate some ill masters that are readier to chastise their scholars than to teach them. There are dreadful punishments enacted against thieves, but it were much better to make such good provisions by which every man might be put in a method how to live, and so be preserved from the fatal necessity of stealing and of dying for it.'—'There has been care enough taken for that,' said he, 'there are many handicrafts, and there is husbandry, by which they may make a shift to live unless they have a greater mind to follow ill courses.'—'That will not serve your turn,' said I, 'for many lose their limbs in civil or foreign wars, as lately in the Cornish rebellion, and some time ago in your wars with France, who being thus mutilated in the service of their king and country, can no more follow their old trades, and are too old to learn new ones: but since wars are only accidental things, and have intervals, let us consider those things that fall out every day. There is a great number of noblemen among you, that are themselves as idle as drones, that subsist on other men's labour, on the labour of their tenants, whom, to raise their revenues, they pare to the quick. This indeed is the only instance of their frugality, for in all other things they are prodigal, even to the beggaring of themselves: but besides this, they carry about with them a great number of idle fellows, who never learned any art by which they may gain their living; and these, as soon as either their lord dies, or they themselves fall sick, are turned out of doors; for your lords are readier to feed idle people, than to take care of the sick; and often the heir is not able to keep together so great a family as his predecessor did. Now when the stomachs of those that are thus turned out of doors, grow keen, they rob no less keenly; and what else can they do? for when, by wandering about, they have worn out both their health and their clothes, and are tattered, and look ghastly, men of quality will not entertain them, and poor men dare not do it; knowing that one who has been bred up in idleness and pleasure, and who was used to walk about with his sword and buckler, despising all the neighbourhood with an insolent scorn, as far below him, is not fit for the spade and mattock: nor will he serve a poor man for so small a hire, and in so low a diet as he can afford to give him.' To this he answered, 'This sort of men ought to be particularly cherished, for in them consists the force of the armies for which we have occasion; since their birth inspires them with a nobler sense of honour, than is to be found among tradesmen or ploughmen.'—'You may as well say,' replied I, 'that you must cherish thieves on the account of wars, for you will never want the one, as long as you have the other; and as robbers prove sometimes gallant soldiers, so soldiers often prove brave robbers; so near an alliance there is between those two sorts of life. But this bad custom, so common among you, of keeping many servants, is not peculiar to this nation. In France there is yet a more pestiferous sort of people, for the whole country is full of soldiers, still kept up in time of peace; if such a state of a nation can be called a peace: and these are kept in pay upon the same account that you plead for those idle retainers about noblemen; this being a maxim of those pretended statesmen that it is necessary for the public safety, to have a good body of veteran soldiers ever in readiness. They think raw men are not to be depended on, and they sometimes seek occasions for making war, that they may train up their soldiers in the art of cutting throats; or as Sallust observed, for keeping their hands in use, that they may not grow dull by too long an intermission. But France has learned to its cost, how dangerous it is to feed such beasts. The fate of the Romans, Carthaginians, and Syrians, and many other nations and cities, which were both overturned and quite ruined by those standing armies, should make others wiser: and the folly of this maxim of the French, appears plainly even from this, that their trained soldiers often find your raw men prove too hard for them; of which I will not say much, lest you may think I flatter the English. Every day's experience shows, that the mechanics in the towns, or the clowns in the country, are not afraid of fighting with those idle gentlemen, if they are not disabled by some misfortune in their body, or dispirited by extreme want, so that you need not fear that those well-shaped and strong men (for it is only such that noblemen love to keep about them, till they spoil them) who now grow feeble with ease, and are softened with their effeminate manner of life, would be less fit for action if they were well bred and well employed. And it seems very unreasonable, that for the prospect of a war, which you need never have but when you please, you should maintain so many idle men, as will always disturb you in time of peace, which is ever to be more considered than war. But I do not think that this necessity of stealing arises only from hence; there is another cause of it more peculiar to England.'—'What is that?' said the Cardinal.—'The increase of pasture,' said I, 'by which your sheep, which are naturally mild, and easily kept in order, may be said now to devour men, and unpeople, not only villages, but towns; for wherever it is found that the sheep of any soil yield a softer and richer wool than ordinary, there the nobility and gentry, and even those holy men the abbots, not contented with the old rents which their farms yielded, nor thinking it enough that they, living at their ease, do no good to the public, resolve to do it hurt instead of good. They stop the course of agriculture, destroying houses and towns, reserving only the churches, and enclose grounds that they may lodge their sheep in them. As if forests and parks had swallowed up too little of the land, those worthy countrymen turn the best inhabited places in solitudes; for when an insatiable wretch, who is a plague to his country, resolves to inclose many thousand acres of ground, the owners, as well as tenants, are turned out of their possessions, by tricks, or by main force, or being wearied out with ill usage, they are forced to sell them. By which means those miserable people, both men and women, married and unmarried, old and young, with their poor but numerous families (since country business requires many hands), are all forced to change their seats, not knowing whither to go; and they must sell almost for nothing their household stuff, which could not bring them much money, even though they might stay for a buyer. When that little money is at an end, for it will be soon spent; what is left for them to do, but either to steal and so to be hanged (God knows how justly), or to go about and beg? And if they do this, they are put in prison as idle vagabonds; while they would willingly work, but can find none that will hire them; for there is no more occasion for country labour, to which they have been bred, when there is no arable ground left. One shepherd can look after a flock, which will stock an extent of ground that would require many hands, if it were to be ploughed and reaped. This likewise in many places raises the price of corn. The price of wool is also so risen, that the poor people who were wont to make cloth are no more able to buy it; and this likewise makes many of them idle. For since the increase of pasture, God has punished the avarice of the owners, by a rot among the sheep, which has destroyed vast numbers of them; to us it might have seemed more just had it fell on the owners themselves. But suppose the sheep should increase ever so much, their price is not like to fall; since though they cannot be called a monopoly, because they are not engrossed by one person, yet they are in so few hands, and these are so rich, that as they are not pressed to sell them sooner than they have a mind to it, so they never do it till they have raised the price as high as possible. And on the same account it is, that the other kinds of cattle are so dear, because many villages being pulled down, and all country labour being much neglected, there are none who make it their business to breed them. The rich do not breed cattle as they do sheep, but buy them lean, and at low prices; and after they have fattened them on their grounds, sell them again at high rates. And I do not think that all the inconveniences this will produce are yet observed; for as they sell the cattle dear, so if they are consumed faster than the breeding countries from which they are brought can afford them, then the stock must decrease, and this must needs end in great scarcity; and by these means this your island, which seemed as to this particular the happiest in the world, will suffer much by the cursed avarice of a few persons; besides this, the rising of corn makes all people lessen their families as much as they can; and what can those who are dismissed by them do, but either beg or rob? And to this last, a man of a great mind is much sooner drawn than to the former. Luxury likewise breaks in apace upon you, to set forward your poverty and misery; there is an excessive vanity in apparel, and great cost in diet; and that not only in noblemen's families, but even among tradesmen, among the farmers themselves, and among all ranks of persons. You have also many infamous houses, and besides those that are known, the taverns and alehouses are no better; add to these, dice, cards, tables, foot-ball, tennis, and quoits, in which money runs fast away; and those that are initiated into them, must in the conclusion betake themselves to robbing for a supply. Banish these plagues, and give orders that those who have dispeopled so much soil, may either rebuild the villages they have pulled down, or let out their grounds to such as will do it: restrain those engrossings of the rich, that are as bad almost as monopolies; leave fewer occasions to idleness; let agriculture be set up again, and the manufacture of the wool be regulated, that so there may be work found for those companies of idle people whom want forces to be thieves, or who now being idle vagabonds, or useless servants, will certainly grow thieves at last. If you do not find a remedy to these evils, it is a vain thing to boast of your severity in punishing theft, which though it may have the appearance of justice, yet in itself is neither just nor convenient. For if you suffer your people to be ill educated, and their manners to be corrupted from their infancy, and then punish them for those crimes to which their first education disposed them, what else is to be concluded from this, but that you first make thieves and then punish them?'

"While I was talking thus, the counsellor who was present had prepared an answer, and had resolved to resume all I had said, according to the formality of a debate, in which things are generally repeated more faithfully than they are answered; as if the chief trial to be made were of men's memories. 'You have talked prettily for a stranger,' said he, 'having heard of many things among us which you have not been able to consider well; but I will make the whole matter plain to you, and will first repeat in order all that you have said, then I will show how much your ignorance of our affairs has misled you, and will in the last place answer all your arguments. And that I may begin where I promised, there were four things——' 'Hold your peace,' said the Cardinal, 'this will take up too much time; therefore we will at present ease you of the trouble of answering, and reserve it to our next meeting, which shall be to-morrow, if Raphael's affairs and yours can admit of it. But, Raphael,' said he to me, 'I would gladly know upon what reason it is that you think theft ought not to be punished by death? Would you give way to it? Or do you propose any other punishment that will be more useful to the public? For since death does not restrain theft, if men thought their lives would be safe, what fear or force could restrain ill men? On the contrary, they would look on the mitigation of the punishment as an invitation to commit more crimes.' I answered, 'It seems to me a very unjust thing to take away a man's life for a little money; for nothing in the world can be of equal value with a man's life: and if it is said, that it is not for the money that one suffers, but for his breaking the law, I must say, extreme justice is an extreme injury; for we ought not to approve of these terrible laws that make the smallest offences capital, nor of that opinion of the

Stoics, that makes all crimes equal, as if there were no difference to be made between the killing a man and the taking his purse, between which, if we examine things impartially, there is no likeness nor proportion. God has commanded us not to kill, and shall we kill so easily for a little money? But if one shall say, that by that law we are only forbid to kill any, except when the laws of the land allow of it; upon the same grounds, laws may be made in some cases to allow of adultery and perjury: for God having taken from us the right of disposing, either of our own or of other people's lives, if it is pretended that the mutual consent of man in making laws can authorize man-slaughter in cases in which God has given us no example, that it frees people from the obligation of the divine law, and so makes murder a lawful action; what is this, but to give a preference to human laws before the divine? And if this is once admitted, by the same rule men may in all other things put what restrictions they please upon the laws of God. If by the Mosaical law, though it was rough and severe, as being a yoke laid on an obstinate and servile nation, men were only fined, and not put to death for theft, we cannot imagine that in this new law of mercy, in which God treats us with the tenderness of a father, He has given us a greater license to cruelty than He did to the Jews. Upon these reasons it is, that I think putting thieves to death is not lawful; and it is plain and obvious that it is absurd, and of ill consequence to the commonwealth, that a thief and a murderer should be equally punished; for if a robber sees that his danger is the same, if he is convicted of theft as if he were guilty of murder, this will naturally incite him to kill the person whom otherwise he would only have robbed, since if the punishment is the same, there is more security, and less danger of discovery, when he that can best make it is put out of the way; so that terrifying thieves too much, provokes them to cruelty.

"'But as to the question, what more convenient way of punishment can be found? I think it is much more easier to find out that, than to invent anything that is worse; why should we doubt but the way that was so long in use among the old Romans, who understood so well the arts of government, was very proper for their punishment? They condemned such as they found guilty of great crimes, to work their whole lives in quarries, or to dig in mines with chains about them. But the method that I liked best, was that which I observed in my travels in Persia, among the Polylerits, who are a considerable and well-governed people. They pay a yearly tribute to the King of Persia; but in all other respects they are a free nation, and governed by their own laws. They lie far from the sea, and are environed with hills; and being contented with the productions of their own country, which is very fruitful, they have little commerce with any other nation; and as they, according to the genius of their country, have no inclination to enlarge their borders; so their mountains, and the pension they pay to the Persian, secure them from all invasions. Thus they have no wars among them: they live rather conveniently than with splendour, and may be rather called a happy nation, than either eminent or famous; for I do not think that they are known so much as by name to any but their next neighbours. Those that are found guilty of theft among them, are bound to make restitution to the owner, and not as it is in other places, to the prince, for they reckon that the prince has no more right to the stolen goods than the thief; but if that which was stolen is no more in being, then the goods of the thieves are estimated, and restitution being made out of them, the remainder is given to their wives and children: and they themselves are condemned to serve in the public works, but are neither imprisoned, nor chained, unless there happened to be some extraordinary circumstances in their crimes. They go about loose and free, working for the public. If they are idle or backward to work, they are whipped; but if they work hard, they are well used and treated without any mark of reproach, only the lists of them are called always at night, and then they are shut up. They suffer no other uneasiness, but this of constant labour; for as they work for the public, so they are well entertained out of the public stock, which is done differently in different places. In some places, whatever is bestowed on them, is raised by a charitable contribution; and though this way may seem uncertain, yet so merciful are the inclinations of that people, that they are plentifully supplied by it; but in other places, public revenues are set aside for them; or there is a constant tax of a poll-money raised for their maintenance. In some places they are set to no public work, but every private man that has occasion to hire workmen, goes to the market-places and hires them of the public, a little lower than he would do a freeman: if they go lazily about their task, he may quicken them with the whip. By this means there is always some piece of work or other to be done by them; and beside their livelihood, they earn somewhat still to the public. They all wear a peculiar habit, of one certain colour, and their hair is cropped a little above their ears, and a piece of one of their ears is cut off. Their friends are allowed to give them either meat, drink, or clothes, so they are of their proper colour; but it is death, both to the giver and taker, if they give them money; nor is it less penal for any freeman to take money from them, upon any account whatsoever: and it is also death for any of these slaves (so they are called) to handle arms. Those of every division of the country are distinguished by a peculiar mark; which it is capital for them to lay aside, to go out of their bounds, or to talk with a slave of another jurisdiction; and the very attempt of an escape is no less penal than an escape itself; it is death for any other slave to be accessory to it; and if a freeman engages in it he is condemned to slavery. Those that discover it are rewarded; if freemen, in money; and if slaves, with liberty, together with a pardon for being accessory to it; that so they might find their account, rather in repenting of their engaging in such a design, than in persisting in it.

"These are their laws and rules in relation to robbery; and it is obvious that they are as advantageous as they are mild and gentle; since vice is not only destroyed, and men preserved, but they treated in such a manner as to make them see the necessity of being honest, and of employing the rest of their lives in repairing the injuries they have formerly done to society. Nor is there any hazard of their falling back to their old customs: and so little do travellers apprehend mischief from them, that they generally make use of them for guides, from one jurisdiction to another; for there is nothing left them by which they can rob, or be the better for it, since as they are disarmed, so the very having of money is a sufficient conviction: and as they are certainly punished if discovered, so they cannot hope to escape; for their habit being in all the parts of it different from what is commonly worn, they cannot fly away, unless they would go naked, and even then their cropped ear would betray them. The only danger to be feared from them, is their conspiring against the government: but those of one division and neighbourhood can do nothing to any purpose, unless a general conspiracy were laid amongst all the slaves of the several jurisdictions, which cannot be done, since they cannot meet or talk together; nor will any venture on a design where the concealment would be so dangerous, and the discovery so profitable. None are quite hopeless of recovering their freedom, since by their obedience and patience, and by giving good grounds to believe that they will change their manner of life for the future, they may expect at last to obtain their liberty: and some are every year restored to it, upon the good character that is given of them.—When I had related all this, I added, that I did not see why such a method might not be followed with more advantage, than could ever be expected from that severe justice which the counsellor magnified so much. To this he answered, that it could never take place in England, without endangering the whole nation. As he said this, he shook his head, made some grimaces, and held his peace, while all the company seemed of his opinion, except the Cardinal, who said that it was not easy to form a judgment of its success, since it was a method that never yet had been tried. 'But if,' said he, 'when the sentence of death was passed upon a thief, the prince would reprieve him for a while, and make the experiment upon him, denying him the privilege of a sanctuary; and then if it had a good effect upon him, it might take place; and if it did not succeed, the worst would be, to execute the sentence on the condemned persons at last. And I do not see,' added he, 'why it would be either unjust, inconvenient, or at all dangerous, to admit of such a delay: in my opinion, the vagabonds ought to be treated in the same manner; against whom, though we have made many laws, yet we have not been able to gain our end.' When the Cardinal had done, they all commended the motion, though they had despised it when it came from me; but more particularly commended what related to the vagabonds, because it was his own observation.

"I do not know whether it be worth while to tell what followed, for it was very ridiculous; but I shall venture at it, for as it is not foreign to this matter, so some good use may be made of it. There was a jester standing by, that counterfeited the fool so naturally, that he seemed to be really one. The jests which he offered were so cold and dull, that we laughed more at him than at them; yet sometimes he said, as it were by chance, things that were not unpleasant; so as to justify the old proverb, 'That he who throws the dice often, will sometimes have a lucky hit.' When one of the company had said, that I had taken care of the thieves, and the Cardinal had taken care of the vagabonds, so that there remained nothing but that some public provision might be made for the poor, whom sickness or old age had disabled from labour. 'Leave that to me,' said the fool, 'and I shall take care of them; for there is no sort of people whose sight I abhor more, having been so often vexed with them, and with their sad complaints; but as dolefully soever as they have told their tale, they could never prevail so far as to draw one penny from me: for either I had no mind to give them anything, or when I had a mind to do it, I had nothing to give them: and they now know me so well, that they will not lose their labour, but let me pass without giving me any trouble, because they hope for nothing, no more in faith than if I were a priest: but I would have a law made, for sending all these beggars to monasteries, the men to the Benedictines to be made lay-brothers, and the women to be nuns.' The Cardinal smiled, and approved of it in jest; but the rest liked it in earnest. There was a divine present, who though he was a grave morose man, yet he was so pleased with this reflection that was made on the priests and the monks, that he began to play with the fool, and said to him, 'This will not deliver you from all beggars, except you take care of us friars.'—'That is done already,' answered the fool, 'for the Cardinal has provided for you, by what he proposed for restraining vagabonds, and setting them to work, for I know no vagabonds like you.' This was well entertained by the whole company, who looking at the Cardinal, perceived that he was not ill pleased at it; only the friar himself was vexed, as may be easily imagined, and fell into such a passion, that he could not forbear railing at the fool, and calling him knave, slanderer, back-biter, and son of perdition, and then cited some dreadful threatenings out of the Scriptures against him. Now the jester thought he was in his element, and laid about him freely. 'Good friar,' said he, 'be not angry, for it is written, "In patience possess your soul."'—The friar answered (for I shall give you his own words), 'I am not angry, you hangman; at least I do not sin in it, for the Psalmist says, "Be ye angry, and sin not."'—Upon this the Cardinal admonished him gently, and wished him to govern his passions. 'No, my lord,' said he, 'I speak not but from a good zeal, which I ought to have; for holy men have had a good zeal, as it is said, "The zeal of thy house hath eaten me up;" and we sing in our church, that those who mocked Elisha as he went up to the house of God, felt the effects of his zeal; which that mocker, that rogue, that scoundrel, will perhaps feel.'—'You do this perhaps with a good intention,' said the Cardinal; 'but in my opinion, it were wiser in you, and perhaps better for you, not to engage in so ridiculous a contest with a fool.'—'No, my lord,' answered he, 'that were not wisely done; for Solomon, the wisest of men, said, "Answer a fool according to his folly;" which I now do, and show him the ditch into which he will fall, if he is not aware of it; for if the many mockers of Elisha, who was but one bald man, felt the effect of his zeal, what will become of one mocker of so many friars, among whom there are so many bald men? We have likewise a Bull, by which all that jeer us are excommunicated.'—When the Cardinal saw that there was no end of this matter, he made a sign to the fool to withdraw, turned the discourse another way; and soon after rose from the table, and dismissing us, went to hear causes.

"Thus, Mr. More, I have run out into a tedious story, of the length of which I had been ashamed, if, as you earnestly begged it of me, I had not observed you to hearken to it, as if you had no mind to lose any part of it. I might have contracted it, but I resolved to give it you at large, that you might observe how those that despised what I had proposed, no sooner perceived that the Cardinal did not dislike it, but presently approved of it, fawned so on him, and flattered him to such a degree, that they in good earnest applauded those things that he only liked in jest. And from hence you may gather, how little courtiers would value either me or my counsels."

To this I answered, "You have done me a great kindness in this relation; for as everything has been related by you, both wisely and pleasantly, so you have made me imagine that I was in my own country, and grown young again, by recalling that good Cardinal to my thoughts, in whose family I was bred from my childhood: and though you are upon other accounts very dear to me, yet you are the dearer, because you honour his memory so much; but after all this I cannot change my opinion; for I still think that if you could overcome that aversion which you have to the Courts of Princes, you might, by the advice which it is in your power to give, do a great deal of good to mankind; and this is the chief design that every good man ought to propose to himself in living: for your friend Plato thinks that nations will be happy, when either philosophers become kings, or kings become philosophers; it is no wonder if we are so far from that happiness, while philosophers will not think it their duty to assist kings with their councils."—"They are not so base-minded," said he, "but that they would willingly do it; many of them have already done it by their books, if those that are in power would but hearken to their good advice. But Plato judged right, that except kings themselves became philosophers, they who from their childhood are corrupted with false notions, would never fall in entirely with the councils of philosophers, and this he himself found to be true in the person of Dionysius.

"Do not you think, that if I were about any king, proposing good laws to him, and endeavouring to root out all the cursed seeds of evil that I found in him, I should either be turned out of his Court, or at least be laughed at for my pains? For instance, what could it signify if I were about the King of France, and were called into his cabinet-council, where several wise men, in his hearing, were proposing many expedients; as by what arts and practices Milan may be kept; and Naples, that had so oft slipped out of their hands, recovered; how the Venetians, and after them the rest of Italy, may be subdued; and then how Flanders, Brabant, and all Burgundy, and some other kingdoms which he has swallowed already in his designs, may be added to his empire. One proposes a league with the Venetians, to be kept as long as he finds his account in it, and that he ought to communicate councils with them, and give them some share of the spoil, till his success makes him need or fear them less, and then it will be easily taken out of their hands. Another proposes the hiring the Germans, and the securing the Switzers by pensions. Another proposes the gaining the Emperor by money, which is omnipotent with him. Another proposes a peace with the King of Arragon, and in order to cement it, the yielding up the King of Navarre's pretensions. Another thinks the Prince of Castile is to be wrought on, by the hope of an alliance; and that some of his courtiers are to be gained to the French faction by pensions. The hardest point of all is what to do with England: a treaty of peace is to be set on foot, and if their alliance is not to be depended on, yet it is to be made as firm as possible; and they are to be called friends, but suspected as enemies: therefore the Scots are to be kept in readiness, to be let loose upon England on every occasion: and some banished nobleman is to be supported underhand (for by the league it cannot be done avowedly) who has a pretension to the crown, by which means that suspected prince may be kept in awe. Now when things are in so great a fermentation, and so many gallant men are joining councils, how to carry on the war, if so mean a man as I should stand up, and wish them to change all their councils, to let Italy alone, and stay at home, since the kingdom of France was indeed greater than could be well governed by one man; that therefore he ought not to think of adding others to it: and if after this, I should propose to them the resolutions of the Achorians, a people that lie on the south-east of Utopia, who long ago engaged in war, in order to add to the dominions of their prince another kingdom, to which he had some pretensions by an ancient alliance. This they conquered, but found that the trouble of keeping it was equal to that by which it was gained; that the conquered people were always either in rebellion or exposed to foreign invasions, while they were obliged to be incessantly at war, either for or against them, and consequently could never disband their army; that in the meantime they were oppressed with taxes, their money went out of the kingdom, their blood was spilt for the glory of their king, without procuring the least advantage to the people, who received not the smallest benefit from it even in time of peace; and that their manners being corrupted by a long war, robbery and murders everywhere abounded, and their laws fell into contempt; while their king, distracted with the care of two kingdoms, was the less able to apply his mind to the interests of either. When they saw this, and that there would be no end to these evils, they by joint councils made an humble address to their king, desiring him to choose which of the two kingdoms he had the greatest mind to keep, since he could not hold both; for they were too great a people to be governed by a divided king, since no man would willingly have a groom that should be in common between him and another. Upon which the good prince was forced to quit his new kingdom to one of his friends (who was not long after dethroned), and to be contented with his old one. To this I would add, that after all those warlike attempts, the vast confusions, and the consumption both of treasure and of people that must follow them; perhaps upon some misfortune, they might be forced to throw up all at last; therefore it seemed much more eligible that the king should improve his ancient kingdom all he could, and make it flourish as much as possible; that he should love his people, and be beloved of them; that he should live among them, govern them gently, and let other kingdoms alone, since that which had fallen to his share was big enough, if not too big for him. Pray how do you think would such a speech as this be heard?"—"I confess," said I, "I think not very well."

"But what," said he, "if I should sort with another kind of ministers, whose chief contrivances and consultations were, by what art the prince's treasures might be increased. Where one proposes raising the value of specie when the king's debts are large, and lowering it when his revenues were to come in, that so he might both pay much with a little, and in a little receive a great deal: another proposes a pretence of a war, that money might be raised in order to carry it on, and that a peace be concluded as soon as that was done; and this with such appearances of religion as might work on the people, and make them impute it to the piety of their prince, and to his tenderness for the lives of his subjects. A third offers some old musty laws, that have been antiquated by a long disuse; and which, as they had been forgotten by all the subjects, so they had been also broken by them; and proposes the levying the penalties of these laws, that as it would bring in a vast treasure, so there might be a very good pretence for it, since it would look like the executing a law, and the doing of justice. A fourth proposes the prohibiting of many things under severe penalties, especially such as were against the interest of the people, and then the dispensing with these prohibitions upon great compositions, to those who might find their advantage in breaking them. This would serve two ends, both of them acceptable to many; for as those whose avarice led them to transgress would be severely fined, so the selling licenses dear would look as if a prince were tender of his people, and would not easily, or at low rates, dispense with anything that might be against the public good. Another proposes that the judges must be made sure, that they may declare always in favour of the prerogative, that they must be often sent for to Court, that the king may hear them argue those points in which he is concerned; since how unjust soever any of his pretensions may be, yet still some one or other of them, either out of contradiction to others, or the pride of singularity, or to make their court, would find out some pretence or other to give the king a fair colour to carry the point: for if the judges but differ in opinion, the clearest thing in the world is made by that means disputable, and truth being once brought in question, the king may then take advantage to expound the law for his own profit; while the judges that stand out will be brought over, either out of fear or modesty; and they being thus gained, all of them may be sent to the bench to give sentence boldly, as the king would have it: for fair pretences will never be wanting when sentence is to be given in the prince's favour. It will either be said that equity lies of his side, or some words in the law will be found sounding that way, or some forced sense will be put on them; and when all other things fail, the king's undoubted prerogative will be pretended, as that which is above all law; and to which a religious judge ought to have a special regard. Thus all consent to that maxim of Crassus, that a prince cannot have treasure enough, since he must maintain his armies out of it: that a king, even though he would, can do nothing unjustly; that all property is in him, not excepting the very persons of his subjects: and that no man has any other property, but that which the king out of his goodness thinks fit to leave him. And they think it is the prince's interest, that there be as little of this left as may be, as if it were his advantage that his people should have neither riches nor liberty; since these things make them less easy and less willing to submit to a cruel and unjust government; whereas necessity and poverty blunts them, makes them patient, beats them down, and breaks that height of spirit, that might otherwise dispose them to rebel. Now what if after all these propositions were made, I should rise up and assert, that such councils were both unbecoming a king, and mischievous to him: and that not only his honour but his safety consisted more in his people's wealth, than in his own; if I should show that they choose a king for their own sake, and not for his; that by his care and endeavours they may be both easy and safe; and that therefore a prince ought to take more care of his people's happiness than of his own, as a shepherd is to take more care of his flock than of himself. It is also certain, that they are much mistaken that think the poverty of a nation is a means of the public safety. Who quarrel more than beggars? Who does more earnestly long for a change, than he that is uneasy in his present circumstances? And who run to create confusions with so desperate a boldness, as those who have nothing to lose, hope to gain by them? If a king should fall under such contempt or envy, that he could not keep his subjects in their duty, but by oppression and ill usage, and by rendering them poor and miserable, it were certainly better for him to quit his kingdom, than to retain it by such methods, as makes him while he keeps the name of authority, lose the majesty due to it. Nor is it so becoming the dignity of a king to reign over beggars, as over rich and happy subjects. And therefore Fabricius, a man of a noble and exalted temper, said, he would rather govern rich men, than be rich himself; since for one man to abound in wealth and pleasure, when all about him are mourning and groaning, is to be a gaoler and not a king. He is an unskilful physician, that cannot cure one disease without casting his patient into another: so he that can find no other way for correcting the errors of his people, but by taking from them the conveniences of life, shows that he knows not what it is to govern a free nation. He himself ought rather to shake off his sloth, or to lay down his pride; for the contempt or hatred that his people have for him, takes its rise from the vices in himself. Let him live upon what belongs to him, without wronging others, and accommodate his expense to his revenue. Let him punish crimes, and by his wise conduct let him endeavour to prevent them, rather than be severe when he has suffered them to be too common: let him not rashly revive laws that are abrogated by disuse, especially if they have been long forgotten, and never wanted; and let him never take any penalty for the breach of them, to which a judge would not give way in a private man, but would look on him as a crafty and unjust person for pretending to it. To these things I would add, that law among the Macarians, a people that lie not far from Utopia, by which their king, on the day on which he begins to reign, is tied by an oath confirmed by solemn sacrifices, never to have at once above a thousand pounds of gold in his treasures, or so much silver as is equal to that in value. This law, they tell us, was made by an excellent king, who had more regard to the riches of his country than to his own wealth; and therefore provided against the heaping up of so much treasure, as might impoverish the people. He thought that moderate sum might be sufficient for any accident; if either the king had occasion for it against rebels, or the kingdom against the invasion of an enemy; but that it was not enough to encourage a prince to invade other men's rights, a circumstance that was the chief cause of his making that law. He also thought that it was a good provision for that free circulation of money, so necessary for the course of commerce and exchange: and when a king must distribute all those extraordinary accessions that increase treasure beyond the due pitch, it makes him less disposed to oppress his subjects. Such a king as this will be the terror of ill men, and will be beloved by all the good.

"If, I say, I should talk of these or such like things, to men that had taken their bias another way, how deaf would they be to all I could say?"—"No doubt, very deaf," answered I; and no wonder, for one is never to offer at propositions or advice that we are certain will not be entertained. Discourses so much out of the road could not avail anything, nor have any effect on men whose minds were prepossessed with different sentiments. This philosophical way of speculation is not unpleasant among friends in a free conversation, but there is no room for it in the Courts of Princes where great affairs are carried on by authority."—"That is what I was saying," replied he, "that there is no room for philosophy in the Courts of Princes."—"Yes, there is," said I, "but not for this speculative philosophy that makes everything to be alike fitting at all times: but there is another philosophy that is more pliable, that knows its proper scene, accommodates itself to it, and teaches a man with propriety and decency to act that part which has fallen to his share. If when one of Plautus's comedies is upon the stage and a company of servants are acting their parts, you should come out in the garb of a philosopher, and repeat out of 'Octavia' a discourse of Seneca's to Nero, would it not be better for you to say nothing than by mixing things of such different natures to make an impertinent tragi-comedy? For you spoil and corrupt the play that is in hand when you mix with it things of an opposite nature, even though they are much better. Therefore go through with the play that is acting the best you can, and do not confound it because another that is pleasanter comes into your thoughts. It is even so in a commonwealth, and in the councils of princes; if ill opinions cannot be quite rooted out, and you cannot cure some received vice according to your wishes, you must not therefore abandon the commonwealth, for the same reasons you should not forsake the ship in a storm because you cannot command the winds. You are not obliged to assault people with discourses that are out of their road, when you see that their received notions must prevent your making an impression upon them. You ought rather to cast about and to manage things with all the dexterity in your power, so that if you are not able to make them go well they may be as little ill as possible; for except all men were good everything cannot be right, and that is a blessing that I do not at present hope to see. According to your arguments," answered he, "all that I could be able to do would be to preserve myself from being mad while I endeavoured to cure the madness of others; for if I speak truth, I must repeat what I have said to you; and as for lying, whether a philosopher can do it or not, I cannot tell, I am sure I cannot do it. But though these discourses may be uneasy and ungrateful to them, I do not see why they should seem foolish or extravagant: indeed if I should either propose such things as Plato has contrived in his commonwealth, or as the Utopians practise in theirs, though they might seem better, as certainly they are, yet they are so different from our establishment, which is founded on property, there being no such thing among them, that I could not expect that it would have any effect on them; but such discourses as mine, which only call past evils to mind and give warning of what may follow, have nothing in them that is so absurd that they may not be used at any time, for they can only be unpleasant to those who are resolved to run headlong the contrary way; and if we must let alone everything as absurd or extravagant which by reason of the wicked lives of many may seem uncouth, we must, even among Christians, give over pressing the greatest part of those things that Christ hath taught us, though He has commanded us not to conceal them, but to proclaim on the house-tops that which He taught in secret. The greatest parts of His precepts are more opposite to the lives of the men of this age than any part of my discourse has been; but the preachers seemed to have learned that craft to which you advise me, for they observing that the world would not willingly suit their lives to the rules that Christ has given, have fitted His doctrine as if it had been a leaden rule, to their lives, that so some way or other they might agree with one another. But I see no other effect of this compliance except it be that men become more secure in their wickedness by it. And this is all the success that I can have in a Court, for I must always differ from the rest, and then I shall signify nothing; or if I agree with them, I shall then only help forward their madness. I do not comprehend what you mean by your casting about, or by the bending and handling things so dexterously, that if they go not well they may go as little ill as may be; for in Courts they will not bear with a man's holding his peace or conniving at what others do. A man must barefacedly approve of the worst counsels, and consent to the blackest designs: so that he would pass for a spy, or possibly for a traitor, that did but coldly approve of such wicked practices: and therefore when a man is engaged in such a society, he will be so far from being able to mend matters by his casting about, as you call it, that he will find no occasions of doing any good: the ill company will sooner corrupt him, than be the better for him: or if notwithstanding all their ill company, he still remains steady and innocent, yet their follies and knavery will be imputed to him; and by mixing counsels with them, he must bear his share of all the blame that belongs wholly to others.

"It was no ill simile by which Plato set forth the unreasonableness of a philosopher's meddling with government. If a man, says he, was to see a great company run out every day into the rain, and take delight in being wet; if he knew that it would be to no purpose for him to go and persuade them to return to their houses, in order to avoid the storm, and that all that could be expected by his going to speak to them would be that he himself should be as wet as they, it would be best for him to keep within doors; and since he had not influence enough to correct other people's folly, to take care to preserve himself.

"Though to speak plainly my real sentiments, I must freely own, that as long as there is any property, and while money is the standard of all other things, I cannot think that a nation can be governed either justly or happily: not justly, because the best things will fall to the share of the worst men; nor happily, because all things will be divided among a few (and even these are not in all respects happy), the rest being left to be absolutely miserable. Therefore when I reflect on the wise and good constitution of the Utopians, among whom all things are so well governed, and with so few laws; where virtue hath its due reward, and yet there is such an equality, that every man lives in plenty; when I compare with them so many other nations that are still making new laws, and yet can never bring their constitution to a right regulation, where notwithstanding every one has his property; yet all the laws that they can invent have not the power either to obtain or preserve it, or even to enable men certainly to distinguish what is their own from what is another's; of which the many lawsuits that every day break out, and are eternally depending, give too plain a demonstration; when, I say, I balance all these things in my thoughts, I grow more favourable to Plato, and do not wonder that he resolved not to make any laws for such as would not submit to a community of all things: for so wise a man could not but foresee that the setting all upon a level was the only way to make a nation happy, which cannot be obtained so long as there is property: for when every man draws to himself all that he can compass, by one title or another, it must needs follow, that how plentiful soever a nation may be, yet a few dividing the wealth of it among themselves, the rest must fall into indigence. So that there will be two sorts of people among them, who deserve that their fortunes should be interchanged; the former useless, but wicked and ravenous; and the latter, who by their constant industry serve the public more than themselves, sincere and modest men. From whence I am persuaded, that till property is taken away there can be no equitable or just distribution of things, nor can the world be happily governed: for as long as that is maintained, the greatest and the far best part of mankind will be still oppressed with a load of cares and anxieties. I confess without taking it quite away, those pressures that lie on a great part of mankind may be made lighter; but they can never be quite removed. For if laws were made to determine at how great an extent in soil, and at how much money every man must stop, to limit the prince that he might not grow too great, and to restrain the people that they might not become too insolent, and that none might factiously aspire to public employments; which ought neither to be sold, nor made burthensome by a great expense; since otherwise those that serve in them would be tempted to reimburse themselves by cheats and violence, and it would become necessary to find out rich men for undergoing those employments which ought rather to be trusted to the wise. These laws, I say, might have such effects, as good diet and care might have on a sick man, whose recovery is desperate: they might allay and mitigate the disease, but it could never be quite healed, nor the body politic be brought again to a good habit, as long as property remains; and it will fall out as in a complication of diseases, that by applying a remedy to one sore, you will provoke another; and that which removes the one ill symptom produces others, while the strengthening one part of the body weakens the rest."—"On the contrary," answered I, "it seems to me that men cannot live conveniently, where all things are common: how can there be any plenty, where every man will excuse himself from labour? For as the hope of gain doth not excite him, so the confidence that he has in other men's industry may make him slothful: if people come to be pinched with want, and yet cannot dispose of anything as their own; what can follow upon this but perpetual sedition and bloodshed, especially when the reverence and authority due to magistrates falls to the ground? For I cannot imagine how that can be kept up among those that are in all things equal to one another."—"I do not wonder," said he, "that it appears so to you, since you have no notion, or at least no right one, of such a constitution: but if you had been in Utopia with me, and had seen their laws and rules, as I did, for the space of five years, in which I lived among them; and during which time I was so delighted with them, that indeed I should never have left them, if it had not been to make the discovery of that new world to the Europeans; you would then confess that you had never seen a people so well constituted as they,"—"You will not easily persuade me," said Peter, "that any nation in that new world is better governed than those among us. For as our understandings are not worse than theirs, so our government, if I mistake not, being more ancient, a long practice has helped us to find out many conveniences of life: and some happy chances have discovered other things to us, which no man's understanding could ever have invented."—"As for the antiquity, either of their government, or of ours," said he, "you cannot pass a true judgment of it, unless you had read their histories; for if they are to be believed, they had towns among them before these parts were so much as inhabited. And as for those discoveries, that have been either hit on by chance, or made by ingenious men, these might have happened there as well as here. I do not deny but we are more ingenious than they are, but they exceed us much in industry and application. They knew little concerning us before our arrival among them; they call us all by a general name of the nations that lie beyond the Equinoctial Line; for their Chronicle mentions a shipwreck that was made on their coast 1,200 years ago; and that some Romans and Egyptians that were in the ship, getting safe ashore, spent the rest of their days amongst them; and such was their ingenuity, that from this single opportunity they drew the advantage of learning from those unlooked-for guests, and acquired all the useful arts that were then among the Romans, and which were known to these shipwrecked men: and by the hints that they gave them, they themselves found out even some of those arts which they could not fully explain; so happily did they improve that accident, of having some of our people cast upon their shore. But if such an accident has at any time brought any from thence into Europe, we have been so far from improving it, that we do not so much as remember it; as in after-times perhaps it will be forgot by our people that I was ever there. For though they from one such accident made themselves masters of all the good inventions that were among us; yet I believe it would be long before we should learn or put in practice any of the good institutions that are among them. And this is the true cause of their being better governed, and living happier than we, though we come not short of them in point of understanding or outward advantages."—Upon this I said to him, "I earnestly beg you would describe that island very particularly to us. Be not too short, but set out in order all things relating to their soil, their rivers, their towns, their people, their manners, constitution, laws, and, in a word, all that you imagine we desire to know. And you may well imagine that we desire to know everything concerning them, of which we are hitherto ignorant."—"I will do it very willingly," said he, "for I have digested the whole matter carefully; but it will take up some time,"—"Let us go then," said I, "first and dine, and then we shall have leisure enough." He consented. We went in and dined, and after dinner came back, and sat down in the same place. I ordered my servants to take care that none might come and interrupt us. And both Peter and I desired Raphael to be as good as his word. When he saw that we were very intent upon it, he paused a little to recollect himself, and began in this manner.

BOOK II.

The island of Utopia is in the middle two hundred miles broad, and holds almost at the same breadth over a great part of it; but it grows narrower towards both ends. Its figure is not unlike a crescent: between its horns, the sea comes in eleven miles broad, and spreads itself into a great bay, which is environed with land to the compass of about five hundred miles, and is well secured from winds. In this bay there is no great current, the whole coast is, as it were, one continued harbour, which gives all that live in the island great convenience for mutual commerce; but the entry into the bay, occasioned by rocks on the one hand, and shallows on the other, is very dangerous. In the middle of it there is one single rock which appears above water, and may therefore be easily avoided, and on the top of it there is a tower in which a garrison is kept, the other rocks lie under water, and are very dangerous. The channel is known only to the natives, so that if any stranger should enter into the bay, without one of their pilots, he would run great danger of shipwreck; for even they themselves could not pass it safe, if some marks that are on the coast did not direct their way; and if these should be but a little shifted, any fleet that might come against them, how great soever it were, would be certainly lost. On the other side of the island there are likewise many harbours; and the coast is so fortified, both by nature and art, that a small number of men can hinder the descent of a great army. But they report (and there remains good marks of it to make it credible) that this was no island at first, but a part of the continent. Utopus that conquered it (whose name it still carries, for Abraxa was its first name) brought the rude and uncivilized inhabitants into such a good government, and to that measure of politeness, that they now far excel all the rest of mankind; having soon subdued them, he designed to separate them from the continent, and to bring the sea quite round them. To accomplish this, he ordered a deep channel to be dug fifteen miles long; and that the natives might not think he treated them like slaves, he not only forced the inhabitants, but also his own soldiers, to labour in carrying it on. As he set a vast number of men to work, he beyond all men's expectations brought it to a speedy conclusion. And his neighbours who at first laughed at the folly of the undertaking, no sooner saw it brought to perfection, than they were struck with admiration and terror.

There are fifty-four cities in the island, all large and well built: the manners, customs, and laws of which are the same, and they are all contrived as near in the same manner as the ground on which they stand will allow. The nearest lie at least twenty-four miles distance from one another, and the most remote are not so far distant, but that a man can go on foot in one day from it, to that which lies next it. Every city sends three of their wisest senators once a year to Amaurot, to consult about their common concerns; for that is chief town of the island, being situated near the centre of it, so that it is the most convenient place for their assemblies. The jurisdiction of every city extends at least twenty miles: and where the towns lie wider, they have much more ground: no town desires to enlarge its bounds, for the people consider themselves rather as tenants than landlords. They have built over all the country, farmhouses for husbandmen, which are well contrived, and are furnished with all things necessary for country labour. Inhabitants are sent by turns from the cities to dwell in them; no country family has fewer than forty men and women in it, besides two slaves. There is a master and a mistress set over every family; and over thirty families there is a magistrate. Every year twenty of this family come back to the town, after they have stayed two years in the country; and in their room there are other twenty sent from the town, that they may learn country work from those that have been already one year in the country, as they must teach those that come to them the next from the town. By this means such as dwell in those country farms are never ignorant of agriculture, and so commit no errors, which might otherwise be fatal, and bring them under a scarcity of corn. But though there is every year such a shifting of the husbandmen, to prevent any man being forced against his will to follow that hard course of life too long; yet many among them take such pleasure in it, that they desire leave to continue in it many years. These husbandmen till the ground, breed cattle, hew wood, and convey it to the towns, either by land or water, as is most convenient. They breed an infinite multitude of chickens in a very curious manner; for the hens do not sit and hatch them, but vast number of eggs are laid in a gentle and equal heat, in order to be hatched, and they are no sooner out of the shell, and able to stir about, but they seem to consider those that feed them as their mothers, and follow them as other chickens do the hen that hatched them. They breed very few horses, but those they have are full of mettle, and are kept only for exercising their youth in the art of sitting and riding them; for they do not put them to any work, either of ploughing or carriage, in which they employ oxen; for though their horses are stronger, yet they find oxen can hold out longer; and as they are not subject to so many diseases, so they are kept upon a less charge, and with less trouble; and even when they are so worn out, that they are no more fit for labour, they are good meat at last. They sow no corn, but that which is to be their bread; for they drink either wine, cyder, or perry, and often water, sometimes boiled with honey or liquorice, with which they abound; and though they know exactly how much corn will serve every town, and all that tract of country which belongs to it, yet they sow much more, and breed more cattle than are necessary for their consumption; and they give that overplus of which they make no use to their neighbours. When they want anything in the country which it does not produce, they fetch that from the town, without carrying anything in exchange for it. And the magistrates of the town take care to see it given them; for they meet generally in the town once a month, upon a festival day. When the time of harvest comes, the magistrates in the country send to those in the towns, and let them know how many hands they will need for reaping the harvest; and the number they call for being sent to them, they commonly despatch it all in one day.

OF THEIR TOWNS, PARTICULARLY OF AMAUROT.

He that knows one of their towns, knows them all, they are so like one another, except where the situation makes some difference. I shall therefore describe one of them; and none is so proper as Amaurot; for as none is more eminent, all the rest yielding in precedence to this, because it is the seat of their supreme council; so there was none of them better known to me, I having lived five years altogether in it.

It lies upon the side of a hill, or rather a rising ground: its figure is almost square, for from the one side of it, which shoots up almost to the top of the hill, it runs down in a descent for two miles to the river Anider; but it is a little broader the other way that runs along by the bank of that river. The Anider rises about eighty miles above Amaurot in a small spring at first; but other brooks falling into it, of which two are more considerable than the rest. As it runs by Amaurot, it is grown half a mile broad; but it still grows larger and larger, till after sixty miles course below it, it is lost in the ocean, between the town and the sea, and for some miles above the town, it ebbs and flows every six hours, with a strong current. The tide comes up for about thirty miles so full, that there is nothing but salt water in the river, the fresh water being driven back with its force; and above that, for some miles, the water is brackish; but a little higher, as it runs by the town, it is quite fresh; and when the tide ebbs, it continues fresh all along to the sea. There is a bridge cast over the river, not of timber, but of fair stone, consisting of many stately arches; it lies at that part of the town which is farthest from the sea, so that ships without any hindrance lie all along the side of the town. There is likewise another river that runs by it, which though it is not great, yet it runs pleasantly, for it rises out of the same hill on which the town stands, and so runs down through it, and falls into the Anider. The inhabitants have fortified the fountain-head of this river, which springs a little without the towns; that so if they should happen to be besieged, the enemy might not be able to stop or divert the course of the water, nor poison it; from thence it is carried in earthen pipes to the lower streets; and for those places of the town to which the water of that small river cannot be conveyed, they have great cisterns for receiving the rain-water, which supplies the want of the other. The town is compassed with a high and thick wall, in which there are many towers and forts; there is also a broad and deep dry ditch, set thick with thorns, cast round three sides of the town, and the river is instead of a ditch on the fourth side. The streets are very convenient for all carriage, and are well sheltered from the winds. Their buildings are good, and are so uniform, that a whole side of a street looks like one house. The streets are twenty feet broad; there lie gardens behind all their houses; these are large but enclosed with buildings, that on all hands face the streets; so that every house has both a door to the street, and a back door to the garden. Their doors have all two leaves, which, as they are easily opened, so they shut of their own accord; and there being no property among them, every man may freely enter into any house whatsoever. At every ten years end they shift their houses by lots. They cultivate their gardens with great care, so that they have both vines, fruits, herbs, and flowers in them; and all is so well ordered, and so finely kept, that I never saw gardens anywhere that were both so fruitful and so beautiful as theirs. And this humour of ordering their gardens so well, is not only kept up by the pleasure they find in it, but also by an emulation between the inhabitants of the several streets, who vie with each other; and there is indeed nothing belonging to the whole town that is both more useful and more pleasant. So that he who founded the town, seems to have taken care of nothing more than of their gardens; for they say, the whole scheme of the town was designed at first by Utopus, but he left all that belonged to the ornament and improvement of it, to be added by those that should come after him, that being too much for one man to bring to perfection. Their records, that contain the history of their town and state, are preserved with an exact care, and run backwards 1,760 years. From these it appears that their houses were at first low and mean, like cottages, made of any sort of timber, and were built with mud walls and thatched with straw. But now their houses are three stories high: the fronts of them are faced either with stone, plastering, or brick; and between the facings of their walls they throw in their rubbish. Their roofs are flat, and on them they lay a sort of plaster, which costs very little, and yet is so tempered that it is not apt to take fire, and yet resists the weather more than lead. They have great quantities of glass among them, with which they glaze their windows. They use also in their windows a thin linen cloth, that is so oiled or gummed that it both keeps out the wind and gives free admission to the light.

OF THEIR MAGISTRATES.

Thirty families choose every year a magistrate, who was anciently called the Syphogrant, but is now called the Philarch; and over every ten Syphogrants, with the families subject to them, there is another magistrate, who was anciently called the Tranibor, but of late the Archphilarch. All the Syphogrants, who are in number 200, choose the Prince out of a list of four, who are named by the people of the four divisions of the city; but they take an oath before they proceed to an election, that they will choose him whom they think most fit for the office. They give their voices secretly, so that it is not known for whom every one gives his suffrage. The Prince is for life, unless he is removed upon suspicion of some design to enslave the people. The Tranibors are new chosen every year, but yet they are for the most part continued. All their other magistrates are only annual. The Tranibors meet every third day, and oftener if necessary, and consult with the Prince, either concerning the affairs of the state in general, or such private differences as may arise sometimes among the people; though that falls out but seldom. There are always two Syphogrants called into the council-chamber, and these are changed every day. It is a fundamental rule of their government, that no conclusion can be made in anything that relates to the public, till it has been first debated three several days in their council. It is death for any to meet and consult concerning the state, unless it be either in their ordinary council, or in the assembly of the whole body of the people.

These things have been so provided among them, that the Prince and the Tranibors may not conspire together to change the government, and enslave the people; and therefore when anything of great importance is set on foot, it is sent to the Syphogrants; who after they have communicated it to the families that belong to their divisions, and have considered it among themselves, make report to the senate; and upon great occasions, the matter is referred to the council of the whole island. One rule observed in their council, is, never to debate a thing on the same day in which it is first proposed; for that is always referred to the next meeting, that so men may not rashly, and in the heat of discourse, engage themselves too soon, which might bias them so much, that instead of consulting the good of the public, they might rather study to support their first opinions, and by a perverse and preposterous sort of shame, hazard their country rather than endanger their own reputation, or venture the being suspected to have wanted foresight in the expedients that they at first proposed. And therefore to prevent this, they take care that they may rather be deliberate than sudden in their motions.

OF THEIR TRADES, AND MANNER OF LIFE.

Agriculture is that which is so universally understood among them, that no person, either man or woman, is ignorant of it; they are instructed in it from their childhood, partly by what they learn at school, and partly by practice; they being led out often into the fields, about the town, where they not only see others at work, but are likewise exercised in it themselves. Besides agriculture, which is so common to them all, every man has some peculiar trade to which he applies himself, such as the manufacture of wool, or flax, masonry, smith's work, or carpenter's work; for there is no sort of trade that is in great esteem among them. Throughout the island they wear the same sort of clothes without any other distinction, except what is necessary to distinguish the two sexes, and the married and unmarried. The fashion never alters; and as it is neither disagreeable nor uneasy, so it is suited to the climate, and calculated both for their summers and winters. Every family makes their own clothes; but all among them, women as well men, learn one or other of the trades formerly mentioned. Women, for the most part, deal in wool and flax, which suit best with their weakness, leaving the ruder trades to the men. The same trade generally passes down from father to son, inclinations often following descent; but if any man's genius lies another way, he is by adoption translated into a family that deals in the trade to which he is inclined: and when that is to be done, care is taken not only by his father, but by the magistrate, that he may be put to a discreet and good man. And if after a person has learned one trade, he desires to acquire another, that is also allowed, and is managed in the same manner as the former. When he has learned both, he follows that which he likes best, unless the public has more occasion for the other.

The chief, and almost the only business of the Syphogrants, is to take care that no man may live idle, but that every one may follow his trade diligently: yet they do not wear themselves out with perpetual toil, from morning to night, as if they were beasts of burden, which as it is indeed a heavy slavery, so it is everywhere the common course of life amongst all mechanics except the Utopians; but they dividing the day and night into twenty-four hours, appoint six of these for work; three of which are before dinner; and three after. They then sup, and at eight o'clock, counting from noon, go to bed and sleep eight hours. The rest of their time besides that taken up in work, eating and sleeping, is left to every man's discretion; yet they are not to abuse that interval to luxury and idleness, but must employ it in some proper exercise according to their various inclinations, which is for the most part reading. It is ordinary to have public lectures every morning before daybreak; at which none are obliged to appear but those who are marked out for literature; yet a great many, both men and women of all ranks, go to hear lectures of one sort or other, according to their inclinations. But if others, that are not made for contemplation, choose rather to employ themselves at that time in their trades, as many of them do, they are not hindered, but are rather commended, as men that take care to serve their country. After supper, they spend an hour in some diversion, in summer in their gardens, and in winter in the halls where they eat; where they entertain each other, either with music or discourse. They do not so much as know dice, or any such foolish and mischievous games: they have, however, two sorts of games not unlike our chess; the one is between several numbers, in which one number, as it were, consumes another: the other resembles a battle between the virtues and the vices, in which the enmity in the vices among themselves, and their agreement against virtue, is not unpleasantly represented; together with the special oppositions between the particular virtues and vices; as also the methods by which vice either openly assaults or secretly undermines virtue; and virtue on the other hand resists it. But the time appointed for labour is to be narrowly examined, otherwise you may imagine, that since there are only six hours appointed for work, they may fall under a scarcity of necessary provisions. But it is so far from being true, that this time is not sufficient for supplying them with plenty of all things, either necessary or convenient; that it is rather too much; and this you will easily apprehend, if you consider how great a part of all other nations is quite idle. First, women generally do little, who are the half of mankind; and if some few women are diligent, their husbands are idle: then consider the great company of idle priests, and of those that are called religious men; add to these all rich men, chiefly those that have estates in land, who are called noblemen and gentlemen, together with their families, made up of idle persons, that are kept more for show than use; add to these, all those strong and lusty beggars, that go about pretending some disease, in excuse for their begging; and upon the whole account you will find that the number of those by whose labours mankind is supplied, is much less than you perhaps imagined. Then consider how few of those that work are employed in labours that are of real service; for we who measure all things by money, give rise to many trades that are both vain and superfluous, and serve only to support riot and luxury. For if those who work were employed only in such things as the conveniences of life require, there would be such an abundance of them, that the prices of them would so sink, that tradesmen could not be maintained by their gains; if all those who labour about useless things, were set to more profitable employments, and if all they that languish out their lives in sloth and idleness, every one of whom consumes as much as any two of the men that are at work, were forced to labour, you may easily imagine that a small proportion of time would serve for doing all that is either necessary, profitable, or pleasant to mankind, especially while pleasure is kept within its due bounds. This appears very plainly in Utopia, for there, in a great city, and in all the territory that lies round it, you can scarce find five hundred, either men or women, by their age and strength, are capable of labour, that are not engaged in it; even the Syphogrants, though excused by the law, yet do not excuse themselves, but work, that by their examples they may excite the industry of the rest of the people. The like exemption is allowed to those, who being recommended to the people by the priests, are by the secret suffrages of the Syphogrants privileged from labour, that they may apply themselves wholly to study; and if any of these fall short of those hopes that they seemed at first to give, they are obliged to return to work. And sometimes a mechanic, that so employs his leisure hours, as to make a considerable advancement in learning, is eased from being a tradesman, and ranked among their learned men. Out of these they choose their ambassadors, their priests, their Tranibors, and the Prince himself; anciently called their Barzenes, but is called of late their Ademus.

And thus from the great numbers among them that are neither suffered to be idle, nor to be employed in any fruitless labour, you may easily make the estimate how much may be done in those few hours in which they are obliged to labour. But besides all that has been already said, it is to be considered that the needful arts among them are managed with less labour than anywhere else. The building or the repairing of houses among us employ many hands, because often a thriftless heir suffers a house that his father built to fall into decay, so that his successor must, at a great cost, repair that which he might have kept up with a small charge: it frequently happens, that the same house which one person built at a vast expense, is neglected by another, who thinks he has a more delicate sense of the beauties of architecture; and he suffering it to fall to ruin, builds another at no less charge. But among the Utopians, all things are so regulated that men very seldom build upon a new piece of ground; and are not only very quick in repairing their houses, but show their foresight in preventing their decay: so that their buildings are preserved very long, with but little labour; and thus the builders to whom that care belongs are often without employment, except the hewing of timber, and the squaring of stones, that the materials may be in readiness for raising a building very suddenly, when there is any occasion for it. As to their clothes, observe how little work is spent in them: while they are at labour, they are clothed with leather and skins, cast carelessly about them, which will last seven years; and when they appear in public they put on an upper garment, which hides the other; and these are all of one colour, and that is the natural colour of the wool. As they need less woollen cloth than is used anywhere else, so that which they make use of is much less costly. They use linen cloth more; but that is prepared with less labour, and they value cloth only by the whiteness of the linen, or the cleanness of the wool, without much regard to the fineness of the thread: while in other places, four or five upper garments of woollen cloth, of different colours, and as many vests of silk, will scarce serve one man; and while those that are nicer think ten too few, every man there is content with one, which very often serves him two years. Nor is there anything that can tempt a man to desire more; for if he had them, he would neither be the warmer, nor would he make one jot the better appearance for it. And thus, since they are all employed in some useful labour, and since they content themselves with fewer things, it falls out that there is a great abundance of all things among them: so that it frequently happens, that for want of other work, vast numbers are sent out to mend the highways. But when no public undertaking is to be performed, the hours of working are lessened. The magistrates never engage the people in unnecessary labour, since the chief end of the constitution is to regulate labour by the necessities of the public, and to allow all the people as much time as is necessary for the improvement of their minds, in which they think the happiness of life consists.

OF THEIR TRAFFIC.

But it is now time to explain to you the mutual intercourse of this people, their commerce, and the rules by which all things are distributed among them.

As their cities are composed of families, so their families are made up of those that are nearly related to one another. Their women, when they grow up, are married out; but all the males, both children and grandchildren, live still in the same house, in great obedience to their common parent, unless age has weakened his understanding; and in that case, he that is next to him in age comes in his room. But lest any city should become either too great, or by any accident be dispeopled, provision is made that none of their cities may contain above six thousand families, besides those of the country round it. No family may have less than ten, and more than sixteen persons in it; but there can be no determined number for the children under age. This rule is easily observed, by removing some of the children of a more fruitful couple to any other family that does not abound so much in them. By the same rule, they supply cities that do not increase so fast, from others that breed faster; and if there is any increase over the whole island, then they draw out a number of their citizens out of the several towns, and send them over to the neighbouring continent; where, if they find that the inhabitants have more soil than they can well cultivate, they fix a colony, taking the inhabitants into their society, if they are willing to live with them; and where they do that of their own accord, they quickly enter into their method of life, and conform to their rules, and this proves a happiness to both nations: for according to their constitution, such care is taken of the soil, that it becomes fruitful enough for both, though it might be otherwise too narrow and barren for any one of them. But if the natives refuse to conform themselves to their laws, they drive them out of those bounds which they mark out for themselves, and use force if they resist. For they account it a very just cause of war, for a nation to hinder others from possessing a part of that soil, of which they make no use, but which is suffered to lie idle and uncultivated; since every man has by the law of Nature a right to such a waste portion of the earth as is necessary for his subsistence. If an accident has so lessened the number of the inhabitants of any of their towns, that it cannot be made up from the other towns of the island, without diminishing them too much, which is said to have fallen out but twice since they were first a people, when great numbers were carried off by the plague; the loss is then supplied by recalling as many as are wanted from their colonies; for they will abandon these, rather than suffer the towns in the island to sink too low.

But to return to their manner of living in society, the oldest man of every family, as has been already said, is its governor. Wives serve their husbands, and children their parents, and always the younger serves the elder. Every city is divided into four equal parts, and in the middle of each there is a market-place: what is brought thither, and manufactured by the several families, is carried from thence to houses appointed for that purpose, in which all things of a sort are laid by themselves; and thither every father goes and takes whatsoever he or his family stand in need of, without either paying for it, or leaving anything in exchange. There is no reason for giving a denial to any person, since there is such plenty of everything among them; and there is no danger of a man's asking for more than he needs; they have no inducements to do this, since they are sure that they shall always be supplied. It is the fear of want that makes any of the whole race of animals either greedy or ravenous; but besides fear, there is in man a pride that makes him fancy it a particular glory to excel others in pomp and excess. But by the laws of the Utopians, there is no room for this. Near these markets there are others for all sorts of provisions, where there are not only herbs, fruits, and bread, but also fish, fowl, and cattle. There are also, without their towns, places appointed near some running water, for killing their beasts, and for washing away their filth; which is done by their slaves: for they suffer none of their citizens to kill their cattle, because they think that pity and good-nature, which are among the best of those affections that are born with us, are much impaired by the butchering of animals: nor do they suffer anything that is foul or unclean to be brought within their towns, lest the air should be infected by ill smells which might prejudice their health. In every street there are great halls that lie at an equal distance from each other, distinguished by particular names. The Syphogrants dwell in those that are set over thirty families, fifteen lying on one side of it, and as many on the other. In these halls they all meet and have their repasts. The stewards of every one of them come to the market-place at an appointed hour; and according to the number of those that belong to the hall, they carry home provisions. But they take more care of their sick than of any others: these are lodged and provided for in public hospitals: they have belonging to every town four hospitals, that are built without their walls, and are so large that they may pass for little towns: by this means, if they had ever such a number of sick persons, they could lodge them conveniently, and at such a distance, that such of them as are sick of infectious diseases may be kept so far from the rest that there can be no danger of contagion. The hospitals are furnished and stored with all things that are convenient for the ease and recovery of the sick; and those that are put in them are looked after with such tender and watchful care, and are so constantly attended by their skilful physicians, that as none is sent to them against their will, so there is scarce one in a whole town that, if he should fall ill, would not choose rather to go thither than lie sick at home.

After the steward of the hospitals has taken for the sick whatsoever the physician prescribes, then the best things that are left in the market are distributed equally among the halls, in proportion to their numbers, only, in the first place, they serve the

Prince, the chief priest, the Tranibors, the ambassadors, and strangers, if there are any, which indeed falls out but seldom, and for whom there are houses well furnished, particularly appointed for their reception when they come among them. At the hours of dinner and supper, the whole Syphogranty being called together by sound of trumpet, they meet and eat together, except only such as are in the hospitals, or lie sick at home. Yet after the halls are served, no man is hindered to carry provisions home from the market-place; for they know that none does that but for some good reason; for though any that will may eat at home, yet none does it willingly, since it is both ridiculous and foolish for any to give themselves the trouble to make ready an ill dinner at home, when there is a much more plentiful one made ready for him so near hand. All the uneasy and sordid services about these halls are performed by their slaves; but the dressing and cooking their meat, and the ordering their tables, belong only to the women, all those of every family taking it by turns. They sit at three or more tables, according to their number; the men sit towards the wall, and the women sit on the other side, that if any of them should be taken suddenly ill, which is no uncommon case amongst women with child, she may, without disturbing the rest, rise and go to the nurse's room, who are there with the sucking children; where there is always clean water at hand, and cradles in which they may lay the young children, if there is occasion for it, and a fire that they may shift and dress them before it. Every child is nursed by its own mother, if death or sickness does not intervene; and in that case the Syphogrants' wives find out a nurse quickly, which is no hard matter; for any one that can do it, offers herself cheerfully; for as they are much inclined to that piece of mercy, so the child whom they nurse considers the nurse as its mother. All the children under five years old sit among the nurses, the rest of the younger sort of both sexes, till they are fit for marriage, either serve those that sit at table; or if they are not strong enough for that, stand by them in great silence, and eat what is given them; nor have they any other formality of dining. In the middle of the first table, which stands across the upper end of the hall, sit the

Syphogrant and his wife; for that is the chief and most conspicuous place; next to him sit two of the most ancient, for there go always four to a mess. If there is a temple within that Syphogranty, the priest and his wife sit with the Syphogrant above all the rest: next them there is a mixture of old and young, who are so placed, that as the young are set near others, so they are mixed with the more ancient; which they say was appointed on this account, that the gravity of the old people, and the reverence that is due to them, might restrain the younger from all indecent words and gestures. Dishes are not served up to the whole table at first, but the best are first set before the old, whose seats are distinguished from the young, and after them all the rest are served alike. The old men distribute to the younger any curious meats that happen to be set before them, if there is not such an abundance of them that the whole company may be served alike.

Thus old men are honoured with a particular respect; yet all the rest fare as well as they. Both dinner and supper are begun with some lecture of morality that is read to them; but it is so short, that it is not tedious nor uneasy to them to hear it: from hence the old men take occasion to entertain those about them, with some useful and pleasant enlargements; but they do not engross the whole discourse so to themselves, during their meals, that the younger may not put in for a share: on the contrary, they engage them to talk, that so they may in that free way of conversation find out the force of every one's spirit, and observe his temper. They despatch their dinners quickly, but sit long at supper; because they go to work after the one, and are to sleep after the other, during which they think the stomach carries on the concoction more vigorously. They never sup without music; and there is always fruit served up after meat; while they are at table, some burn perfumes, and sprinkle about fragrant ointments and sweet waters: in short, they want nothing that may cheer up their spirits: they give themselves a large allowance that way, and indulge themselves in all such pleasures as are attended with no inconvenience. Thus do those that are in the towns live together;

but in the country, where they live at great distance, every one eats at home, and no family wants any necessary sort of provision, for it is from them that provisions are sent unto those that live in the towns.

OF THE TRAVELLING OF THE UTOPIANS.

If any man has a mind to visit his friends that live in some other town, or desires to travel and see the rest of the country, he obtains leave very easily from the Syphogrant and Tranibors, when there is no particular occasion for him at home: such as travel, carry with them a passport from the Prince, which both certifies the license that is granted for travelling, and limits the time of their return. They are furnished with a waggon and a slave, who drives the oxen, and looks after them: but unless there are women in the company, the waggon is sent back at the end of the journey as a needless encumbrance: while they are on the road, they carry no provisions with them; yet they want nothing, but are everywhere treated as if they were at home. If they stay in any place longer than a night, every one follows his proper occupation, and is very well used by those of his own trade: but if any man goes out of the city to which he belongs, without leave, and is found rambling without a passport, he is severely treated, he is punished as a fugitive, and sent home disgracefully; and if he falls again into the like fault, is condemned to slavery. If any man has a mind to travel only over the precinct of his own city, he may freely do it, with his father's permission and his wife's consent; but when he comes into any of the country houses, if he expects to be entertained by them, he must labour with them and conform to their rules: and if he does this, he may freely go over the whole precinct; being thus as useful to the city to which he belongs, as if he were still within it. Thus you see that there are no idle persons among them, nor pretences of excusing any from labour. There are no taverns, no alehouses nor stews among them; nor any other occasions of corrupting each other, of getting into corners, or forming themselves into parties: all men live in full view, so that all are obliged, both to perform their ordinary task, and to employ themselves well in their spare hours. And it is certain that a people thus ordered must live in great abundance of all things; and these being equally distributed among them, no man can want, or be obliged to beg.

In their great council at Amaurot, to which there are three sent from every town once a year, they examine what towns abound in provisions, and what are under any scarcity, that so the one may be furnished from the other; and this is done freely, without any sort of exchange; for according to their plenty or scarcity, they supply, or are supplied from one another; so that indeed the whole island is, as it were, one family. When they have thus taken care of their whole country, and laid up stores for two years, which they do to prevent the ill consequences of an unfavourable season, they order an exportation of the overplus, both of corn, honey, wool, flax, wood, wax, tallow, leather, and cattle; which they send out commonly in great quantities to other nations. They order a seventh part of all these goods to be freely given to the poor of the countries to which they send them, and sell the rest at moderate rates. And by this exchange, they not only bring back those few things that they need at home (for indeed they scarce need anything but iron), but likewise a great deal of gold and silver; and by their driving this trade so long, it is not to be imagined how vast a treasure they have got among them: so that now they do not much care whether they sell off their merchandise for money in hand, or upon trust. A great part of their treasure is now in bonds; but in all their contracts no private man stands bound, but the writing runs in the name of the town; and the towns that owe them money, raise it from those private hands that owe it to them, lay it up in their public chamber, or enjoy the profit of it till the Utopians call for it; and they choose rather to let the greatest part of it lie in their hands who make advantage by it, than to call for it themselves: but if they see that any of their other neighbours stand more in need of it, then they call it in and lend it to them: whenever they are engaged in war, which is the only occasion in which their treasure can be usefully employed, they make use of it themselves. In great extremities or sudden accidents they employ it in hiring foreign troops, whom they more willingly expose to danger than their own people: they give them great pay, knowing well that this will work even on their enemies, that it will engage them either to betray their own side, or at least to desert it, and that it is the best means of raising mutual jealousies among them: for this end they have an incredible treasure; but they do not keep it as a treasure, but in such a manner as I am almost afraid to tell, lest you think it so extravagant, as to be hardly credible. This I have the more reason to apprehend, because if I had not seen it myself, I could not have been easily persuaded to have believed it upon any man's report.

It is certain that all things appear incredible to us, in proportion as they differ from own customs. But one who can judge aright, will not wonder to find, that since their constitution differs so much from ours, their value of gold and silver should be measured by a very different standard; for since they have no use for money among themselves, but keep it as a provision against events which seldom happen, and between which there are generally long intervening intervals; they value it no farther than it deserves, that is, in proportion to its use. So that it is plain, they must prefer iron either to gold or silver: for men can no more live without iron, than without fire or water; but Nature has marked out no use for the other metals, so essential as not easily to be dispensed with. The folly of men has enhanced the value of gold and silver, because of their scarcity. Whereas, on the contrary, it is their opinion that Nature, as an indulgent parent, has freely given us all the best things in great abundance, such as water and earth, but has laid up and hid from us the things that are vain and useless.

If these metals were laid up in any tower in the kingdom, it would raise a jealousy of the Prince and Senate, and give birth to that foolish mistrust into which the people are apt to fall, a jealousy of their intending to sacrifice the interest of the public to their own private advantage. If they should work it into vessels, or any sort of plate, they fear that the people might grow too fond of it, and so be unwilling to let the plate be run down, if a war made it necessary to employ it in paying their soldiers. To prevent all these inconveniences, they have fallen upon an expedient, which as it agrees with their other policy, so is it very different from ours, and will scarce gain belief among us, who value gold so much, and lay it up so carefully. They eat and drink out of vessels of earth, or glass, which make an agreeable appearance though formed of brittle materials: while they make their chamber-pots and close-stools of gold and silver; and that not only in their public halls, but in their private houses: of the same metals they likewise make chains and fetters for their slaves; to some of which, as a badge of infamy, they hang an ear-ring of gold, and make others wear a chain or a coronet of the same metal; and thus they take care, by all possible means, to render gold and silver of no esteem. And from hence it is, that while other nations part with their gold and silver, as unwillingly as if one tore out their bowels, those of Utopia would look on their giving in all they possess of those (metals, when there were any use for them) but as the parting with a trifle, or as we would esteem the loss of a penny. They find pearls on their coast; and diamonds and carbuncles on their rocks; they do not look after them, but if they find them by chance, they polish them, and with them they adorn their children, who are delighted with them, and glory in them during their childhood; but when they grow to years, and see that none but children use such baubles, they of their own accord, without being bid by their parents, lay them aside; and would be as much ashamed to use them afterwards, as children among us, when they come to years, are of their puppets and other toys.

I never saw a clearer instance of the opposite impressions that different customs make on people, than I observed in the ambassadors of the Anemolians, who came to Amaurot when I was there. As they came to treat of affairs of great consequence, the deputies from several towns met together to wait for their coming. The ambassadors of the nations that lie near Utopia, knowing their customs, and that fine clothes are in no esteem among them, that silk is despised, and gold is a badge of infamy, use to come very modestly clothed; but the Anemolians lying more remote, and having had little commerce with them, understanding that they were coarsely clothed, and all in the same manner, took it for granted that they had none of those fine things among them of which they made no use; and they being a vain-glorious rather than a wise people, resolved to set themselves out with so much pomp, that they should look like gods, and strike the eyes of the poor Utopians with their splendour. Thus three ambassadors made their entry with an hundred attendants, all clad in garments of different colours, and the greater part in silk; the ambassadors themselves, who were of the nobility of their country, were in cloth of gold, and adorned with massy chains, ear-rings and rings of gold: their caps were covered with bracelets set full of pearls and other gems: in a word, they were set out with all those things that, among the Utopians, were either the badges of slavery, the marks of infamy, or the playthings of children. It was not unpleasant to see, on the one side, how they looked big, when they compared their rich habits with the plain clothes of the Utopians, who were come out in great numbers to see them make their entry: and, on the other, to observe how much they were mistaken in the impression which they hoped this pomp would have made on them. It appeared so ridiculous a show to all that had never stirred out of their country, and had not seen the customs of other nations, that though they paid some reverence to those that were the most meanly clad, as if they had been the ambassadors, yet when they saw the ambassadors themselves, so full of gold and chains, they looked upon them as slaves, and forbore to treat them with reverence. You might have seen the children, who were grown big enough to despise their playthings, and who had thrown away their jewels, call to their mothers, push them gently, and cry out, "See that great fool that wears pearls and gems, as if he were yet a child." While their mothers very innocently replied, "Hold your peace, this I believe is one of the ambassador's fools." Others censured the fashion of their chains, and observed that they were of no use; for they were too slight to bind their slaves, who could easily break them; and besides hung so loose about them, that they thought it easy to throw them away, and so get from them. But after the ambassadors had stayed a day among them, and saw so vast a quantity of gold in their houses, which was as much despised by them as it was esteemed in other nations, and beheld more gold and silver in the chains and fetters of one slave than all their ornaments amounted to, their plumes fell, and they were ashamed of all that glory for which they had formerly valued themselves, and accordingly laid it aside; a resolution that they immediately took, when on their engaging in some free discourse with the Utopians, they discovered their sense of such things and their other customs. The Utopians wonder how any man should be so much taken with the glaring doubtful lustre of a jewel or a stone, that can look up to a star, or to the sun himself; or how any should value himself because his cloth is made of a finer thread: for how fine soever that thread may be, it was once no better than the fleece of a sheep, and that sheep was a sheep still for all its wearing it. They wonder much to hear that gold which in itself is so useless a thing, should be everywhere so much esteemed, that even men for whom it was made, and by whom it has its value, should yet be thought of less value than this metal. That a man of lead, who has no more sense than a log of wood, and is as bad as he is foolish, should have many wise and good men to serve him, only because he has a great heap of that metal; and that if it should happen that by some accident or trick of law (which sometimes produces as great changes as chance itself) all this wealth should pass from the master to the meanest varlet of his whole family, he himself would very soon become one of his servants, as if he were a thing that belonged to his wealth, and so were bound to follow its fortune. But they much more admire and detest the folly of those who when they see a rich man, though they neither owe him anything, nor are in any sort dependent on his bounty, yet merely because he is rich give him little less than divine honours; even though they know him to be so covetous and base-minded, that notwithstanding all his wealth, he will not part with one farthing of it to them as long as he lives.

These and such like notions has that people imbibed, partly from their education, being bred in a country whose customs and laws are opposite to all such foolish maxims, and partly from their learning and studies; for though there are but few in any town that are so wholly excused from labour as to give themselves entirely up to their studies, these being only such persons as discover from their childhood an extraordinary capacity and disposition for letters; yet their children, and a great part of the nation, both men and women, are taught to spend those hours in which they are not obliged to work in reading: and this they do through the whole progress of life. They have all their learning in their own tongue, which is both a copious and pleasant language, and in which a man can fully express his mind. It runs over a great tract of many countries, but it is not equally pure in all places. They had never so much as heard of the names of any of those philosophers that are so famous in these parts of the world, before we went among them; and yet they had made the same discoveries as the Greeks, both in music, logic, arithmetic, and geometry. But as they are almost in everything equal to the ancient philosophers, so they far exceed our modern logicians; for they have never yet fallen upon the barbarous niceties that our youth are forced to learn in those trifling logical schools that are among us; they are so far from minding chimeras, and fantastical images made in the mind, that none of them could comprehend what we meant when we talked to them of a man in the abstract, as common to all men in particular (so that though we spoke of him as a thing that we could point at with our fingers, yet none of them could perceive him), and yet distinct from every one, as if he were some monstrous Colossus or giant. Yet for all this ignorance of these empty notions, they knew astronomy, and were perfectly acquainted with the motions of the heavenly bodies, and have many instruments, well contrived and divided, by which they very accurately compute the course and positions of the sun, moon, and stars. But for the cheat, of divining by the stars by their oppositions or conjunctions, it has not so much as entered into their thoughts. They have a particular sagacity, founded upon much observation, in judging of the weather, by which they know when they may look for rain, wind, or other alterations in the air; but as to the philosophy of these things, the causes of the saltness of the sea, of its ebbing and flowing, and of the original and nature both of the heavens and the earth; they dispute of them, partly as our ancient philosophers have done, and partly upon some new hypothesis, in which, as they differ from them, so they do not in all things agree among themselves.

As to moral philosophy, they have the same disputes among them as we have here: they examine what are properly good both for the body and the mind, and whether any outward thing can be called truly good, or if that term belong only to the endowments of the soul. They inquire likewise into the nature of virtue and pleasure; but their chief dispute is concerning the happiness of a man, and wherein it consists? Whether in some one thing, or in a great many? They seem, indeed, more inclinable to that opinion that places, if not the whole, yet the chief part of a man's happiness in pleasure; and, what may seem more strange, they make use of arguments even from religion, notwithstanding its severity and roughness, for the support of that opinion so indulgent to pleasure; for they never dispute concerning happiness without fetching some arguments from the principles of religion, as well as from natural reason, since without the former they reckon that all our inquiries after happiness must be but conjectural and defective.

These are their religious principles, that the soul of man is immortal, and that God of His goodness has designed that it should be happy; and that He has therefore appointed rewards for good and virtuous actions, and punishments for vice, to be distributed after this life. Though these principles of religion are conveyed down among them by tradition, they think that even reason itself determines a man to believe and acknowledge them, and freely confess that if these were taken away no man would be so insensible as not to seek after pleasure by all possible means, lawful or unlawful; using only this caution, that a lesser pleasure might not stand in the way of a greater, and that no pleasure ought to be pursued that should draw a great deal of pain after it; for they think it the maddest thing in the world to pursue virtue, that is a sour and difficult thing; and not only to renounce the pleasures of life, but willingly to undergo much pain and trouble, if a man has no prospect of a reward. And what reward can there be for one that has passed his whole life, not only without pleasure, but in pain, if there is nothing to be expected after death? Yet they do not place happiness in all sorts of pleasures, but only in those that in themselves are good and honest. There is a party among them who place happiness in bare virtue; others think that our natures are conducted by virtue to happiness, as that which is the chief good of man. They define virtue thus, that it is a living according to Nature, and think that we are made by God for that end; they believe that a man then follows the dictates of Nature when he pursues or avoids things according to the direction of reason; they say that the first dictate of reason is the kindling in us a love and reverence for the Divine Majesty, to whom we owe both all that we have, and all that we can ever hope for. In the next place, reason directs us to keep our minds as free from passion and as cheerful as we can, and that we should consider ourselves as bound by the ties of good-nature and humanity to use our utmost endeavours to help forward the happiness of all other persons; for there never was any man such a morose and severe pursuer of virtue, such an enemy to pleasure, that though he set hard rules for men to undergo much pain, many watchings, and other rigours, yet did not at the same time advise them to do all they could, in order to relieve and ease the miserable, and who did not represent gentleness and good-nature as amiable dispositions. And from thence they infer that if a man ought to advance the welfare and comfort of the rest of mankind, there being no virtue more proper and peculiar to our nature, than to ease the miseries of others, to free from trouble and anxiety, in furnishing them with the comforts of life, in which pleasure consists, Nature much more vigorously leads them to do all this for himself. A life of pleasure is either a real evil, and in that case we ought not to assist others in their pursuit of it, but on the contrary, to keep them from it all we can, as from that which is most hurtful and deadly; or if it is a good thing, so that we not only may, but ought to help others to it, why then ought not a man to begin with himself? Since no man can be more bound to look after the good of another than after his own; for Nature cannot direct us to be good and kind to others, and yet at the same time to be unmerciful and cruel to ourselves. Thus, as they define virtue to be living according to Nature, so they imagine that Nature prompts all people on to seek after pleasure, as the end of all they do. They also observe that in order to our supporting the pleasures of life, Nature inclines us to enter into society; for there is no man so much raised above the rest of mankind as to be the only favourite of Nature, who, on the contrary, seems to have placed on a level all those that belong to the same species. Upon this they infer that no man ought to seek his own conveniences so eagerly as to prejudice others; and therefore they think that not only all agreements between private persons ought to be observed; but likewise that all those laws ought to be kept, which either a good prince has published in due form, or to which a people, that is neither oppressed with tyranny nor circumvented by fraud, has consented, for distributing those conveniences of life which afford us all our pleasures.

They think it is an evidence of true wisdom for a man to pursue his own advantages, as far as the laws allow it. They account it piety to prefer the public good to one's private concerns; but they think it unjust for a man to seek for pleasure, by snatching another man's pleasures from him. And on the contrary, they think it a sign of a gentle and good soul, for a man to dispense with his own advantage for the good of others; and that by this means a good man finds as much pleasure one way, as he parts with another; for as he may expect the like from others when he may come to need it, so if that should fail him, yet the sense of a good action, and the reflections that he makes on the love and gratitude of those whom he has so obliged, gives the mind more pleasure than the body could have found in that from which it had restrained itself. They are also persuaded that God will make up the loss of those small pleasures, with a vast and endless joy, of which religion easily convinces a good soul.

Thus upon an inquiry into the whole matter, they reckon that all our actions, and even all our virtues, terminate in pleasure, as in our chief end and greatest happiness; and they call every motion or state, either of body or mind, in which Nature teaches us to delight, a pleasure. Thus they cautiously limit pleasure only to those appetites to which Nature leads us; for they say that Nature leads us only to those delights to which reason as well as sense carries us, and by which we neither injure any other person, nor lose the possession of greater pleasures, and of such as draw no troubles after them; but they look upon those delights which men by a foolish, though common, mistake call pleasure, as if they could change as easily the nature of things as the use of words; as things that greatly obstruct their real happiness, instead of advancing it, because they so entirely possess the minds of those that are once captivated by them with a false notion of pleasure, that there is no room left for pleasures of a truer or purer kind.

There are many things that in themselves have nothing that is truly delightful; on the contrary, they have a good deal of bitterness in them; and yet from our perverse appetites after forbidden objects, are not only ranked among the pleasures, but are made even the greatest designs of life. Among those who pursue these sophisticated pleasures, they reckon such as I mentioned before, who think themselves really the better for having fine clothes; in which they think they are doubly mistaken, both in the opinion that they have of their clothes, and in that they have of themselves; for if you consider the use of clothes, why should a fine thread be thought better than a coarse one? And yet these men, as if they had some real advantages beyond others, and did not owe them wholly to their mistakes, look big, seem to fancy themselves to be more valuable, and imagine that a respect is due to them for the sake of a rich garment, to which they would not have pretended if they had been more meanly clothed; and even resent it as an affront, if that respect is not paid them. It is also a great folly to be taken with outward marks of respect, which signify nothing: for what true or real pleasure can one man find in another's standing bare, or making legs to him? Will the bending another man's knees give ease to yours? And will the head's being bare cure the madness of yours? And yet it is wonderful to see how this false notion of pleasure bewitches many who delight themselves with the fancy of their nobility, and are pleased with this conceit, that they are descended from ancestors, who have been held for some successions rich, and who have had great possessions; for this is all that makes nobility at present; yet they do not think themselves a whit the less noble, though their immediate parents have left none of this wealth to them, or though they themselves have squandered it away. The Utopians have no better opinion of those who are much taken with gems and precious stones, and who account it a degree of happiness, next to a divine one, if they can purchase one that is very extraordinary; especially if it be of that sort of stones that is then in greatest request; for the same sort is not at all times universally of the same value; nor will men buy it unless it be dismounted and taken out of the gold; the jeweller is then made to give good security, and required solemnly to swear that the stone is true, that by such an exact caution a false one might not be bought instead of a true: though if you were to examine it, your eye could find no difference between the counterfeit and that which is true; so that they are all one to you as much as if you were blind. Or can it be thought that they who heap up an useless mass of wealth, not for any use that it is to bring them, but merely to please themselves with the contemplation of it, enjoy any true pleasure in it? The delight they find is only a false shadow of joy. Those are no better whose error is somewhat different from the former, and who hide it, out of their fear of losing it; for what other name can fit the hiding it in the earth, or rather the restoring it to it again, it being thus cut off from being useful, either to its owner or to the rest of mankind? And yet the owner having hid it carefully, is glad, because he thinks he is now sure of it. If it should be stole, the owner, though he might live perhaps ten years after the theft, of which he knew nothing, would find no difference between his having or losing it; for both ways it was equally useless to him.

Among those foolish pursuers of pleasure, they reckon all that delight in hunting, in fowling, or gaming: of whose madness they have only heard, for they have no such things among them. But they have asked us, what sort of pleasure is it that men can find in throwing the dice? For if there were any pleasure in it, they think the doing of it so often should give one a surfeit of it: and what pleasure can one find in hearing the barking and howling of dogs, which seem rather odious than pleasant sounds? Nor can they comprehend the pleasure of seeing dogs run after a hare, more than of seeing one dog run after another; for if the seeing them run is that which gives the pleasure, you have the same entertainment to the eye on both these occasions; since that is the same in both cases: but if the pleasure lies in seeing the hare killed and torn by the dogs, this ought rather to stir pity, that a weak, harmless and fearful hare should be devoured by strong, fierce, and cruel dogs. Therefore all this business of hunting is, among the Utopians, turned over to their butchers; and those, as has been already said, are all slaves; and they look on hunting as one of the basest parts of a butcher's work: for they account it both more profitable and more decent to kill those beasts that are more necessary and useful to mankind; whereas the killing and tearing of so small and miserable an animal can only attract the huntsman with a false show of pleasure, from which he can reap but small advantage. They look on the desire of the bloodshed, even of beasts, as a mark of a mind that is already corrupted with cruelty, or that at least by the frequent returns of so brutal a pleasure must degenerate into it.

Thus, though the rabble of mankind look upon these, and on innumerable other things of the same nature, as pleasures; the Utopians, on the contrary, observing that there is nothing in them truly pleasant, conclude that they are not to be reckoned among pleasures: for though these things may create some tickling in the senses (which seems to be a true notion of pleasure), yet they imagine that this does not arise from the thing itself, but from a depraved custom, which may so vitiate a man's taste, that bitter things may pass for sweet; as women with child think pitch or tallow taste sweeter than honey; but as a man's sense when corrupted, either by a disease or some ill habit, does not change the nature of other things, so neither can it change the nature of pleasure.

They reckon up several sorts of pleasures, which they call true ones: some belong to the body and others to the mind. The pleasures of the mind lie in knowledge, and in that delight which the contemplation of truth carries with it; to which they add the joyful reflections on a well-spent life, and the assured hopes of a future happiness. They divide the pleasures of the body into two sorts; the one is that which gives our senses some real delight, and is performed, either by recruiting nature, and supplying those parts which feed the internal heat of life by eating and drinking; or when nature is eased of any surcharge that oppresses it; when we are relieved from sudden pain, or that which arises from satisfying the appetite which Nature has wisely given to lead us to the propagation of the species. There is another kind of pleasure that arises neither from our receiving what the body requires, nor its being relieved when overcharged, and yet by a secret, unseen virtue affects the senses, raises the passions, and strikes the mind with generous impressions; this is the pleasure that arises from music. Another kind of bodily pleasure is that which results from an undisturbed and vigorous constitution of body, when life and active spirits seem to actuate every part. This lively health, when entirely free from all mixture of pain, of itself gives an inward pleasure, independent of all external objects of delight; and though this pleasure does not so powerfully affect us, nor act so strongly on the senses as some of the others, yet it may be esteemed as the greatest of all pleasures, and almost all the Utopians reckon it the foundation and basis of all the other joys of life; since this alone makes the state of life easy and desirable; and when this is wanting, a man is really capable of no other pleasure. They look upon freedom from pain, if it does not rise from perfect health, to be a state of stupidity rather than of pleasure. This subject has been very narrowly canvassed among them; and it has been debated whether a firm and entire health could be called a pleasure or not? Some have thought that there was no pleasure but what was excited by some sensible motion in the body. But this opinion has been long ago excluded from among them, so that now they almost universally agree that health is the greatest of all bodily pleasures; and that as there is a pain in sickness, which is as opposite in its nature to pleasure as sickness itself is to health; so they hold, that health is accompanied with pleasure: and if any should say that sickness is not really pain, but that it only carries pain along with it, they look upon that as a fetch of subtilty, that does not much alter the matter. It is all one, in their opinion, whether it be said that health is in itself a pleasure, or that it begets a pleasure, as fire gives heat; so it be granted, that all those whose health is entire have a true pleasure in the enjoyment of it: and they reason thus—what is the pleasure of eating, but that a man's health which had been weakened, does, with the assistance of food, drive away hunger, and so recruiting itself recovers its former vigour? And being thus refreshed, it finds a pleasure in that conflict; and if the conflict is pleasure, the victory must yet breed a greater pleasure, except we fancy that it becomes stupid as soon as it has obtained that which it pursued, and so neither knows nor rejoices in its own welfare. If it is said that health cannot be felt, they absolutely deny it; for what man is in health that does not perceive it when he is awake? Is there any man that is so dull and stupid as not to acknowledge that he feels a delight in health? And what is delight but another name for pleasure?

But of all pleasures, they esteem those to be most valuable that lie in the mind; the chief of which arises out of true virtue, and the witness of a good conscience. They account health the chief pleasure that belongs to the body; for they think that the pleasure of eating and drinking, and all the other delights of sense, are only so far desirable as they give or maintain health. But they are not pleasant in themselves, otherwise than as they resist those impressions that our natural infirmities are still making upon us: for as a wise man desires rather to avoid diseases than to take physic; and to be freed from pain, rather than to find ease by remedies; so it is more desirable not to need this sort of pleasure, than to be obliged to indulge it. If any man imagines that there is a real happiness in these enjoyments, he must then confess that he would be the happiest of all men if he were to lead his life in perpetual hunger, thirst, and itching, and by consequence in perpetual eating, drinking, and scratching himself; which any one may easily see would be not only a base, but a miserable state of a life. These are indeed the lowest of pleasures, and the least pure; for we can never relish them, but when they are mixed with the contrary pains. The pain of hunger must give us the pleasure of eating; and here the pain out-balances the pleasure; and as the pain is more vehement, so it lasts much longer; for as it begins before the pleasure, so it does not cease but with the pleasure that extinguishes it, and both expire together. They think, therefore, none of those pleasures are to be valued any further than as they are necessary; yet they rejoice in them, and with due gratitude acknowledge the tenderness of the great Author of Nature, who has planted in us appetites, by which those things that are necessary for our preservation are likewise made pleasant to us. For how miserable a thing would life be, if those daily diseases of hunger and thirst were to be carried off by such bitter drugs as we must use for those diseases that return seldomer upon us? And thus these pleasant as well as proper gifts of Nature maintain the strength and the sprightliness of our bodies.

They also entertain themselves with the other delights let in at their eyes, their ears, and their nostrils, as the pleasant relishes and seasonings of life, which Nature seems to have marked out peculiarly for man; since no other sort of animals contemplates the figure and beauty of the universe; nor is delighted with smells, any farther than as they distinguish meats by them; not do they apprehend the concords or discords of sound; yet in all pleasures whatsoever they take care that a lesser joy does not hinder a greater, and that pleasure may never breed pain, which they think always follows dishonest pleasures. But they think it madness for a man to wear out the beauty of his face, or the force of his natural strength; to corrupt the sprightliness of his body by sloth and laziness, or to waste it by fasting; that it is madness to weaken the strength of his constitution, and reject the other delights of life; unless by renouncing his own satisfaction, he can either serve the public or promote the happiness of others, for which he expects a greater recompense from God. So that they look on such a course of life as the mark of a mind that is both cruel to itself, and ungrateful to the Author of Nature, as if we would not be beholden to Him for His favours, and therefore rejects all His blessings; as one who should afflict himself for the empty shadow of virtue; or for no better end than to render himself capable of bearing those misfortunes which possibly will never happen.

This is their notion of virtue and of pleasure; they think that no man's reason can carry him to a truer idea of them, unless some discovery from Heaven should inspire him with sublimer notions. I have not now the leisure to examine whether they think right or wrong in this matter: nor do I judge it necessary, for I have only undertaken to give you an account of their constitution, but not to defend all their principles. I am sure, that whatsoever may be said of their notions, there is not in the whole world either a better people or a happier government: their bodies are vigorous and lively; and though they are but of a middle stature, and have neither the fruitfullest soil nor the purest air in the world, yet they fortify themselves so well by their temperate course of life, against the unhealthiness of their air, and by their industry they so cultivate their soil, that there is nowhere to be seen a greater increase both of corn and cattle, nor are there anywhere healthier men, and freer from diseases: for one may there see reduced to practice, not only all the art that the husbandman employs in manuring and improving an ill soil, but whole woods plucked up by the roots, and in other places new ones planted, where there were none before. Their principal motive for this is the convenience of carriage, that their timber may be either near their towns, or growing on the banks of the sea, or of some rivers, so as to be floated to them; for it is a harder work to carry wood at any distance over land, than corn. The people are industrious, apt to learn, as well as cheerful and pleasant; and none can endure more labour, when it is necessary; but except in that case they love their ease. They are unwearied pursuers of knowledge; for when we had given them some hints of the learning and discipline of the Greeks, concerning whom we only instructed them (for we know that there was nothing among the Romans, except their historians and their poets, that they would value much), it was strange to see how eagerly they were set on learning that language. We began to read a little of it to them, rather in compliance with their importunity, than out of any hopes of their reaping from it any great advantage. But after a very short trial, we found they made such progress, that we saw our labour was like to be more successful than we could have expected. They learned to write their characters, and to pronounce their language so exactly, had so quick an apprehension, they remembered it so faithfully, and became so ready and correct in the use of it, that it would have looked like a miracle if the greater part of those whom we taught had not been men both of extraordinary capacity and of a fit age for instruction. They were for the greatest part chosen from among their learned men, by their chief council, though some studied it of their own accord. In three years' time they became masters of the whole language, so that they read the best of the Greek authors very exactly. I am indeed apt to think that they learned that language the more easily, from its having some relation to their own. I believe that they were a colony of the Greeks; for though their language comes nearer the Persian, yet they retain many names, both for their towns and magistrates, that are of Greek derivation. I happened to carry a great many books with me, instead of merchandise, when I sailed my fourth voyage; for I was so far from thinking of soon coming back, that I rather thought never to have returned at all, and I gave them all my books, among which were many of Plato's and some of Aristotle's works. I had also Theophrastus on Plants, which, to my great regret, was imperfect; for having laid it carelessly by, while we were at sea, a monkey had seized upon it, and in many places torn out the leaves. They have no books of grammar but Lascares, for I did not carry Theodorus with me; nor have they any dictionaries but Hesichius and Dioscorides. They esteem Plutarch highly, and were much taken with Lucian's wit, and with his pleasant way of writing. As for the poets, they have Aristophanes, Homer, Euripides, and Sophocles of Aldus's edition; and for historians Thucydides, Herodotus and Herodian. One of my companions, Thricius Apinatus, happened to carry with him some of Hippocrates's works, and Galen's Microtechne, which they hold in great estimation; for though there is no nation in the world that needs physic so little as they do, yet there is not any that honours it so much: they reckon the knowledge of it one of the pleasantest and most profitable parts of philosophy, by which, as they search into the secrets of Nature, so they not only find this study highly agreeable, but think that such inquiries are very acceptable to the Author of Nature; and imagine that as He, like the inventors of curious engines amongst mankind, has exposed this great machine of the universe to the view of the only creatures capable of contemplating it, so an exact and curious observer, who admires His workmanship, is much more acceptable to Him than one of the herd, who like a beast incapable of reason, looks on this glorious scene with the eyes of a dull and unconcerned spectator.

The minds of the Utopians when fenced with a love for learning, are very ingenious in discovering all such arts as are necessary to carry it to perfection. Two things they owe to us, the manufacture of paper, and the art of printing: yet they are not so entirely indebted to us for these discoveries, but that a great part of the invention was their own. We showed them some books printed by Aldus, we explained to them the way of making paper, and the mystery of printing; but as we had never practised these arts, we described them in a crude and superficial manner. They seized the hints we gave them, and though at first they could not arrive at perfection, yet by making many essays they at last found out and corrected all their errors, and conquered every difficulty. Before this they only wrote on parchment, on reeds, or on the barks of trees; but now they have established the manufactures of paper, and set up printing-presses, so that if they had but a good number of Greek authors they would be quickly supplied with many copies of them: at present, though they have no more than those I have mentioned, yet by several impressions they have multiplied them into many thousands. If any man was to go among them that had some extraordinary talent, or that by much travelling had observed the customs of many nations (which made us to be so well received), he would receive a hearty welcome; for they are very desirous to know the state of the whole world. Very few go among them on the account of traffic, for what can a man carry to them but iron, or gold, or silver, which merchants desire rather to export than import to a strange country: and as for their exportation, they think it better to manage that themselves than to leave it to foreigners, for by this means, as they understand the state of the neighbouring countries better, so they keep up the art of navigation, which cannot be maintained but by much practice.

OF THEIR SLAVES, AND OF THEIR MARRIAGES.

They do not make slaves of prisoners of war, except those that are taken in battle; nor of the sons of their slaves, nor of those of other nations: the slaves among them are only such as are condemned to that state of life for the commission of some crime, or, which is more common, such as their merchants find condemned to die in those parts to which they trade, whom they sometimes redeem at low rates; and in other places have them for nothing. They are kept at perpetual labour, and are always chained, but with this difference, that their own natives are treated much worse than others; they are considered as more profligate than the rest, and since they could not be restrained by the advantages of so excellent an education, are judged worthy of harder usage. Another sort of slaves are the poor of the neighbouring countries, who offer of their own accord to come and serve them; they treat these better, and use them in all other respects as well as their own countrymen, except their imposing more labour upon them, which is no hard task to those that have been accustomed to it; and if any of these have a mind to go back to their own country, which indeed falls out but seldom, as they do not force them to stay, so they do not send them away empty-handed.

I have already told you with what care they look after their sick, so that nothing is left undone that can contribute either to their ease or health: and for those who are taken with fixed and incurable diseases, they use all possible ways to cherish them, and to make their lives as comfortable as possible. They visit them often, and take great pains to make their time pass off easily: but when any is taken with a torturing and lingering pain, so that there is no hope, either of recovery or ease, the priests and magistrates come and exhort them, that since they are now unable to go on with the business of life, are become a burden to themselves and to all about them, and they have really outlived themselves, they should no longer nourish such a rooted distemper, but choose rather to die, since they cannot live but in much misery: being assured, that if they thus deliver themselves from torture, or are willing that others should do it, they shall be happy after death. Since by their acting thus, they lose none of the pleasures, but only the troubles of life; they think they behave not only reasonably, but in a manner consistent with religion and piety; because they follow the advice given them by their priests, who are the expounders of the will of God. Such as are wrought on by these persuasions, either starve themselves of their own accord, or take opium, and by that means die without pain. But no man is forced on this way of ending his life; and if they cannot be persuaded to it, this does not induce them to fail in their attendance and care of them; but as they believe that a voluntary death, when it is chosen upon such an authority, is very honourable, so if any man takes away his own life, without the approbation of the priests and the Senate, they give him none of the honours of a decent funeral, but throw his body into a ditch.

Their women are not married before eighteen, nor their men before two-and-twenty, and if any of them run into forbidden embraces before marriage they are severely punished, and the privilege of marriage is denied them, unless they can obtain a special warrant from the Prince. Such disorders cast a great reproach upon the master and mistress of the family in which they happen, for it is supposed that they have failed in their duty. The reason of punishing this so severely is, because they think that if they were not strictly restrained from all vagrant appetites, very few would engage in a state in which they venture the quiet of their whole lives, by being confined to one person, and are obliged to endure all the inconveniences with which it is accompanied. In choosing their wives they use a method that would appear to us very absurd and ridiculous, but it is constantly observed among them, and is accounted perfectly consistent with wisdom. Before marriage some grave matron presents the bride naked, whether she is a virgin or a widow, to the bridegroom; and after that some grave man presents the bridegroom naked to the bride. We indeed both laughed at this, and condemned it as very indecent. But they, on the other hand, wondered at the folly of the men of all other nations, who, if they are but to buy a horse of a small value, are so cautious that they will see every part of him, and take off both his saddle and all his other tackle, that there may be no secret ulcer hid under any of them; and that yet in the choice of a wife, on which depends the happiness or unhappiness of the rest of his life, a man should venture upon trust, and only see about a hand's-breadth of the face, all the rest of the body being covered, under which there may lie hid what may be contagious, as well as loathsome. All men are not so wise as to choose a woman only for her good qualities; and even wise men consider the body as that which adds not a little to the mind: and it is certain there may be some such deformity covered with the clothes as may totally alienate a man from his wife when it is too late to part with her. If such a thing is discovered after marriage, a man has no remedy but patience. They therefore think it is reasonable that there should be good provision made against such mischievous frauds.

There was so much the more reason for them to make a regulation in this matter, because they are the only people of those parts that neither allow of polygamy, nor of divorces, except in the case of adultery, or insufferable perverseness; for in these cases the Senate dissolves the marriage, and grants the injured person leave to marry again; but the guilty are made infamous, and are never allowed the privilege of a second marriage. None are suffered to put away their wives against their wills, from any great calamity that may have fallen on their persons; for they look on it as the height of cruelty and treachery to abandon either of the married persons when they need most the tender care of their comfort, and that chiefly in the case of old age, which as it carries many diseases along with it, so it is a disease of itself. But it frequently falls out that when a married couple do not well agree, they by mutual consent separate, and find out other persons with whom they hope they may live more happily. Yet this is not done without obtaining leave of the Senate, which never admits of a divorce, but upon a strict inquiry made, both by the senators and their wives, into the grounds upon which it is desired; and even when they are satisfied concerning the reasons of it, they go on but slowly, for they imagine that too great easiness in granting leave for new marriages would very much shake the kindness of married people. They punish severely those that defile the marriage-bed. If both parties are married they are divorced, and the injured persons may marry one another, or whom they please; but the adulterer and the adulteress are condemned to slavery. Yet if either of the injured persons cannot shake off the love of the married person, they may live with them still in that state, but they must follow them to that labour to which the slaves are condemned; and sometimes the repentance of the condemned, together with the unshaken kindness of the innocent and injured person, has prevailed so far with the Prince that he has taken off the sentence; but those that relapse after they are once pardoned are punished with death.

Their law does not determine the punishment for other crimes; but that is left to the Senate, to temper it according to the circumstances of the fact. Husbands have power to correct their wives, and parents to chastise their children, unless the fault is so great that a public punishment is thought necessary for striking terror into others. For the most part, slavery is the punishment even of the greatest crimes; for as that is no less terrible to the criminals themselves than death, so they think the preserving them in a state of servitude is more for the interest of the commonwealth than killing them; since as their labour is a greater benefit to the public than their death could be, so the sight of their misery is a more lasting terror to other men than that which would be given by their death. If their slaves rebel, and will not bear their yoke, and submit to the labour that is enjoined them, they are treated as wild beasts that cannot be kept in order, neither by a prison, nor by their chains; and are at last put to death. But those who bear their punishment patiently, and are so much wrought on by that pressure that lies so hard on them that it appears they are really more troubled for the crimes they have committed than for the miseries they suffer, are not out of hope but that at last either the Prince will, by his prerogative, or the people by their intercession, restore them again to their liberty, or at least very much mitigate their slavery. He that tempts a married woman to adultery, is no less severely punished than he that commits it; for they believe that a deliberate design to commit a crime, is equal to the fact itself: since its not taking effect does not make the person that miscarried in his attempt at all the less guilty.

They take great pleasure in fools, and as it is thought a base and unbecoming thing to use them ill, so they do not think it amiss for people to divert themselves with their folly: and, in their opinion, this is a great advantage to the fools themselves: for if men were so sullen and severe as not at all to please themselves with their ridiculous behaviour and foolish sayings, which is all that they can do to recommend themselves to others, it could not be expected that they would be so well provided for, nor so tenderly used as they must otherwise be. If any man should reproach another for his being misshaped or imperfect in any part of his body, it would not at all be thought a reflection on the person so treated, but it would be accounted scandalous in him that had upbraided another with what he could not help. It is thought a sign of a sluggish and sordid mind not to preserve carefully one's natural beauty; but it is likewise infamous among them to use paint. They all see that no beauty recommends a wife so much to her husband as the probity of her life, and her obedience: for as some few are catched and held only by beauty, so all are attracted by the other excellences which charm all the world.

As they fright men from committing crimes by punishments, so they invite them to the love of virtue by public honours: therefore they erect statues to the memories of such worthy men as have deserved well of their country, and set these in their market-places, both to perpetuate the remembrance of their actions, and to be an incitement to their posterity to follow their example.

If any man aspires to any office, he is sure never to compass it: they all live easily together, for none of the magistrates are either insolent or cruel to the people: they affect rather to be called fathers, and by being really so, they well deserve the name; and the people pay them all the marks of honour the more freely, because none are exacted from them. The Prince himself has no distinction, either of garments, or of a crown; but is only distinguished by a sheaf of corn carried before him; as the high priest is also known by his being preceded by a person carrying a wax light.

They have but few laws, and such is their constitution that they need not many. They very much condemn other nations, whose laws, together with the commentaries on them, swell up to so many volumes; for they think it an unreasonable thing to oblige men to obey a body of laws that are both of such a bulk, and so dark as not to be read and understood by every one of the subjects.

They have no lawyers among them, for they consider them as a sort of people whose profession it is to disguise matters, and to wrest the laws; and therefore they think it is much better that every man should plead his own cause, and trust it to the judge, as in other places the client trusts it to a counsellor. By this means they both cut off many delays, and find out truth more certainly: for after the parties have laid open the merits of the cause, without those artifices which lawyers are apt to suggest, the judge examines the whole matter, and supports the simplicity of such well-meaning persons, whom otherwise crafty men would be sure to run down: and thus they avoid those evils which appear very remarkably among all those nations that labour under a vast load of laws. Every one of them is skilled in their law, for as it is a very short study, so the plainest meaning of which words are capable is always the sense of their laws. And they argue thus: all laws are promulgated for this end, that every man may know his duty; and therefore the plainest and most obvious sense of the words is that which ought to be put upon them; since a more refined exposition cannot be easily comprehended, and would only serve to make the laws become useless to the greater part of mankind, and especially to those who need most the direction of them: for it is all one, not to make a law at all, or to couch it in such terms that without a quick apprehension, and much study, a man cannot find out the true meaning of it; since the generality of mankind are both so dull, and so much employed in their several trades, that they have neither the leisure nor the capacity requisite for such an inquiry.

Some of their neighbours, who are masters of their own liberties, having long ago, by the assistance of the Utopians, shaken off the yoke of tyranny, and being much taken with those virtues which they observe among them, have come to desire that they would send magistrates to govern them; some changing them every year, and others every five years. At the end of their government they bring them back to Utopia, with great expressions of honour and esteem, and carry away others to govern in their stead. In this they seem to have fallen upon a very good expedient for their own happiness and safety; for since the good or ill condition of a nation depends so much upon their magistrates, they could not have made a better choice than by pitching on men whom no advantages can bias; for wealth is of no use to them, since they must so soon go back to their own country; and they being strangers among them, are not engaged in any of their heats or animosities; and it is certain that when public judicatories are swayed, either by avarice or partial affections, there must follow a dissolution of justice, the chief sinew of society.

The Utopians call those nations that come and ask magistrates from them, neighbours; but those to whom they have been of more particular service, friends. And as all other nations are perpetually either making leagues or breaking them, they never enter into an alliance with any state. They think leagues are useless things, and believe that if the common ties of humanity do not knit men together, the faith of promises will have no great effect; and they are the more confirmed in this by what they see among the nations round about them, who are no strict observers of leagues and treaties. We know how religiously they are observed in Europe, more particularly where the Christian doctrine is received, among whom they are sacred and inviolable. Which is partly owing to the justice and goodness of the princes themselves, and partly to the reverence they pay to the popes; who as they are most religious observers of their own promises, so they exhort all other princes to perform theirs; and when fainter methods do not prevail, they compel them to it by the severity of the pastoral censure, and think that it would be the most indecent thing possible if men who are particularly distinguished by the title of the faithful, should not religiously keep the faith of their treaties. But in that new-found world, which is not more distant from us in situation than the people are in their manners and course of life, there is no trusting to leagues, even though they were made with all the pomp of the most sacred ceremonies; on the contrary, they are on this account the sooner broken, some slight pretence being found in the words of the treaties, which are purposely couched in such ambiguous terms that they can never be so strictly bound but they will always find some loophole to escape at; and thus they break both their leagues and their faith. And this is done with such impudence, that those very men who value themselves on having suggested these expedients to their princes, would with a haughty scorn declaim against such craft, or to speak plainer, such fraud and deceit, if they found private men make use of it in their bargains, and would readily say that they deserved to be hanged.

By this means it is, that all sort of justice passes in the world for a low-spirited and vulgar virtue, far below the dignity of royal greatness. Or at least, there are set up two sorts of justice; the one is mean, and creeps on the ground, and therefore becomes none but the lower part of mankind, and so must be kept in severely by many restraints that it may not break out beyond the bounds that are set to it. The other is the peculiar virtue of princes, which as it is more majestic than that which becomes the rabble, so takes a freer compass; and thus lawful and unlawful are only measured by pleasure and interest. These practices of the princes that lie about Utopia, who make so little account of their faith, seem to be the reasons that determine them to engage in no confederacies; perhaps they would change their mind if they lived among us; but yet though treaties were more religiously observed, they would still dislike the custom of making them; since the world has taken up a false maxim upon it, as if there were no tie of Nature uniting one nation to another, only separated perhaps by a mountain or a river, and that all were born in a state of hostility, and so might lawfully do all that mischief to their neighbours against which there is no provision made by treaties; and that when treaties are made, they do not cut off the enmity, or restrain the license of preying upon each other, if by the unskilfulness of wording them there are not effectual provisoes made against them. They, on the other hand, judge that no man is to be esteemed our enemy that has never injured us; and that the partnership of the human nature is instead of a league. And that kindness and good-nature unite men more effectually and with greater strength than any agreements whatsoever; since thereby the engagements of men's hearts become stronger than the bond and obligation of words.

OF THEIR MILITARY DISCIPLINE.

They detest war as a very brutal thing; and which, to the reproach of human nature, is more practised by men than by any sort of beasts. They, in opposition to the sentiments of almost all other nations, think that there is nothing more inglorious than that glory that is gained by war. And therefore though they accustom themselves daily to military exercises and the discipline of war, in which not only their men but their women likewise are trained up, that in cases of necessity they may not be quite useless; yet they do not rashly engage in war, unless it be either to defend themselves, or their friends, from any unjust aggressors; or out of good-nature or in compassion assist an oppressed nation in shaking off the yoke of tyranny. They indeed help their friends, not only in defensive, but also in offensive wars; but they never do that unless they had been consulted before the breach was made, and being satisfied with the grounds on which they went, they had found that all demands of reparation were rejected, so that a war was unavoidable. This they think to be not only just, when one neighbour makes an inroad on another, by public order, and carry away the spoils; but when the merchants of one country are oppressed in another, either under pretence of some unjust laws, or by the perverse wresting of good ones. This they count a juster cause of war than the other, because those injuries are done under some colour of laws. This was the only ground of that war in which they engaged with the Nephelogetes against the Aleopolitanes, a little before our time; for the merchants of the former having, as they thought, met with great injustice among the latter, which, whether it was in itself right or wrong, drew on a terrible war, in which many of their neighbours were engaged; and their keenness in carrying it on being supported by their strength in maintaining it, it not only shook some very flourishing states, and very much afflicted others, but after a series of much mischief ended in the entire conquest and slavery of the Aleopolitanes, who though before the war they were in all respects much superior to the Nephelogetes, were yet subdued; but though the Utopians had assisted them in the war, yet they pretended to no share of the spoil.

But though they so vigorously assist their friends in obtaining reparation for the injuries they have received in affairs of this nature, yet if any such frauds was committed against themselves, provided no violence was done to their persons, they would only on their being refused satisfaction forbear trading with such a people. This is not because they consider their neighbours more than their own citizens; but since their neighbours trade every one upon his own stock, fraud is a more sensible injury to them than it is to the Utopians, among whom the public in such a case only suffers. As they expect nothing in return for the merchandises they export but that in which they so much abound, and is of little use to them, the loss does not much affect them; they think therefore it would be too severe to revenge a loss attended with so little inconvenience either to their lives, or their subsistence, with the death of many persons; but if any of their people is either killed or wounded wrongfully, whether it be done by public authority or only by private men, as soon as they hear of it they send ambassadors, and demand that the guilty persons may be delivered up to them; and if that is denied, they declare war; but if it be complied with, the offenders are condemned either to death or slavery.

They would be both troubled and ashamed of a bloody victory over their enemies, and think it would be as foolish a purchase as to buy the most valuable goods at too high a rate. And in no victory do they glory so much as in that which is gained by dexterity and good conduct, without bloodshed. In such cases they appoint public triumphs, and erect trophies to the honour of those who have succeeded; for then do they reckon that a man acts suitably to his nature when he conquers his enemy in such a way as that no other creature but a man could be capable of, and that is by the strength of his understanding. Bears, lions, boars, wolves, and dogs, and all other animals employ their bodily force one against another, in which as many of them are superior to men, both in strength and fierceness, so they are all subdued by his reason and understanding.

The only design of the Utopians in war is to obtain that by force, which if it had been granted them in time would have prevented the war; or if that cannot be done, to take so severe a revenge on those that have injured them that they may be terrified from doing the like for the time to come. By these ends they measure all their designs, and manage them so that it is visible that the appetite of fame or vain-glory does not work so much on them as a just care of their own security.

As soon as they declare war, they take care to have a great many schedules, that are sealed with their common seal, affixed in the most conspicuous places of their enemies' country. This is carried secretly, and done in many places all at once. In these they promise great rewards to such as shall kill the prince, and lesser in proportion to such as shall kill any other persons, who are those on whom, next to the prince himself, they cast the chief balance of the war. And they double the sum to him that, instead of killing the person so marked out, shall take him alive and put him in their hands. They offer not only indemnity, but rewards, to such of the persons themselves that are so marked, if they will act against their countrymen: by this means those that are named in their schedules become not only distrustful of their fellow-citizens, but are jealous of one another, and are much distracted by fear and danger; for it has often fallen out that many of them, and even the Prince himself, have been betrayed by those in whom they have trusted most: for the rewards that the Utopians offer are so unmeasurably great, that there is no sort of crime to which men cannot be drawn by them. They consider the risk that those run who undertake such services, and offer a recompense proportioned to the danger; not only a vast deal of gold, but great revenues in lands, that lie among other nations that are their friends, where they may go and enjoy them very securely; and they observe the promises they make of this kind most religiously.

They very much approve of this way of corrupting their enemies, though it appears to others to be base and cruel; but they look on it as a wise course, to make an end of what would be otherwise a long war, without so much as hazarding one battle to decide it. They think it likewise an act of mercy and love to mankind to prevent the great slaughter of those that must otherwise be killed in the progress of the war, both on their own side and on that of their enemies, by the death of a few that are most guilty; and that in so doing they are kind even to their enemies, and pity them no less than their own people, as knowing that the greater part of them do not engage in the war of their own accord, but are driven into it by the passions of their prince.

If this method does not succeed with them, then they sow seeds of contention among their enemies, and animate the prince's brother, or some of the nobility, to aspire to the crown. If they cannot disunite them by domestic broils, then they engage their neighbours against them, and make them set on foot some old pretensions, which are never wanting to princes when they have occasion for them. These they plentifully supply with money, though but very sparingly with any auxiliary troops: for they are so tender of their own people, that they would not willingly exchange one of them, even with the prince of their enemies' country.

But as they keep their gold and silver only for such an occasion, so when that offers itself they easily part with it, since it would be no inconvenience to them though they should reserve nothing of it to themselves. For besides the wealth that they have among them at home, they have a vast treasure abroad, many nations round about them being deep in their debt: so that they hire soldiers from all places for carrying on their wars, but chiefly from the Zapolets, who live five hundred miles east of Utopia. They are a rude, wild, and fierce nation, who delight in the woods and rocks, among which they were born and bred up. They are hardened both against heat, cold and labour, and know nothing of the delicacies of life. They do not apply themselves to agriculture, nor do they care either for their houses or their clothes. Cattle is all that they look after; and for the greatest part they live either by hunting, or upon rapine; and are made, as it were, only for war. They watch all opportunities of engaging in it, and very readily embrace such as are offered them. Great numbers of them will frequently go out, and offer themselves for a very low pay, to serve any that will employ them: they know none of the arts of life, but those that lead to the taking it away; they serve those that hire them, both with much courage and great fidelity; but will not engage to serve for any determined time, and agree upon such terms, that the next day they may go over to the enemies of those whom they serve, if they offer them a greater encouragement: and will perhaps return to them the day after that, upon a higher advance of their pay. There are few wars in which they make not a considerable part of the armies of both sides: so it often falls out that they who are related, and were hired in the same country, and so have lived long and familiarly together, forgetting both their relations and former friendship, kill one another upon no other consideration than that of being hired to it for a little money, by princes of different interests; and such a regard have they for money, that they are easily wrought on by the difference of one penny a day to change sides. So entirely does their avarice influence them; and yet this money, which they value so highly, is of little use to them; for what they purchase thus with their blood, they quickly waste on luxury, which among them is but of a poor and miserable form.

This nation serves the Utopians against all people whatsoever, for they pay higher than any other. The Utopians hold this for a maxim, that as they seek out the best sort of men for their own use at home, so they make use of this worst sort of men for the consumption of war, and therefore they hire them with the offers of vast rewards, to expose themselves to all sorts of hazards, out of which the greater part never returns to claim their promises. Yet they make them good most religiously to such as escape. This animates them to adventure again, whenever there is occasion for it; for the Utopians are not at all troubled how many of these happen to be killed, and reckon it a service done to mankind if they could be a means to deliver the world from such a lewd and vicious sort of people, that seem to have run together as to the drain of human nature. Next to these they are served in their wars with those upon whose account they undertake them, and with the auxiliary troops of their other friends, to whom they join a few of their own people, and send some men of eminent and approved virtue to command in chief. There are two sent with him, who during his command are but private men, but the first is to succeed him if he should happen to be either killed or taken; and in case of the like misfortune to him, the third comes in his place; and thus they provide against ill events, that such accidents as may befall their generals may not endanger their armies. When they draw out troops of their own people, they take such out of every city as freely offer themselves, for none are forced to go against their wills, since they think that if any man is pressed that wants courage, he will not only act faintly, but by his cowardice dishearten others. But if an invasion is made on their country they make use of such men, if they have good bodies, though they are not brave; and either put them aboard their ships or place them on the walls of their towns, that being so posted they may find no opportunity of flying away; and thus either shame, the heat of action, or the impossibility of flying, bears down their cowardice; they often make a virtue of necessity and behave themselves well, because nothing else is left them. But as they force no man to go into any foreign war against his will, so they do not hinder those women who are willing to go along with their husbands; on the contrary, they encourage and praise them, and they stand often next their husbands in the front of the army. They also place together those who are related, parents and children, kindred, and those that are mutually allied, near one another; that those whom Nature has inspired with the greatest zeal for assisting one another, may be the nearest and readiest to do it; and it is matter of great reproach if husband or wife survive one another, or if a child survives his parents, and therefore when they come to be engaged in action they continue to fight to the last man, if their enemies stand before them. And as they use all prudent methods to avoid the endangering their own men, and if it is possible let all the action and danger fall upon the troops that they hire, so if it becomes necessary for themselves to engage, they then charge with as much courage as they avoided it before with prudence: nor is it a fierce charge at first, but it increases by degrees; and as they continue in action, they grow more obstinate and press harder upon the enemy, insomuch that they will much sooner die than give ground; for the certainty that their children will be well looked after when they are dead, frees them from all that anxiety concerning them which often masters men of great courage; and thus they are animated by a noble and invincible resolution. Their skill in military affairs increases their courage; and the wise sentiments which, according to the laws of their country are instilled into them in their education, give additional vigour to their minds: for as they do not undervalue life so as prodigally to throw it away, they are not so indecently fond of it as to preserve it by base and unbecoming methods. In the greatest heat of action, the bravest of their youth, who have devoted themselves to that service, single out the general of their enemies, set on him either openly or by ambuscade, pursue him everywhere, and when spent and wearied out, are relieved by others, who never give over the pursuit; either attacking him with close weapons when they can get near him, or with those which wound at a distance, when others get in between them; so that unless he secures himself by flight, they seldom fail at last to kill or to take him prisoner. When they have obtained a victory, they kill as few as possible, and are much more bent on taking many prisoners than on killing those that fly before them; nor do they ever let their men so loose in the pursuit of their enemies, as not to retain an entire body still in order; so that if they have been forced to engage the last of their battalions before they could gain the day, they will rather let their enemies all escape than pursue them, when their own army is in disorder; remembering well what has often fallen out to themselves, that when the main body of their army has been quite defeated and broken, when their enemies imagining the victory obtained, have let themselves loose into an irregular pursuit, a few of them that lay for a reserve, waiting a fit opportunity, have fallen on them in their chase, and when straggling in disorder and apprehensive of no danger, but counting the day their own, have turned the whole action, and wresting out of their hands a victory that seemed certain and undoubted, while the vanquished have suddenly become victorious.

It is hard to tell whether they are more dexterous in laying or avoiding ambushes. They sometimes seem to fly when it is far from their thoughts; and when they intend to give ground, they do it so that it is very hard to find out their design. If they see they are ill posted, or are like to be overpowered by numbers, they then either march off in the night with great silence, or by some stratagem delude their enemies: if they retire in the daytime, they do it in such order, that it is no less dangerous to fall upon them in a retreat than in a march. They fortify their camps with a deep and large trench, and throw up the earth that is dug out of it for a wall; nor do they employ only their slaves in this, but the whole army works at it, except those that are then upon the guard; so that when so many hands are at work, a great line and a strong fortification is finished in so short a time that it is scarce credible. Their armour is very strong for defence, and yet is not so heavy as to make them uneasy in their marches; they can even swim with it. All that are trained up to war, practise swimming. Both horse and foot make great use of arrows, and are very expert. They have no swords, but fight with a pole-axe that is both sharp and heavy, by which they thrust or strike down an enemy. They are very good at finding out warlike machines, and disguise them so well, that the enemy does not perceive them till he feels the use of them; so that he cannot prepare such a defence as would render them useless; the chief consideration had in the making them, is that they may be easily carried and managed.

If they agree to a truce, they observe it so religiously that no provocations will make them break it. They never lay their enemies' country waste, nor burn their corn, and even in their marches they take all possible care that neither horse nor foot may tread it down, for they do not know but that they may have use for it themselves. They hurt no man whom they find disarmed, unless he is a spy. When a town is surrendered to them, they take it into their protection: and when they carry a place by storm, they never plunder it, but put those only to the sword that opposed the rendering of it up, and make the rest of the garrison slaves, but for the other inhabitants, they do them no hurt; and if any of them had advised a surrender, they give them good rewards out of the estates of those that they condemn, and distribute the rest among their auxiliary troops, but they themselves take no share of the spoil.

When a war is ended, they do not oblige their friends to reimburse their expenses; but they obtain them of the conquered, either in money, which they keep for the next occasion, or in lands, out of which a constant revenue is to be paid them; by many increases, the revenue which they draw out from several countries on such occasions, is now risen to above 700,000 ducats a year. They send some of their own people to receive these revenues, who have orders to live magnificently, and like princes, by which means they consume much of it upon the place; and either bring over the rest to Utopia, or lend it to that nation in which it lies. This they most commonly do, unless some great occasion, which falls out but very seldom, should oblige them to call for it all. It is out of these lands that they assign rewards to such as they encourage to adventure on desperate attempts. If any prince that engages in war with them is making preparations for invading their country, they prevent him, and make his country the seat of the war; for they do not willingly suffer any war to break in upon their island; and if that should happen, they would only defend themselves by their own people, but would not call for auxiliary troops to their assistance.

OF THE RELIGIONS OF THE UTOPIANS.

There are several sorts of religions, not only in different parts of the island, but even in every town; some worshipping the sun, others the moon, or one of the planets; some worship such men as have been eminent in former times for virtue, or glory, not only as ordinary deities, but as the supreme God: yet the greater and wiser sort of them worship none of these, but adore one eternal, invisible, infinite, and incomprehensible Deity; as a Being that is far above all our apprehensions, that is spread over the whole universe, not by His bulk, but by His power and virtue; Him they call the Father of All, and acknowledge that the beginnings, the increase, the progress, the vicissitudes, and the end of all things come only from Him; nor do they offer divine honours to any but to Him alone. And indeed, though they differ concerning other things, yet all agree in this, that they think there is one supreme Being that made and governs the world, whom they call in the language of their country Mithras. They differ in this, that one thinks the God whom he worships is this supreme Being, and another thinks that his idol is that God; but they all agree in one principle, that whoever is this supreme Being, He is also that great Essence to whose glory and majesty all honours are ascribed by the consent of all nations.

By degrees, they fall off from the various superstitions that are among them, and grow up to that one religion that is the best and most in request; and there is no doubt to be made but that all the others had vanished long ago, if some of those who advised them to lay aside their superstitions had not met with some unhappy accident, which being considered as inflicted by Heaven, made them afraid that the God whose worship had like to have been abandoned, had interposed, and revenged themselves on those who despised their authority.

After they had heard from us an account of the doctrine, the course of life, and the miracles of Christ, and of the wonderful constancy of so many martyrs, whose blood, so willingly offered up by them, was the chief occasion of spreading their religion over a vast number of nations; it is not to be imagined how inclined they were to receive it. I shall not determine whether this proceeded from any secret inspiration of God, or whether it was because it seemed so favourable to that community of goods, which is an opinion so particular as well as so dear to them; since they perceived that Christ and His followers lived by that rule, and that it was still kept up in some communities among the sincerest sort of Christians. From whichsoever of these motives it might be, true it is that many of them came over to our religion, and were initiated into it by baptism. But as two of our number were dead, so none of the four that survived were in priest's orders; we therefore could only baptize them; so that to our great regret they could not partake of the other sacraments, that can only be administered by priests; but they are instructed concerning them, and long most vehemently for them. They have had great disputes among themselves, whether one chosen by them to be a priest would not be thereby qualified to do all the things that belong to that character, even though he had no authority derived from the Pope; and they seemed to be resolved to choose some for that employment, but they had not done it when I left them.

Those among them that have not received our religion, do not fright any from it, and use none ill that goes over to it; so that all the while I was there, one man was only punished on this occasion. He being newly baptized, did, notwithstanding all that we could say to the contrary, dispute publicly concerning the Christian religion with more zeal than discretion; and with so much heat, that he not only preferred our worship to theirs, but condemned all their rites as profane; and cried out against all that adhered to them, as impious and sacrilegious persons, that were to be damned to everlasting burnings. Upon his having frequently preached in this manner, he was seized, and after trial he was condemned to banishment, not for having disparaged their religion, but for his inflaming the people to sedition: for this is one of their most ancient laws, that no man ought to be punished for his religion. At the first constitution of their government, Utopus having understood that before his coming among them the old inhabitants had been engaged in great quarrels concerning religion, by which they were so divided among themselves, that he found it an easy thing to conquer them, since instead of uniting their forces against him, every different party in religion fought by themselves; after he had subdued them, he made a law that every man might be of what religion he pleased, and might endeavour to draw others to it by the force of argument, and by amicable and modest ways, but without bitterness against those of other opinions; but that he ought to use no other force but that of persuasion, and was neither to mix with it reproaches nor violence; and such as did otherwise were to be condemned to banishment or slavery.

This law was made by Utopus, not only for preserving the public peace, which he saw suffered much by daily contentions and irreconcilable heats, but because he thought the interest of religion itself required it. He judged it not fit to determine anything rashly, and seemed to doubt whether those different forms of religion might not all come from God, who might inspire men in a different manner, and be pleased with this variety; he therefore thought it indecent and foolish for any man to threaten and terrify another to make him believe what did not appear to him to be true. And supposing that only one religion was really true, and the rest false, he imagined that the native force of truth would at last break forth and shine bright, if supported only by the strength of argument, and attended to with a gentle and unprejudiced mind; while, on the other hand, if such debates were carried on with violence and tumults, as the most wicked are always the most obstinate, so the best and most holy religion might be choked with superstition, as corn is with briars and thorns; he therefore left men wholly to their liberty, that they might be free to believe as they should see cause; only he made a solemn and severe law against such as should so far degenerate from the dignity of human nature as to think that our souls died with our bodies, or that the world was governed by chance, without a wise overruling Providence: for they all formerly believed that there was a state of rewards and punishments to the good and bad after this life; and they now look on those that think otherwise as scarce fit to be counted men, since they degrade so noble a being as the soul, and reckon it no better than a beast's: thus they are far from looking on such men as fit for human society, or to be citizens of a well-ordered commonwealth; since a man of such principles must needs, as oft as he dares do it, despise all their laws and customs: for there is no doubt to be made that a man who is afraid of nothing but the law, and apprehends nothing after death, will not scruple to break through all the laws of his country, either by fraud or force, when by this means he may satisfy his appetites. They never raise any that hold these maxims, either to honours or offices, nor employ them in any public trust, but despise them, as men of base and sordid minds: yet they do not punish them, because they lay this down as a maxim that a man cannot make himself believe anything he pleases; nor do they drive any to dissemble their thoughts by threatenings, so that men are not tempted to lie or disguise their opinions; which being a sort of fraud, is abhorred by the Utopians. They take care indeed to prevent their disputing in defence of these opinions, especially before the common people; but they suffer, and even encourage them to dispute concerning them in private with their priests and other grave men, being confident that they will be cured of those mad opinions by having reason laid before them. There are many among them that run far to the other extreme, though it is neither thought an ill nor unreasonable opinion, and therefore is not at all discouraged. They think that the souls of beasts are immortal, though far inferior to the dignity of the human soul, and not capable of so great a happiness. They are almost all of them very firmly persuaded that good men will be infinitely happy in another state; so that though they are compassionate to all that are sick, yet they lament no man's death, except they see him loth to depart with life; for they look on this as a very ill presage, as if the soul, conscious to itself of guilt, and quite hopeless, was afraid to leave the body, from some secret hints of approaching misery. They think that such a man's appearance before God cannot be acceptable to Him, who, being called on, does not go out cheerfully, but is backward and unwilling, and is, as it were, dragged to it. They are struck with horror when they see any die in this manner, and carry them out in silence and with sorrow, and praying God that He would be merciful to the errors of the departed soul, they lay the body in the ground; but when any die cheerfully, and full of hope, they do not mourn for them, but sing hymns when they carry out their bodies, and commending their souls very earnestly to God: their whole behaviour is then rather grave than sad, they burn the body, and set up a pillar where the pile was made, with an inscription to the honour of the deceased. When they come from the funeral, they discourse of his good life and worthy actions, but speak of nothing oftener and with more pleasure than of his serenity at the hour of death. They think such respect paid to the memory of good men is both the greatest incitement to engage others to follow their example, and the most acceptable worship that can be offered them; for they believe that though by the imperfection of human sight they are invisible to us, yet they are present among us, and hear those discourses that pass concerning themselves. They believe it inconsistent, with the happiness of departed souls not to be at liberty to be where they will, and do not imagine them capable of the ingratitude of not desiring to see those friends with whom they lived on earth in the strictest bonds of love and kindness: besides they are persuaded that good men after death have these affections and all other good dispositions increased rather than diminished, and therefore conclude that they are still among the living, and observe all they say or do. From hence they engage in all their affairs with the greater confidence of success, as trusting to their protection; while this opinion of the presence of their ancestors is a restraint that prevents their engaging in ill designs.

They despise and laugh at auguries, and the other vain and superstitious ways of divination, so much observed among other nations; but have great reverence for such miracles as cannot flow from any of the powers of Nature, and look on them as effects and indications of the presence of the supreme Being, of which they say many instances have occurred among them; and that sometimes their public prayers, which upon great and dangerous occasions they have solemnly put up to God, with assured confidence of being heard, have been answered in a miraculous manner.

They think the contemplating God in His works, and the adoring Him for them, is a very acceptable piece of worship to Him.

There are many among them, that upon a motive of religion neglect learning, and apply themselves to no sort of study; nor do they allow themselves any leisure time, but are perpetually employed, believing that by the good things that a man does he secures to himself that happiness that comes after death. Some of these visit the sick; others mend highways, cleanse ditches, repair bridges, or dig turf, gravel, or stones. Others fell and cleave timber, and bring wood, corn, and other necessaries on carts into their towns. Nor do these only serve the public, but they serve even private men, more than the slaves themselves do; for if there is anywhere a rough, hard, and sordid piece of work to be done, from which many are frightened by the labour and loathsomeness of it, if not the despair of accomplishing it, they cheerfully, and of their own accord, take that to their share; and by that means, as they ease others very much, so they afflict themselves, and spend their whole life in hard labour; and yet they do not value themselves upon this, nor lessen other people's credit to raise their own; but by their stooping to such servile employments, they are so far from being despised, that they are so much the more esteemed by the whole nation.

Of these there are two sorts; some live unmarried and chaste, and abstain from eating any sort of flesh; and thus weaning themselves from all the pleasures of the present life, which they account hurtful, they pursue, even by the hardest and painfullest methods possible, that blessedness which they hope for hereafter; and the nearer they approach to it, they are the more cheerful and earnest in their endeavours after it. Another sort of them is less willing to put themselves to much toil, and therefore prefer a married state to a single one; and as they do not deny themselves the pleasure of it, so they think the begetting of children is a debt which they owe to human nature and to their country; nor do they avoid any pleasure that does not hinder labour, and therefore eat flesh so much the more willingly, as they find that by this means they are the more able to work; the Utopians look upon these as the wiser sect, but they esteem the others as the most holy. They would indeed laugh at any man, who from the principles of reason would prefer an unmarried state to a married, or a life of labour to an easy life; but they reverence and admire such as do it from the motives of religion. There is nothing in which they are more cautious than in giving their opinion positively concerning any sort of religion. The men that lead those severe lives are called in the language of their country Brutheskas, which answers to those we call religious orders.

Their priests are men of eminent piety, and therefore they are but few, for there are only thirteen in every town, one for every temple; but when they go to war, seven of these go out with their forces, and seven others are chosen to supply their room in their absence; but these enter again upon their employment when they return; and those who served in their absence attend upon the high-priest, till vacancies fall by death; for there is one set over all the rest. They are chosen by the people as the other magistrates are, by suffrages given in secret, for preventing of factions; and when they are chosen they are consecrated by the college of priests. The care of all sacred things, the worship of God, and an inspection into the manners of the people, are committed to them. It is a reproach to a man to be sent for by any of them, or for them to speak to him in secret, for that always gives some suspicion. All that is incumbent on them is only to exhort and admonish the people; for the power of correcting and punishing ill men belongs wholly to the Prince and to the other magistrates. The severest thing that the priest does, is the excluding those that are desperately wicked from joining in their worship. There is not any sort of punishment more dreaded by them than this, for as it loads them with infamy, so it fills them with secret horrors, such is their reverence to their religion; nor will their bodies be long exempted from their share of trouble; for if they do not very quickly satisfy the priests of the truth of their repentance, they are seized on by the Senate, and punished for their impiety. The education of youth belongs to the priests, yet they do not take so much care of instructing them in letters as in forming their minds and manners aright; they use all possible methods to infuse very early into the tender and flexible minds of children such opinions as are both good in themselves and will be useful to their country. For when deep impressions of these things are made at that age, they follow men through the whole course of their lives, and conduce much to preserve the peace of the government, which suffers by nothing more than by vices that rise out of ill opinions. The wives of their priests are the most extraordinary women of the whole country; sometimes the women themselves are made priests, though that falls out but seldom, nor are any but ancient widows chosen into that order.

None of the magistrates have greater honour paid them than is paid the priests; and if they should happen to commit any crime, they would not be questioned for it. Their punishment is left to God, and to their own consciences; for they do not think it lawful to lay hands on any man, how wicked soever he is, that has been in a peculiar manner dedicated to God; nor do they find any great inconvenience in this, both because they have so few priests, and because these are chosen with much caution, so that it must be a very unusual thing to find one who merely out of regard to his virtue, and for his being esteemed a singularly good man, was raised up to so great a dignity, degenerate into corruption and vice. And if such a thing should fall out, for man is a changeable creature, yet there being few priests, and these having no authority but what rises out of the respect that is paid them, nothing of great consequence to the public can proceed from the indemnity that the priests enjoy.

They have indeed very few of them, lest greater numbers sharing in the same honour might make the dignity of that order which they esteem so highly to sink in its reputation. They also think it difficult to find out many of such an exalted pitch of goodness, as to be equal to that dignity which demands the exercise of more than ordinary virtues. Nor are the priests in greater veneration among them than they are among their neighbouring nations, as you may imagine by that which I think gives occasion for it.

When the Utopians engage in battle, the priests who accompany them to the war, apparelled in their sacred vestments, kneel down during the action, in a place not far from the field; and lifting up their hands to heaven, pray, first for peace, and then for victory to their own side, and particularly that it may be gained without the effusion of much blood on either side; and when the victory turns to their side, they run in among their own men to restrain their fury; and if any of their enemies see them, or call to them, they are preserved by that means; and such as can come so near them as to touch their garments, have not only their lives, but their fortunes secured to them; it is upon this account that all the nations roundabout consider them so much, and treat them with such reverence, that they have been often no less able to preserve their own people from the fury of their enemies, than to save their enemies from their rage; for it has sometimes fallen out, that when their armies have been in disorder, and forced to fly, so that their enemies were running upon the slaughter and spoil, the priests by interposing have separated them from one another, and stopped the effusion of more blood; so that by their mediation a peace has been concluded on very reasonable terms; nor is there any nation about them so fierce, cruel, or barbarous as not to look upon their persons as sacred and inviolable.

The first and the last day of the month, and of the year, is a festival. They measure their months by the course of the moon, and their years by the course of the sun. The first days are called in their language the Cynemernes, and the last the Trapemernes; which answers in our language to the festival that begins, or ends the season.

They have magnificent temples, that are not only nobly built, but extremely spacious; which is the more necessary, as they have so few of them; they are a little dark within, which proceeds not from any error in the architecture, but is done with design; for their priests think that too much light dissipates the thoughts, and that a more moderate degree of it both recollects the mind and raises devotion. Though there are many different forms of religion among them, yet all these, how various soever, agree in the main point, which is the worshipping the Divine Essence; and therefore there is nothing to be seen or heard in their temples in which the several persuasions among them may not agree; for every sect performs those rites that are peculiar to it, in their private houses, nor is there anything in the public worship that contradicts the particular ways of those different sects. There are no images for God in their temples, so that every one may represent Him to his thoughts, according to the way of his religion; nor do they call this one God by any other name but that of Mithras, which is the common name by which they all express the Divine Essence, whatsoever otherwise they think it to be; nor are there any prayers among them but such as every one of them may use without prejudice to his own opinion.

They meet in their temples on the evening of the festival that concludes a season: and not having yet broke their fast, they thank God for their good success during that year or month, which is then at an end; and the next day being that which begins the new season, they meet early in their temples, to pray for the happy progress of all their affairs during that period upon which they then enter. In the festival which concludes the period, before they go to the temple, both wives and children fall on their knees before their husbands or parents, and confess everything in which they have either erred or failed in their duty, and beg pardon for it. Thus all little discontents in families are removed, that they may offer up their devotions with a pure and serene mind; for they hold it a great impiety to enter upon them with disturbed thoughts, or with a consciousness of their bearing hatred or anger in their hearts to any person whatsoever; and think that they should become liable to severe punishments if they presumed to offer sacrifices without cleansing their hearts, and reconciling all their differences. In the temples, the two sexes are separated, the men go to the right hand, and the women to the left; and the males and females all place themselves before the head and master or mistress of that family to which they belong; so that those who have the government of them at home may see their deportment in public; and they intermingle them so, that the younger and the older may be set by one another; for if the younger sort were all set together, they would perhaps trifle away that time too much in which they ought to beget in themselves that religious dread of the supreme Being, which is the greatest and almost the only incitement to virtue.

They offer up no living creature in sacrifice, nor do they think it suitable to the divine Being, from whose bounty it is that these creatures have derived their lives, to take pleasure in their deaths, or the offering up their blood. They burn incense and other sweet odours, and have a great number of wax lights during their worship; not out of any imagination that such oblations can add anything to the divine Nature, which even prayers cannot do; but as it is a harmless and pure way of worshipping God, so they think those sweet savours and lights, together with some other ceremonies, by a secret and unaccountable virtue, elevate men's souls, and inflame them with greater energy and cheerfulness during the divine worship.

All the people appear in the temples in white garments, but the priest's vestments are parti-coloured, and both the work and colours are wonderful. They are made of no rich materials, for they are neither embroidered nor set with precious stones, but are composed of the plumes of several birds, laid together with so much art and so neatly, that the true value of them is far beyond the costliest materials. They say that in the ordering and placing those plumes some dark mysteries are represented, which pass down among their priests in a secret tradition concerning them; and that they are as hieroglyphics, putting them in mind of the blessings that they have received from God, and of their duties both to Him and to their neighbours. As soon as the priest appears in those ornaments, they all fall prostrate on the ground, with so much reverence and so deep a silence that such as look on cannot but be struck with it, as if it were the effect of the appearance of a Deity. After they have been for some time in this posture, they all stand up, upon a sign given by the priest, and sing hymns to the honour of God, some musical instruments playing all the while. These are quite of another form than those used among us: but as many of them are much sweeter than ours, so others are made use of by us. Yet in one thing they very much exceed us; all their music, both vocal and instrumental, is adapted to imitate and express the passions, and is so happily suited to every occasion, that whether the subject of the hymn be cheerful or formed to soothe or trouble the mind, or to express grief or remorse, the music takes the impression of whatever is represented, affects and kindles the passions, and works the sentiments deep into the hearts of the hearers. When this is done, both priests and people offer up very solemn prayers to God in a set form of words; and these are so composed, that whatsoever is pronounced by the whole assembly may be likewise applied by every man in particular to his own condition; in these they acknowledge God to be the author and governor of the world, and the fountain of all the good they receive, and therefore offer up to Him their thanksgiving; and in particular bless Him for His goodness in ordering it so, that they are born under the happiest government in the world, and are of a religion which they hope is the truest of all others: but if they are mistaken, and if there is either a better government or a religion more acceptable to God, they implore His goodness to let them know it, vowing that they resolve to follow Him whithersoever He leads them. But if their government is the best, and their religion the truest, then they pray that He may fortify them in it, and bring all the world both to the same rules of life, and to the same opinions concerning himself; unless, according to the unsearchableness of His mind, He is pleased with a variety of religions. Then they pray that God may give them an easy passage at last to himself; not presuming to set limits to Him, how early or late it should be; but if it may be wished for, without derogating from His supreme authority, they desire to be quickly delivered, and to be taken to himself, though by the most terrible kind of death, rather than to be detained long from seeing Him by the most prosperous course of life. When this prayer is ended, they all fall down again upon the ground, and after a little while they rise up, go home to dinner, and spend the rest of the day in diversion or military exercises.

Thus have I described to you, as particularly as I could, the constitution of that commonwealth, which I do not only think the best in the world, but indeed the only commonwealth that truly deserves that name. In all other places it is visible, that while people talk of a commonwealth, every man only seeks his own wealth; but there, where no man has any property, all men zealously pursue the good of the public: and, indeed, it is no wonder to see men act so differently; for in other commonwealths, every man knows that unless he provides for himself, how flourishing soever the commonwealth may be, he must die of hunger; so that he sees the necessity of preferring his own concerns to the public; but in Utopia, where every man has a right to everything, they all know that if care is taken to keep the public stores full, no private man can want anything; for among them there is no unequal distribution, so that no man is poor, none in necessity; and though no man has anything, yet they are all rich; for what can make a man so rich as to lead a serene and cheerful life, free from anxieties; neither apprehending want himself, nor vexed with the endless complaints of his wife? He is not afraid of the misery of his children, nor is he contriving how to raise a portion for his daughters, but is secure in this, that both he and his wife, his children and grandchildren, to as many generations as he can fancy, will all live both plentifully and happily; since among them there is no less care taken of those who were once engaged in labour, but grow afterwards unable to follow it, than there is elsewhere of these that continue still employed. I would gladly hear any man compare the justice that is among them with that of all other nations; among whom, may I perish, if I see anything that looks either like justice or equity: for what justice is there in this, that a nobleman, a goldsmith, a banker, or any other man, that either does nothing at all, or at best is employed in things that are of no use to the public, should live in great luxury and splendour, upon what is so ill acquired;

and a mean man, a carter, a smith, or a ploughman, that works harder even than the beasts themselves, and is employed in labours so necessary, that no commonwealth could hold out a year without them, can only earn so poor a livelihood, and must lead so miserable a life, that the condition of the beasts is much better than theirs? For as the beasts do not work so constantly, so they feed almost as well, and with more pleasure; and have no anxiety about what is to come, whilst these men are depressed by a barren and fruitless employment, and tormented with the apprehensions of want in their old age; since that which they get by their daily labour does but maintain them at present, and is consumed as fast as it comes in, there is no overplus left to lay up for old age.

Is not that government both unjust and ungrateful, that is so prodigal of its favours to those that are called gentlemen, or goldsmiths, or such others who are idle, or live either by flattery, or by contriving the arts of vain pleasure; and on the other hand, takes no care of those of a meaner sort, such as ploughmen, colliers, and smiths, without whom it could not subsist? But after the public has reaped all the advantage of their service, and they come to be oppressed with age, sickness, and want, all their labours and the good they have done is forgotten; and all the recompense given them is that they are left to die in great misery. The richer sort are often endeavouring to bring the hire of labourers lower, not only by their fraudulent practices, but by the laws which they procure to be made to that effect; so that though it is a thing most unjust in itself, to give such small rewards to those who deserve so well of the public, yet they have given those hardships the name and colour of justice, by procuring laws to be made for regulating them.

Therefore I must say that, as I hope for mercy, I can have no other notion of all the other governments that I see or know, than that they are a conspiracy of the rich, who on pretence of managing the public only pursue their private ends, and devise all the ways and arts they can find out; first, that they may, without danger, preserve all that they have so ill acquired, and then that they may engage the poor to toil and labour for them at as low rates as possible, and oppress them as much as they please. And if they can but prevail to get these contrivances established by the show of public authority, which is considered as the representative of the whole people, then they are accounted laws. Yet these wicked men after they have, by a most insatiable covetousness, divided that among themselves with which all the rest might have been well supplied, are far from that happiness that is enjoyed among the Utopians: for the use as well as the desire of money being extinguished, much anxiety and great occasions of mischief is cut off with it. And who does not see that the frauds, thefts, robberies, quarrels, tumults, contentions, seditions, murders, treacheries, and witchcrafts, which are indeed rather punished than restrained by the severities of law, would all fall off, if money were not any more valued by the world? Men's fears, solicitudes, cares, labours, and watchings, would all perish in the same moment with the value of money: even poverty itself, for the relief of which money seems most necessary, would fall. But, in order to the apprehending this aright, take one instance.

Consider any year that has been so unfruitful that many thousands have died of hunger; and yet if at the end of that year a survey was made of the granaries of all the rich men that have hoarded up the corn, it would be found that there was enough among them to have prevented all that consumption of men that perished in misery; and that if it had been distributed among them, none would have felt the terrible effects of that scarcity; so easy a thing would it be to supply all the necessities of life, if that blessed thing called money, which is pretended to be invented for procuring them, was not really the only thing that obstructed their being procured!

I do not doubt but rich men are sensible of this, and that they well know how much a greater happiness it is to want nothing necessary than to abound in many superfluities, and to be rescued out of so much misery than to abound with so much wealth; and I cannot think but the sense of every man's interest, added to the authority of Christ's commands, who as He was infinitely wise, knew what was best, and was not less good in discovering it to us, would have drawn all the world over to the laws of the Utopians, if pride, that plague of human nature, that source of so much misery, did not hinder it; for this vice does not measure happiness so much by its own conveniences as by the miseries of others; and would not be satisfied with being thought a goddess, if none were left that were miserable, over whom she might insult. Pride thinks its own happiness shines the brighter by comparing it with the misfortunes of other persons; that by displaying its own wealth, they may feel their poverty the more sensibly. This is that infernal serpent that creeps into the breasts of mortals, and possesses them too much to be easily drawn out; and therefore I am glad that the Utopians have fallen upon this form of government, in which I wish that all the world could be so wise as to imitate them; for they have indeed laid down such a scheme and foundation of policy, that as men live happily under it, so it is like to be of great continuance; for they having rooted out of the minds of their people all the seeds both of ambition and faction, there is no danger of any commotion at home; which alone has been the ruin of many states, that seemed otherwise to be well secured; but as long as they live in peace at home, and are governed by such good laws, the envy of all their neighbouring princes, who have often though in vain attempted their ruin, will never be able to put their state into any commotion or disorder.

When Raphael had thus made an end of speaking, though many things occurred to me, both concerning the manners and laws of that people, that seemed very absurd, as well as their way of making war, as in their notions of religion and divine matters; together with several other particulars, but chiefly what seemed the foundation of all the rest, their living in common, without the use of money, by which all nobility, magnificence, splendour, and majesty, which, according to the common opinion, are the true ornaments of a nation, would be quite taken away; yet since I perceived that Raphael was weary, and was not sure whether he could easily bear contradiction, remembering that he had taken notice of some who seemed to think they were bound in honour to support the credit of their own wisdom, by finding out something to censure in all other men's inventions, besides their own; I only commended their constitution, and the account he had given of it in general; and so taking him by the hand, carried him to supper, and told him I would find out some other time for examining this subject more particularly, and for discoursing more copiously upon it; and indeed I shall be glad to embrace an opportunity of doing it. In the meanwhile, though it must be confessed that he is both a very learned man, and a person who has obtained a great knowledge of the world, I cannot perfectly agree to everything he has related; however, there are many things in the Commonwealth of Utopia that I rather wish, than hope, to see followed in our governments.

BACON'S NEW ATLANTIS.

New Atlantis.

We sailed from Peru, where we had continued by the space of one whole year, for China and Japan, by the South Sea, taking with us victuals for twelve months; and had good winds from the east, though soft and weak, for five months' space and more. But then the wind came about, and settled in the west for many days, so as we could make little or no way, and were sometimes in purpose to turn back. But then again there arose strong and great winds from the south, with a point east; which carried us up, for all that we could do, towards the north: by which time our victuals failed us, though we had made good spare of them. So that finding ourselves, in the midst of the greatest wilderness of waters in the world, without victual, we gave ourselves for lost men, and prepared for death. Yet we did lift up our hearts and voices to God above, who showeth His wonders in the deep; beseeching Him of his mercy, that as in the beginning He discovered the face of the deep, and brought forth dry land, so He would now discover land to us, that we might not perish. And it came to pass, that the next day about evening we saw within a kenning before us, towards the north, as it were thick clouds, which did put us in some hope of land: knowing how that part of the South Sea was utterly unknown: and might have islands or continents, that hitherto were not come to light. Wherefore we bent out course thither, where we saw the appearance of land, all that night: and in the dawning of next day, we might plainly discern that it was a land flat to our sight, and full of boscage, which made it show the more dark. And after an hour and a half's sailing, we entered into a good haven, being the port of a fair city. Not great indeed, but well built, and that gave a pleasant view from the sea. And we thinking every minute long till we were on land, came close to the shore and offered to land. But straightways we saw divers of the people, with bastons in their hands, as it were forbidding us to land: yet without any cries or fierceness, but only as warning us off, by signs that they made. Whereupon being not a little discomfited, we were advising with ourselves what we should do. During which time there made forth to us a small boat, with about eight persons in it, whereof one of them had in his hand a tipstaff of a yellow cane, tipped at both ends with blue, who made aboard our ship, without any show of distrust at all. And when he saw one of our number present himself somewhat afore the rest, he drew forth a little scroll of parchment (somewhat yellower than our parchment, and shining like the leaves of writing tables, but otherwise soft and flexible), and delivered it to our foremost man. In which scroll were written in ancient Hebrew, and in ancient Greek, and in good Latin of the school, and in Spanish these words: "Land ye not, none of you, and provide to be gone from this coast within sixteen days, except you have further time given you; meanwhile, if you want fresh water, or victual, or help for your sick, or that your ship needeth repair, write down your wants, and you shall have that which belongeth to mercy." This scroll was signed with a stamp of cherubim's wings, not spread, but hanging downwards; and by them a cross. This being delivered, the officer returned, and left only a servant with us to receive our answer. Consulting hereupon amongst ourselves, we were much perplexed. The denial of landing, and hasty warning us away, troubled us much: on the other side, to find that the people had languages, and were so full of humanity, did comfort us not a little. And above all, the sign of the cross to that instrument, was to us a great rejoicing, and as it were a certain presage of good. Our answer was in the Spanish tongue, "That for our ship, it was well; for we had rather met with calms and contrary winds, than any tempests. For our sick, they were many, and in very ill case; so that if they were not permitted to land, they ran in danger of their lives." Our other wants we set down in particular, adding, "That we had some little store of merchandise, which if it pleased them to deal for, it might supply our wants, without being chargeable unto them."

We offered some reward in pistolets unto the servant, and a piece of crimson velvet to be presented to the officer; but the servant took them not, nor would scarce look upon them; and so left us, and went back in another little boat which was sent for him.

About three hours after we had despatched our answer there came towards us a person (as it seemed) of a place. He had on him a gown with wide sleeves, of a kind of water chamolet, of an excellent azure colour, far more glossy than ours: his under apparel was green, and so was his hat, being in the form of a turban, daintily made, and not so huge as the Turkish turbans; and the locks of his hair came down below the brims of it. A reverend man was he to behold. He came in a boat, gilt in some part of it, with four persons more only in that boat; and was followed by another boat, wherein were some twenty. When he was come within a flight-shot of our ship, signs were made to us that we should send forth some to meet him upon the water, which we presently did in our ship-boat, sending the principal man amongst us save one, and four of our number with him. When we were come within six yards of their boat, they called to us to stay, and not to approach farther, which we did. And thereupon the man, whom I before described, stood up, and with a loud voice in Spanish, asked, "Are ye Christians?" We answered, "We were;" fearing the less, because of the cross we had seen in the subscription. At which answer the said person lift up his right hand towards heaven, and drew it softly to his mouth (which is the gesture they use, when they thank God), and then said: "If ye will swear, all of you, by the merits of the Saviour, that ye are no pirates; nor have shed blood, lawfully nor unlawfully, within forty days past; you may have license to come on land." We said, "We were all ready to take that oath." Whereupon one of those that were with him, being (as it seemed) a notary, made an entry of this act. Which done, another of the attendants of the great person, which was with him in the same boat, after his lord had spoken a little to him, said aloud: "My lord would have you know, that it is not of pride, or greatness, that he cometh not aboard your ship: but for that, in your answer, you declare that you have many sick amongst you, he was warned by the conservator of health of the city that he should keep a distance." We bowed ourselves towards him, and answered: "We were his humble servants; and accounted for great honour and singular humanity towards us, that which was already done: but hoped well, that the nature of the sickness of our men was not infectious." So he returned; and a while after came the notary to us aboard our ship; holding in his hand a fruit of that country, like an orange, but of colour between orange-tawny and scarlet: which cast a most excellent odour. He used it (as it seemed) for a preservative against infection. He gave us our oath, "By the name of Jesus, and His merits:" and after told us, that the next day by six of the clock in the morning, we should be sent to, and brought to the strangers' house (so he called it), where we should be accommodated of things, both for our whole and for our sick. So he left us; and when we offered him some pistolets, he smiling, said, "He must not be twice paid for one labour:" meaning (as I take it) that he had salary sufficient of the state for his service. For (as I after learned) they call an officer that taketh rewards twice-paid.

The next morning early, there came to us the same officer that came to us at first with his cane, and told us: "He came to conduct us to the strangers' house: and that he had prevented the hour, because we might have the whole day before us for our business. For (said he) if you will follow my advice, there shall first go with me some few of you, and see the place, and how it may be made convenient for you: and then you may send for your sick, and the rest of your number, which ye will bring on land." We thanked him, and said, "That his care which he took of desolate strangers, God would reward." And so six of us went on land with him; and when we were on land, he went before us, and turned to us, and said, "He was but our servant, and our guide." He led us through three fair streets; and all the way we went there were gathered some people on both sides, standing in a row; but in so civil a fashion, as if it had been, not to wonder at us, but to welcome us; and divers of them, as we passed by them, put their arms a little abroad, which is their gesture when they bid any welcome. The strangers' house is a fair and spacious house, built of brick, of somewhat a bluer colour than our brick; and with handsome windows, some of glass, some of a kind of cambric oiled. He brought us first into a fair parlour above stairs, and then asked us, "What number of persons we were? and how many sick?" We answered, "We were in all (sick and whole) one and fifty persons, whereof our sick were seventeen." He desired us to have patience a little, and to stay till he came back to us, which was about an hour after; and then he led us to see the chambers which were provided for us, being in number nineteen. They having cast it (as it seemeth) that four of those chambers, which were better than the rest, might receive four of the principal men of our company; and lodge them alone by themselves; and the other fifteen chambers were to lodge us, two and two together. The chambers were handsome and cheerful chambers, and furnished civilly. Then he led us to a long gallery, like a dorture, where he showed us all along the one side (for the other side was but wall and window) seventeen cells, very neat ones, having partitions of cedar wood. Which gallery and cells, being in all forty (many more than we needed), were instituted as an infirmary for sick persons. And he told us withal, that as any of our sick waxed well, he might be removed from his cell to a chamber: for which purpose there were set forth ten spare chambers, besides the number we spake of before. This done, he brought us back to the parlour, and lifting up his cane a little (as they do when they give any charge or command), said to us, "Ye are to know that the custom of the land requireth, that after this day and to-morrow (which we give you for removing your people from your ship), you are to keep within doors for three days. But let it not trouble you, nor do not think yourselves restrained, but rather left to your rest and ease. You shall want nothing; and there are six of our people appointed to attend you for any business you may have abroad." We gave him thanks with all affection and respect, and said, "God surely is manifested in this land." We offered him also twenty pistolets; but he smiled, and only said: "What? Twice paid!" And so he left us. Soon after our dinner was served in; which was right good viands, both for bread and meat: better than any collegiate diet that I have known in Europe. We had also drink of three sorts, all wholesome and good; wine of the grape; a drink of grain, such as is with us our ale, but more clear; and a kind of cider made of a fruit of that country; a wonderful pleasing and refreshing drink. Besides, there were brought in to us great store of those scarlet oranges for our sick; which (they said) were an assured remedy for sickness taken at sea. There was given us also a box of small grey or whitish pills, which they wished our sick should take, one of the pills every night before sleep; which (they said) would hasten their recovery. The next day, after that our trouble of carriage and removing of our men and goods out of our ship was somewhat settled and quiet, I thought good to call our company together, and when they were assembled, said unto them, "My dear friends, let us know ourselves, and how it standeth with us. We are men cast on land, as Jonas was out of the whale's belly, when we were as buried in the deep; and now we are on land, we are but between death and life, for we are beyond both the old world and the new; and whether ever we shall see Europe, God only knoweth. It is a kind of miracle hath brought us hither, and it must be little less that shall bring us hence. Therefore in regard of our deliverance past, and our danger present and to come, let us look up to God, and every man reform his own ways. Besides we are come here amongst a Christian people, full of piety and humanity. Let us not bring that confusion of face upon ourselves, as to show our vices or unworthiness before them. Yet there is more, for they have by commandment (though in form of courtesy) cloistered us within these walls for three days; who knoweth whether it be not to take some taste of our manners and conditions? And if they find them bad, to banish us straightways; if good, to give us further time. For these men that they have given us for attendance, may withal have an eye upon us. Therefore, for God's love, and as we love the weal of our souls and bodies, let us so behave ourselves, as we may be at peace with God, and may find grace in the eyes of this people." Our company with one voice thanked me for my good admonition, and promised me to live soberly and civilly, and without giving any the least occasion of offence. So we spent our three days joyfully, and without care, in expectation what would be done with us when they were expired. During which time, we had every hour joy of the amendment of our sick, who thought themselves cast into some divine pool of healing, they mended so kindly and so fast.

The morrow after our three days were past, there came to us a new man, that we had not seen before, clothed in blue as the former was, save that his turban was white with a small red cross on the top. He had also a tippet of fine linen. At his coming in, he did bend to us a little, and put his arms abroad. We of our parts saluted him in a very lowly and submissive manner; as looking that from him we should receive sentence of life or death. He desired to speak with some few of us. Whereupon six of us only stayed, and the rest avoided the room. He said, "I am by office governor of this house of strangers, and by vocation I am a Christian priest; and therefore am come to you, to offer you my service, both as strangers, and chiefly as Christians. Some things I may tell you, which I think you will not be unwilling to hear. The state hath given you license to stay on land for the space of six weeks: and let it not trouble you, if your occasions ask further time, for the law in this point is not precise; and I do not doubt, but myself shall be able to obtain for you such further time as shall be convenient. Ye shall also understand, that the strangers' house is at this time rich, and much aforehand; for it hath laid up revenue these thirty-seven years: for so long it is since any stranger arrived in this part; and therefore take ye no care; the state will defray you all the time you stay. Neither shall you stay one day the less for that. As for any merchandise you have brought, ye shall be well used, and have your return, either in merchandise or in gold and silver: for to us it is all one. And if you have any other request to make, hide it not; for ye shall find we will not make your countenance to fall by the answer ye shall receive. Only this I must tell you, that none of you must go above a karan (that is with them a mile and a half) from the walls of the city, without special leave." We answered, after we had looked a while upon one another, admiring this gracious and parent-like usage, that we could not tell what to say, for we wanted words to express our thanks; and his noble free offers left us nothing to ask. It seemed to us, that we had before us a picture of our salvation in heaven; for we that were a while since in the jaws of death, were now brought into a place where we found nothing but consolations. For the commandment laid upon us, we would not fail to obey it, though it was impossible but our hearts should be inflamed to tread further upon this happy and holy ground. We added, that our tongues should first cleave to the roofs of our mouths, ere we should forget, either this reverend person, or this whole nation, in our prayers. We also most humbly besought him to accept of us as his true servants, by as just a right as ever men on earth were bounden; laying and presenting both our persons and all we had at his feet. He said, he was a priest, and looked lot a priest's reward; which was our brotherly love, and the good of our souls and bodies. So he went from us, not without tears of tenderness in his eyes, and left us also confused with joy and kindness, saying amongst ourselves, that we were come into a land of angels, which did appear to us daily, and prevent us with comforts, which we thought not of, much less expected.

The next day, about ten of the clock, the governor came to us again, and after salutations, said familiarly, that he was come to visit us; and called for a chair, and sat him down; and we being some ten of us (the rest were of the meaner sort, or else gone abroad), sat down with him; and when we were set, he began thus: "We of this island of Bensalem (for so they called it in their language) have this: that by means of our solitary situation, and of the laws of secrecy, which we have for our travellers, and our rare admission of strangers; we know well most part of the habitable world, and are ourselves unknown. Therefore because he that knoweth least is fittest to ask questions, it is more reason, for the entertainment of the time, that ye ask me questions, than that I ask you." We answered, that we humbly thanked him, that he would give us leave so to do. And that we conceived by the taste we had already, that there was no worldly thing on earth more worthy to be known than the state of that happy land. But above all (we said) since that we were met from the several ends of the world, and hoped assuredly that we should meet one day in the kingdom of heaven (for that we were both parts Christians), we desired to know (in respect that land was so remote, and so divided by vast and unknown seas from the land where our Saviour walked on earth) who was the apostle of that nation, and how it was converted to the faith? It appeared in his face, that he took great contentment in this our question; he said, "Ye knit my heart to you, by asking this question in the first place: for it showeth that you first seek the kingdom of heaven: and I shall gladly, and briefly, satisfy your demand.

"About twenty years after the ascension of our Saviour it came to pass, that there was seen by the people of Renfusa (a city upon the eastern coast of our island, within sight, the night was cloudy and calm), as it might be some mile in the sea, a great pillar of light; not sharp, but in form of a column, or cylinder, rising from the sea, a great way up towards heaven; and on the top of it was seen a large cross of light, more bright and resplendent than the body of the pillar. Upon which so strange a spectacle, the people of the city gathered apace together upon the sands, to wonder; and so after put themselves into a number of small boats to go nearer to this marvellous sight. But when the boats were come within about sixty yards of the pillar, they found themselves all bound, and could go no further, yet so as they might move to go about, but might not approach nearer; so as the boats stood all as in a theatre, beholding this light, as an heavenly sign. It so fell out, that there was in one of the boats one of the wise men of the Society of Salomon's House; which house or college, my good brethren, is the very eye of this kingdom, who having a while attentively and devoutly viewed and contemplated this pillar and cross, fell down upon his face; and then raised himself upon his knees, and lifting up his hands to heaven, made his prayers in this manner:

"'Lord God of heaven and earth; thou hast vouchsafed of thy grace, to those of our order to know thy works of creation, and true secrets of them; and to discern (as far as appertaineth to the generations of men) between divine miracles, works of Nature, works of art and impostures, and illusions of all sorts. I do here acknowledge and testify before this people, that the thing we now see before our eyes, is thy finger, and a true miracle. And forasmuch as we learn in our books, that thou never workest miracles, but to a divine and excellent end (for the laws of Nature are thine own laws, and thou exceedest them not but upon great cause), we most humbly beseech thee to prosper this great sign, and to give us the interpretation and use of it in mercy; which thou dost in some part secretly promise, by sending it unto us.'

"When he had made his prayer, he presently found the boat he was in movable and unbound; whereas all the rest remained still fast; and taking that for an assurance of leave to approach, he caused the boat to be softly and with silence rowed towards the pillar; but ere he came near it, the pillar and cross of light broke up, and cast itself abroad, as it were into a firmament of many stars, which also vanished soon after; and there was nothing left to be seen but a small ark, or chest of cedar, dry and not wet at all with water, though it swam; and in the fore-end of it, which was towards him, grew a small green branch of palm; and when the wise man had taken it with all reverence into his boat, it opened of itself, and there were found in it a book and a letter, both written in fine parchment, and wrapped in sindons of linen. The book contained all the canonical books of the Old and New Testament, according as you have them (for we know well what the churches with you receive), and the Apocalypse itself; and some other books of the New Testament, which were not at that time written, were nevertheless in the book. And for the letter, it was in these words:

"'I Bartholomew, a servant of the Highest, and apostle of Jesus Christ, was warned by an angel that appeared to me in a vision of glory, that I should commit this ark to the floods of the sea. Therefore I do testify and declare unto that people where

God shall ordain this ark to come to land, that in the same day is come unto them salvation and peace, and goodwill from the Father, and from the Lord Jesus.'

"There was also in both these writings, as well the book as the letter, wrought a great miracle, conform to that of the apostles, in the original gift of tongues. For there being at that time, in this land, Hebrews, Persians, and Indians, besides the natives, every one read upon the book and letter, as if they had been written in his own language. And thus was this land saved from infidelity (as the remain of the old world was from water) by an ark, through the apostolical and miraculous evangelism of St. Bartholomew." And here he paused, and a messenger came, and called him forth from us. So this was all that passed in that conference.

The next day, the same governor came again to us, immediately after dinner, and excused himself, saying, "That the day before he was called from us somewhat abruptly, but now he would make us amends, and spend time with us, if we held his company and conference agreeable." We answered, that we held it so agreeable and pleasing to us, as we forgot both dangers past, and fears to come, for the time we heard him speak; and that we thought an hour spent with him was worth years of our former life. He bowed himself a little to us, and after we were set again, he said, "Well, the questions are on your part." One of our number said, after a little pause, that there was a matter we were no less desirous to know than fearful to ask, lest we might presume too far. But encouraged by his rare humanity towards us (that could scarce think ourselves strangers, being his vowed and professed servants), we would take the hardness to propound it; humbly beseeching him, if he thought it not fit to be answered, that he would pardon it, though he rejected it. We said, we well observed those his words, which he formerly spake, that this happy island, where we now stood, was known to few, and yet knew most of the nations of the world, which we found to be true, considering they had the languages of Europe, and knew much of our state and business; and yet we in Europe (notwithstanding all the remote discoveries and navigations of this last age) never heard any of the least inkling or glimpse of this island. This we found wonderful strange; for that all nations have interknowledge one of another, either by voyage into foreign parts, or by strangers that come to them; and though the traveller into a foreign country doth commonly know more by the eye than he that stayeth at home can by relation of the traveller; yet both ways suffice to make a mutual knowledge, in some degree, on both parts. But for this island, we never heard tell of any ship of theirs, that had been seen to arrive upon any shore of Europe; no, nor of either the East or West Indies, nor yet of any ship of any other part of the world, that had made return for them. And yet the marvel rested not in this. For the situation of it (as his lordship said) in the secret conclave of such a vast sea might cause it. But then, that they should have knowledge of the languages, books, affairs, of those that lie such a distance from them, it was a thing we could not tell what to make of; for that it seemed to us a condition and propriety of divine powers and beings, to be hidden and unseen to others, and yet to have others open, and as in a light to them. At this speech the governor gave a gracious smile and said, that we did well to ask pardon for this question we now asked, for that it imported, as if we thought this land a land of magicians, that sent forth spirits of the air into all parts, to bring them news and intelligence of other countries. It was answered by us all, in all possible humbleness, but yet with a countenance taking knowledge, that we knew that he spake it but merrily. That we were apt enough to think, there was somewhat supernatural in this island, but yet rather as angelical than magical. But to let his lordship know truly what it was that made us tender and doubtful to ask this question, it was not any such conceit, but because we remembered he had given a touch in his former speech, that this land had laws of secrecy touching strangers. To this he said, "You remember it aright; and therefore in that I shall say to you, I must reserve some particulars, which it is not lawful for me to reveal, but there will be enough left to give you satisfaction.

"You shall understand (that which perhaps you will scarce think credible) that about three thousand years ago, or somewhat more, the navigation of the world (especially for remote voyages) was greater than at this day. Do not think with yourselves, that I know not how much it is increased with you, within these threescore years; I know it well, and yet I say, greater then than now; whether it was, that the example of the ark, that saved the remnant of men from the universal deluge, gave men confidence to adventure upon the waters, or what it was; but such is the truth. The Phoenicians, and especially the Tyrians, had great fleets; so had the Carthaginians their colony, which is yet farther west. Toward the east the shipping of Egypt, and of Palestine, was likewise great. China also, and the great Atlantis (that you call America), which have now but junks and canoes, abounded then in tall ships. This island (as appeareth by faithful registers of those times) had then fifteen hundred strong ships, of great content. Of all this there is with you sparing memory, or none; but we have large knowledge thereof.

"At that time, this land was known and frequented by the ships and vessels of all the nations before named. And (as it cometh to pass) they had many times men of other countries, that were no sailors, that came with them; as Persians, Chaldeans, Arabians, so as almost all nations of might and fame resorted hither; of whom we have some stirps and little tribes with us at this day. And for our own ships, they went sundry voyages, as well to your straits, which you call the Pillars of Hercules, as to other parts in the Atlantic and Mediterranean Seas; as to Paguin (which is the same with Cambalaine) and Quinzy, upon the Oriental Seas, as far as to the borders of the East Tartary.

"At the same time, and an age after or more, the inhabitants of the great Atlantis did flourish. For though the narration and description which is made by a great man with you, that the descendants of Neptune planted there, and of the magnificent temple, palace, city and hill; and the manifold streams of goodly navigable rivers, which as so many chains environed the same site and temple; and the several degrees of ascent, whereby men did climb up to the same, as if it had been a Scala Cœli; be all poetical and fabulous; yet so much is true, that the said country of Atlantis, as well that of Peru, then called Coya, as that of Mexico, then named Tyrambel, were mighty and proud kingdoms, in arms, shipping, and riches; so mighty, as at one time, or at least within the space of ten years, they both made two great expeditions; they of Tyrambel through the Atlantic to the Mediterranean Sea; and they of Coya, through the South Sea upon this our island; and for the former of these, which was into Europe, the same author amongst you, as it seemeth, had some relation from the Egyptian priest, whom he citeth. For assuredly, such a thing there was. But whether it were the ancient Athenians that had the glory of the repulse and resistance of those forces, I can say nothing; but certain it is there never came back either ship or man from that voyage. Neither had the other voyage of those of Coya upon us had better fortune, if they had not met with enemies of greater clemency. For the king of this island, by name Altabin, a wise man and a great warrior, knowing well both his own strength and that of his enemies, handled the matter so, as he cut off their land forces from their ships, and entoiled both their navy and their camp with a greater power than theirs, both by sea and land; and compelled them to render themselves without striking a stroke; and after they were at his mercy, contenting himself only with their oath, that they should no more bear arms against him, dismissed them all in safety. But the divine revenge overtook not long after those proud enterprises. For within less than the space of one hundred years the Great Atlantis was utterly lost and destroyed; not by a great earthquake, as your man saith, for that whole tract is little subject to earthquakes, but by a particular deluge, or inundation; those countries having at this day far greater rivers, and far higher mountains to pour down waters, than any part of the old world. But it is true that the same inundation was not deep, not past forty foot, in most places, from the ground, so that although it destroyed man and beast generally, yet some few wild inhabitants of the wood escaped. Birds also were saved by flying to the high trees and woods. For as for men, although they had buildings in many places higher than the depth of the water, yet that inundation, though it were shallow, had a long continuance, whereby they of the vale that were not drowned perished for want of food, and other things necessary. So as marvel you not at the thin population of America, nor at the rudeness and ignorance of the people; for you must account your inhabitants of America as a young people, younger a thousand years at the least than the rest of the world, for that there was so much time between the universal flood and their particular inundation. For the poor remnant of human seed which remained in their mountains, peopled the country again slowly, by little and little, and being simple and a savage people (not like Noah and his sons, which was the chief family of the earth), they were not able to leave letters, arts, and civility to their posterity; and having likewise in their mountainous habitations been used, in respect of the extreme cold of those regions, to clothe themselves with the skins of tigers, bears, and great hairy goats, that they have in those parts; when after they came down into the valley, and found the intolerable heats which are there, and knew no means of lighter apparel, they were forced to begin the custom of going naked, which continueth at this day. Only they take great pride and delight in the feathers of birds, and this also they took from those their ancestors of the mountains, who were invited unto it, by the infinite flight of birds, that came up to the high grounds, while the waters stood below. So you see, by this main accident of time, we lost our traffic with the Americans, with whom of all others, in regard they lay nearest to us, we had most commerce. As for the other parts of the world, it is most manifest that in the ages following (whether it were in respect of wars, or by a natural revolution of time) navigation did everywhere greatly decay, and specially far voyages (the rather by the use of galleys, and such vessels as could hardly brook the ocean) were altogether left and omitted. So then, that part of intercourse which could be from other nations, to sail to us, you see how it hath long since ceased; except it were by some rare accident, as this of yours. But now of the cessation of that other part of intercourse, which might be by our sailing to other nations, I must yield you some other cause. For I cannot say, if I shall say truly, but our shipping, for number, strength, mariners, pilots, and all things that appertain to navigation, is as great as ever; and therefore why we should sit at home, I shall now give you an account by itself; and it will draw nearer, to give you satisfaction, to your principal question.

"There reigned in this island, about 1,900 years ago, a king, whose memory of all others we most adore; not superstitiously, but as a divine instrument, though a mortal man: his name was Salomona; and we esteem him as the lawgiver of our nation. This king had a large heart, inscrutable for good; and was wholly bent to make his kingdom and people happy. He therefore taking into consideration how sufficient and substantive this land was, to maintain itself without any aid at all of the foreigner; being 5,000 miles in circuit, and of rare fertility of soil, in the greatest part thereof; and finding also the shipping of this country might be plentifully set on work, both by fishing and by transportations from port to port, and likewise by sailing unto some small islands that are not far from us, and are under the crown and laws of this state; and recalling into his memory the happy and flourishing estate wherein this land then was, so as it might be a thousand ways altered to the worse, but scarce any one way to the better; though nothing wanted to his noble and heroical intentions, but only (as far as human foresight might reach) to give perpetuity to that which was in his time so happily established, therefore amongst his other fundamental laws of this kingdom he did ordain the interdicts and prohibitions which we have touching entrance of strangers; which at that time (though it was after the calamity of America) was frequent; doubting novelties and commixture of manners. It is true, the like law against the admission of strangers without license is an ancient law in the kingdom of China, and yet continued in use. But there it is a poor thing; and hath made them a curious, ignorant, fearful foolish nation. But our lawgiver made his law of another temper. For first, he hath preserved all points of humanity, in taking order and making provision for the relief of strangers distressed; whereof you have tasted." At which speech (as reason was) we all rose up, and bowed ourselves. He went on: "That king also still desiring to join humanity and policy together; and thinking it against humanity, to detain strangers here against their wills; and against policy, that they should return, and discover their knowledge of this estate, he took this course; he did ordain, that of the strangers that should be permitted to land, as many at all times might depart as many as would; but as many as would stay, should have very good conditions, and means to live from the state. Wherein he saw so far, that now in so many ages since the prohibition, we have memory not of one ship that ever returned, and but of thirteen persons only, at several times, that chose to return in our bottoms. What those few that returned may have reported abroad, I know not. But you must think, whatsoever they have said, could be taken where they came but for a dream. Now for our travelling from hence into parts abroad, our lawgiver thought fit altogether to restrain it. So is it not in China. For the Chinese sail where they will, or can; which showeth, that their law of keeping out strangers is a law of pusillanimity and fear. But this restraint of ours hath one only exception, which is admirable; preserving the good which cometh by communicating with strangers, and avoiding the hurt: and I will now open it to you. And here I shall seem a little to digress, but you will by-and-by find it pertinent. Ye shall understand, my dear friends, that amongst the excellent acts of that king, one above all hath the pre-eminence. It was the erection and institution of an order, or society, which we call Salomon's House; the noblest foundation, as we think, that ever was upon the earth, and the lantern of this kingdom. It is dedicated to the study of the works and creatures of God. Some think it beareth the founder's name a little corrupted, as if it should be Solomon's House. But the records write it as it is spoken. So as I take it to be denominate of the king of the Hebrews, which is famous with you, and no strangers to us; for we have some parts of his works which with you are lost; namely, that natural history which he wrote of all plants, from the cedar of Libanus to the moss that groweth out of the wall; and of all things that have life and motion. This maketh me think that our king finding himself to symbolize, in many things, with that king of the Hebrews, which lived many years before him, honoured him with the title of this foundation. And I am the rather induced to be of this opinion, for that I find in ancient records, this order or society is sometimes called Solomon's House, and sometimes the College of the Six Days' Works; whereby I am satisfied that our excellent king had learned from the Hebrews that God had created the world, and all that therein is, within six days: and therefore he instituted that house, for the finding out of the true nature of all things, whereby God might have the more glory in the workmanship of them, and men the more fruit in their use of them, did give it also that second name. But now to come to our present purpose. When the king had forbidden to all his people navigation into any part that was not under his crown, he made nevertheless this ordinance; that every twelve years there should be set forth out of this kingdom, two ships, appointed to several voyages; that in either of these ships there should be a mission of three of the fellows or brethren of Salomon's House, whose errand was only to give us knowledge of the affairs and state of those countries to which they were designed; and especially of the sciences, arts, manufactures, and inventions of all the world; and withal to bring unto us books, instruments, and patterns in every kind: that the ships, after they had landed the brethren, should return; and that the brethren should stay abroad till the new mission, the ships are not otherwise fraught than with store of victuals, and good quantity of treasure to remain with the brethren, for the buying of such things, and rewarding of such persons, as they should think fit. Now for me to tell you how the vulgar sort of mariners are contained from being discovered at land, and how they that must be put on shore for any time, colour themselves under the names of other nations, and to what places these voyages have been designed; and what places of rendezvous are appointed for the new missions, and the like circumstances of the practice, I may not do it, neither is it much to your desire. But thus you see we maintain a trade, not for gold, silver, or jewels, nor for silks, nor for spices, nor any other commodity of matter; but only for God's first creature, which was light; to have light, I say, of the growth of all parts of the world." And when he had said this, he was silent, and so were we all; for indeed we were all astonished to hear so strange things so probably told. And he perceiving that we were willing to say somewhat, but had it not ready, in great courtesy took us off, and descended to ask us questions of our voyage and fortunes, and in the end concluded that we might do well to think with ourselves, what time of stay we would demand of the state, and bade us not to scant ourselves; for he would procure such time as we desired. Whereupon we all rose up and presented ourselves to kiss the skirt of his tippet, but he would not suffer us, and so took his leave. But when it came once amongst our people, that the state used to offer conditions to strangers that would stay, we had work enough to get any of our men to look to our ship, and to keep them from going presently to the governor, to crave conditions; but with much ado we restrained them, till we might agree what course to take.

We took ourselves now for freemen, seeing there was no danger of our utter perdition, and lived most joyfully, going abroad and seeing what was to be seen in the city and places adjacent, within our tedder; and obtaining acquaintance with many of the city, not of the meanest quality, at whose hands we found such humanity, and such a freedom and desire to take strangers, as it were, into their bosom, as was enough to make us forget all that was dear to us in our own countries; and continually we met with many things, right worthy of observation and relation; as indeed, if there be a mirror in the world, worthy to hold men's eyes, it is that country. One day there were two of our company bidden to a feast of the family, as they call it; a most natural, pious, and reverend custom it is, showing that nation to be compounded of all goodness. This is the manner of it; it is granted to any man that shall live to see thirty persons descended of his body, alive together, and all above three years old, to make this feast, which is done at the cost of the state. The father of the family, whom they call the Tirsan, two days before the feast, taketh to him three of such friends as he liketh to choose, and is assisted also by the governor of the city or place where the feast is celebrated, and all the persons of the family, of both sexes, are summoned to attend him. These two days the Tirsan sitteth in consultation, concerning the good estate of the family. There, if there be any discord or suits between any of the family, they are compounded and appeased. There, if any of the family be distressed or decayed, order is taken for their relief, and competent means to live. There, if any be subject to vice, or take ill courses, they are reproved and censured. So likewise direction is given touching marriages, and the courses of life which any of them should take, with divers other the like orders and advices. The governor assisteth to the end, to put in execution, by his public authority, the decrees and orders of the Tirsan, if they should be disobeyed, though that seldom needeth; such reverence and obedience they give to the order of Nature. The Tirsan doth also then ever choose one man from amongst his sons, to live in house with him; who is called ever after the Son of the Vine. The reason will hereafter appear. On the feast day, the father or Tirsan cometh forth after divine service into a large room where the feast is celebrated; which room hath an half-pace at the upper end. Against the wall, in the middle of the half-pace, is a chair placed for him, with a table and carpet before it. Over the chair is a state, made round or oval, and it is of ivy; an ivy somewhat whiter than ours, like the leaf of a silver asp, but more shining; for it is green all winter. And the state is curiously wrought with silver and silk of divers colours, broiding or binding in the ivy; and is ever of the work of some of the daughters of the family; and veiled over at the top, with a fine net of silk and silver. But the substance of it is true ivy; whereof after it is taken down, the friends of the family are desirous to have some leaf or sprig to keep. The Tirsan cometh forth with all his generation or lineage, the males before him, and the females following him; and if there be a mother, from whose body the whole lineage is descended, there is a traverse placed in a loft above on the right hand of the chair, with a privy door, and a carved window of glass, leaded with gold and blue; where she sitteth, but is not seen. When the Tirsan is come forth, he sitteth down in the chair; and all the lineage place themselves against the wall, both at his back, and upon the return of the half-pace, in order of their years, without difference of sex, and stand upon their feet. When he is set, the room being always full of company, but well kept and without disorder, after some pause there cometh in from the lower end of the room a Taratan (which is as much as an herald), and on either side of him two young lads: whereof one carrieth a scroll of their shining yellow parchment, and the other a cluster of grapes of gold, with a long foot or stalk. The herald and children are clothed with mantles of sea-water green satin; but the herald's mantle is streamed with gold, and hath a train. Then the herald with three curtsies, or rather inclinations, cometh up as far as the half-pace, and there first taketh into his hand the scroll. This scroll is the king's charter, containing gift of revenue, and many privileges, exemptions, and points of honour, granted to the father of the family; and it is ever styled and directed, "To such an one, our well-beloved friend and creditor," which is a title proper only to this case. For they say, the king is debtor to no man, but for propagation of his subjects; the seal set to the king's charter is the king's image, embossed or moulded in gold; and though such charters be expedited of course, and as of right, yet they are varied by discretion, according to the number and dignity of the family. This charter the herald readeth aloud; and while it is read, the father or Tirsan standeth up, supported by two of his sons, such as he chooseth. Then the herald mounteth the half-pace, and delivereth the charter into his hand: and with that there is an acclamation, by all that are present, in their language, which is thus much, "Happy are the people of Bensalem." Then the herald taketh into his hand from the other child the cluster of grapes, which is of gold; both the stalk, and the grapes. But the grapes are daintily enamelled; and if the males of the family be the greater number, the grapes are enamelled purple, with a little sun set on the top; if the females, then they are enamelled into a greenish yellow, with a crescent on the top. The grapes are in number as many as there are descendants of the family. This golden cluster the herald delivereth also to the Tirsan; who presently delivereth it over to that son that he had formerly chosen, to be in house with him: who beareth it before his father, as an ensign of honour, when he goeth in public ever after; and is thereupon called the Son of the Vine. After this ceremony ended the father or Tirsan retireth; and after some time cometh forth again to dinner, where he sitteth alone under the state, as before; and none of his descendants sit with him, of what degree or dignity so ever, except he hap to be of Salomon's House. He is served only by his own children, such as are male; who perform unto him all service of the table upon the knee, and the women only stand about him, leaning against the wall. The room below his half-pace hath tables on the sides for the guests that are bidden; who are served with great and comely order; and towards the end of dinner (which in the greatest feasts with them lasteth never above an hour and a half) there is an hymn sung, varied according to the invention of him that composeth it (for they have excellent poesy), but the subject of it is always the praises of Adam, and Noah, and Abraham; whereof the former two peopled the world, and the last was the father of the faithful: concluding ever with a thanksgiving for the nativity of our Saviour, in whose birth the births of all are only blessed. Dinner being done, the Tirsan retireth again; and having withdrawn himself alone into a place, where he maketh some private prayers, he cometh forth the third time, to give the blessing; with all his descendants, who stand about him as at the first. Then he calleth them forth by one and by one, by name as he pleaseth, though seldom the order of age be inverted. The person that is called (the table being before removed) kneeleth down before the chair, and the father layeth his hand upon his head, or her head, and giveth the blessing in these words: "Son of Bensalem (or daughter of Bensalem), thy father saith it; the man by whom thou hast breath and life speaketh the word; the blessing of the everlasting Father, the Prince of Peace, and the Holy Dove be upon thee, and make the days of thy pilgrimage good and many." This he saith to every of them; and that done, if there be any of his sons of eminent merit and virtue, so they be not above two, he calleth for them again, and saith, laying his arm over their shoulders, they standing: "Sons, it is well you are born, give God the praise, and persevere to the end." And withal delivereth to either of them a jewel, made in the figure of an ear of wheat, which they ever after wear in the front of their turban, or hat; this done, they fall to music and dances, and other recreations, after their manner, for the rest of the day. This is the full order of that feast.

By that time six or seven days were spent, I was fallen into straight acquaintance with a merchant of that city, whose name was Joabin. He was a Jew and circumcised; for they have some few stirps of Jews yet remaining among them, whom they leave to their own religion. Which they may the better do, because they are of a far differing disposition from the Jews in other parts. For whereas they hate the name of Christ, and have a secret inbred rancour against the people amongst whom they live; these, contrariwise, give unto our Saviour many high attributes, and love the nation of Bensalem extremely. Surely this man of whom I speak would ever acknowledge that Christ was born of a Virgin; and that He was more than a man; and he would tell how God made Him ruler of the seraphims, which guard His throne; and they call Him also the Milken Way, and the Eliah of the Messiah, and many other high names, which though they be inferior to His divine majesty, yet they are far from the language of other Jews. And for the country of Bensalem, this man would make no end of commending it, being desirous by tradition among the Jews there to have it believed that the people thereof were of the generations of Abraham, by another son, whom they call Nachoran; and that Moses by a secret cabala ordained the laws of Bensalem which they now use; and that when the Messias should come, and sit in His throne at Hierusalem, the King of Bensalem should sit at His feet, whereas other kings should keep a great distance. But yet setting aside these Jewish dreams, the man was a wise man and learned, and of great policy, and excellently seen in the laws and customs of that nation. Amongst other discourses one day I told him, I was much affected with the relation I had from some of the company of their custom in holding the feast of the family, for that, methought, I had never heard of a solemnity wherein Nature did so much preside. And because propagation of families proceedeth from the nuptial copulation, I desired to know of him what laws and customs they had concerning marriage, and whether they kept marriage well, and whether they were tied to one wife? For that where population is so much affected, and such as with them it seemed to be, there is commonly permission of plurality of wives. To this he said: "You have reason for to commend that excellent institution of the feast of the family; and indeed we have experience, that those families that are partakers of the blessings of that feast, do flourish and prosper ever after, in an extraordinary manner. But hear me now, and I will tell you what I know. You shall understand that there is not under the heavens so chaste a nation as this of Bensalem, nor so free from all pollution or foulness. It is the virgin of the world; I remember, I have read in one of your European books, of an holy hermit amongst you, that desired to see the spirit of fornication, and there appeared to him a little foul ugly Ethiope; but if he had desired to see the spirit of chastity of Bensalem, it would have appeared to him in the likeness of a fair beautiful cherubim. For there is nothing, amongst mortal men, more fair and admirable than the chaste minds of this people. Know, therefore, that with them there are no stews, no dissolute houses, no courtezans, nor anything of that kind. Nay, they wonder, with detestation, at you in Europe, which permit such things. They say ye have put marriage out of office; for marriage is ordained a remedy for unlawful concupiscence; and natural concupiscence seemeth as a spur to marriage. But when men have at hand a remedy, more agreeable to their corrupt will, marriage is almost expulsed. And therefore there are with you seen infinite men that marry not, but choose rather a libertine and impure single life, than to be yoked in marriage; and many that do marry, marry late, when the prime and strength of their years is past. And when they do marry, what is marriage to them but a very bargain; wherein is sought alliance, or portion, or reputation, with some desire (almost indifferent) of issue; and not the faithful nuptial union of man and wife, that was first instituted. Neither is it possible, that those that have cast away so basely so much of their strength, should greatly esteem children (being of the same matter) as chaste men do. So likewise during marriage is the case much amended, as it ought to be if those things were tolerated only for necessity; no, but they remain still as a very affront to marriage. The haunting of those dissolute places, or resort to courtezans, are no more punished in married men than in bachelors. And the depraved custom of change, and the delight in meretricious embracements (where sin is turned into art), maketh marriage a dull thing, and a kind of imposition or tax. They hear you defend these things, as done to avoid greater evils; as advoutries, deflowering of virgins, unnatural lust, and the like. But they say, this is a preposterous wisdom; and they call it Lot's offer, who to save his guests from abusing, offered his daughters; nay, they say further, that there is little gained in this; for that the same vices and appetites do still remain and abound, unlawful lust being like a furnace, that if you stop the flames altogether it will quench, but if you give it any vent it will rage; as for masculine love, they have no touch of it; and yet there are not so faithful and inviolate friendships in the world again as are there, and to speak generally (as I said before) I have not read of any such chastity in any people as theirs. And their usual saying is that whosoever is unchaste cannot reverence himself; and they say that the reverence of a man's self, is, next religion, the chiefest bridle of all vices." And when he had said this the good Jew paused a little; whereupon I, far more willing to hear him speak on than to speak myself; yet thinking it decent that upon his pause of speech I should not be altogether silent, said only this; that I would say to him, as the widow of Sarepta said to Elias: "that he was come to bring to memory our sins;" and that I confess the righteousness of Bensalem was greater than the righteousness of Europe. At which speech he bowed his head, and went on this manner: "They have also many wise and excellent laws, touching marriage. They allow no polygamy. They have ordained that none do intermarry, or contract, until a month be past from their first interview. Marriage without consent of parents they do not make void, but they mulct it in the inheritors; for the children of such marriages are not admitted to inherit above a third part of their parents' inheritance. I have read in a book of one of your men, of a feigned commonwealth, where the married couple are permitted, before they contract, to see one another naked. This they dislike; for they think it a scorn to give a refusal after so familiar knowledge; but because of many hidden defects in men and women's bodies, they have a more civil way; for they have near every town a couple of pools (which they call Adam and Eve's pools), where it is permitted to one of the friends of the man, and another of the friends of the woman, to see them severally bathe naked."

And as we were thus in conference, there came one that seemed to be a messenger, in a rich huke, that spake with the Jew; whereupon he turned to me, and said, "You will pardon me, for I am commanded away in haste." The next morning he came to me again, joyful as it seemed, and said, "There is word come to the governor of the city, that one of the fathers of Salomon's House will be here this day seven-night; we have seen none of them this dozen years. His coming is in state; but the cause of his coming is secret. I will provide you and your fellows of a good standing to see his entry." I thanked him, and told him I was most glad of the news. The day being come he made his entry. He was a man of middle stature and age, comely of person, and had an aspect as if he pitied men. He was clothed in a robe of fine black cloth with wide sleeves, and a cape: his under garment was of excellent white linen down to the foot, girt with a girdle of the same; and a sindon or tippet of the same about his neck. He had gloves that were curious, and set with stone; and shoes of peach-coloured velvet. His neck was bare to the shoulders. His hat was like a helmet, or Spanish montero; and his locks curled below it decently; they were of colour brown. His beard was cut round and of the same colour with his hair, somewhat lighter. He was carried in a rich chariot, without wheels, litter-wise, with two horses at either end, richly trapped in blue velvet embroidered; and two footmen on each side in the like attire. The chariot was all of cedar, gilt and adorned with crystal; save that the fore-end had panels of sapphires, set in borders of gold, and the hinder-end the like of emeralds of the Peru colour. There was also a sun of gold, radiant upon the top, in the midst; and on the top before a small cherub of gold, with wings displayed. The chariot was covered with cloth of gold tissued upon blue. He had before him fifty attendants, young men all, in white satin loose coats up to the mid-leg, and stockings of white silk; and shoes of blue velvet; and hats of blue velvet, with fine plumes of divers colours, set round like hat-bands. Next before the chariot went two men, bare-headed, in linen garments down to the foot, girt, and shoes of blue velvet, who carried the one a crosier, the other a pastoral staff like a sheep-hook; neither of them of metal, but the crosier of balm-wood, the pastoral staff of cedar. Horsemen he had none, neither before nor behind his chariot; as it seemeth, to avoid all tumult and trouble. Behind his chariot went all the officers and principals of the companies of the city. He sat alone, upon cushions, of a kind of excellent plush, blue; and under his foot curious carpets of silk of divers colours, like the Persian, but far finer. He held up his bare hand, as he went, as blessing the people, but in silence. The street was wonderfully well kept; so that there was never any army had their men stand in better battle-array than the people stood. The windows likewise were not crowded, but every one stood in them, as if they had been placed. When the show was passed, the Jew said to me, "I shall not be able to attend you as I would, in regard of some charge the city hath laid upon me for the entertaining of this great person." Three days after the Jew came to me again, and said, "Ye are happy men; for the father of Salomon's House taketh knowledge of your being here, and commanded me to tell you, that he will admit all your company to his presence, and have private conference with one of you, that ye shall choose; and for this hath appointed the next day after to-morrow. And because he meaneth to give you his blessing, he hath appointed it in the forenoon." We came at our day and hour, and I was chosen by my fellows for the private access. We found him in a fair chamber, richly hanged, and carpeted under foot, without any degrees to the state; he was set upon a low throne richly adorned, and a rich cloth of state over his head of blue satin embroidered. He was alone, save that he had two pages of honour, on either hand one, finely attired in white. His under garments were the like that we saw him wear in the chariot; but instead of his gown, he had on him a mantle with a cape, of the same fine black, fastened about him. When we came in, as we were taught, we bowed low at our first entrance; and when we were come near his chair, he stood up, holding forth his hand ungloved, and in posture of blessing; and we every one of us stooped down, and kissed the end of his tippet. That done, the rest departed, and I remained. Then he warned the pages forth of the room, and caused me to sit down beside him, and spake to me thus in the Spanish tongue:

"God bless thee, my son; I will give thee the greatest jewel I have. For I will impart unto thee, for the love of God and men, a relation of the true state of Salomon's House. Son, to make you know the true state of Salomon's House, I will keep this order. First, I will set forth unto you the end of our foundation. Secondly, the preparations and instruments we have for our works. Thirdly, the several employments and functions whereto our fellows are assigned. And fourthly, the ordinances and rites which we observe.

"The end of our foundation is the knowledge of causes, and secret motions of things; and the enlarging of the bounds of human empire, to the effecting of all things possible.

"The preparations and instruments are these. We have large and deep caves of several depths; the deepest are sunk 600 fathoms; and some of them are digged and made under great hills and mountains; so that if you reckon together the depth of the hill, and the depth of the cave, they are, some of them, above three miles deep. For we find that the depth of an hill, and the depth of a cave from the flat, is the same thing; both remote alike from the sun and heaven's beams, and from the open air. These caves we call the lower region. And we use them for all coagulations, indurations, refrigerations, and conservations of bodies. We use them likewise for the imitation of natural mines and the producing also of new artificial metals, by compositions and materials which we use and lay there for many years. We use them also sometimes (which may seem strange) for curing of some diseases, and for prolongation of life, in some hermits that choose to live there, well accommodated of all things necessary, and indeed live very long; by whom also we learn many things.

"We have burials in several earths, where we put divers cements, as the Chinese do their porcelain. But we have them in greater variety, and some of them more fine. We also have great variety of composts and soils, for the making of the earth fruitful.

"We have high towers, the highest about half a mile in height, and some of them likewise set upon high mountains, so that the vantage of the hill with the tower, is in the highest of them three miles at least. And these places we call the upper region, account the air between the high places and the low, as a middle region. We use these towers, according to their several heights and situations, for insulation, refrigeration, conservation, and for the view of divers meteors—as winds, rain, snow, hail; and some of the fiery meteors also. And upon them, in some places, are dwellings of hermits, whom we visit sometimes, and instruct what to observe.

"We have great lakes, both salt and fresh, whereof we have use for the fish and fowl. We use them also for burials of some natural bodies, for we find a difference in things buried in earth, or in air below the earth, and things buried in water. We have also pools, of which some do strain fresh water out of salt, and others by art do turn fresh water into salt. We have also some rocks in the midst of the sea, and some bays upon the shore for some works, wherein is required the air and vapour of the sea. We have likewise violent streams and cataracts, which serve us for many motions; and likewise engines for multiplying and enforcing of winds to set also on divers motions.

"We have also a number of artificial wells and fountains, made in imitation of the natural sources and baths, as tincted upon vitriol, sulphur, steel, brass, lead, nitre, and other minerals; and again, we have little wells for infusions of many things, where the waters take the virtue quicker and better than in vessels or basins. And amongst them we have a water, which we call water of Paradise, being by that we do it made very sovereign for health and prolongation of life.

"We have also great and spacious houses, where we imitate and demonstrate meteors—as snow, hail, rain, some artificial rains of bodies, and not of water, thunders, lightnings; also generations of bodies in air—as frogs, flies, and divers others.

"We have also certain chambers, which we call chambers of health, where we qualify the air as we think good and proper for the cure of divers diseases, and preservation of health.

"We have also fair and large baths, of several mixtures, for the cure of diseases, and the restoring of man's body from arefaction; and others for the confirming of it in strength of sinews, vital parts, and the very juice and substance of the body.

"We have also large and various orchards and gardens, wherein we do not so much respect beauty as variety of ground and soil, proper for divers trees and herbs, and some very spacious, where trees and berries are set, whereof we make divers kinds of drinks, besides the vineyards. In these we practise likewise all conclusions of grafting, and inoculating, as well of wild-trees as fruit-trees, which produceth many effects. And we make by art, in the same orchards and gardens, trees and flowers, to come earlier or later than their seasons, and to come up and bear more speedily than by their natural course they do. We make them also by art greater much than their nature; and their fruit greater and sweeter, and of differing taste, smell, colour, and figure, from their nature. And many of them we so order, as that they become of medicinal use.

"We have also means to make divers plants rise by mixtures of earths without seeds, and likewise to make divers new plants, differing from the vulgar, and to make one tree or plant turn into another.

"We have also parks, and enclosures of all sorts, of beasts and birds; which we use not only for view or rareness, but likewise for dissections and trials, that thereby may take light what may be wrought upon the body of man. Wherein we find many strange effects: as continuing life in them, though divers parts, which you account vital, be perished and taken forth; resuscitating of some that seem dead in appearance, and the like. We try also all poisons, and other medicines upon them, as well of chirurgery as physic. By art likewise we make them greater or smaller than their kind is, and contrariwise dwarf them and stay their growth; we make them more fruitful and bearing than their kind is, and contrariwise barren and not generative. Also we make them differ in colour, shape, activity, many ways. We find means to make commixtures and copulations of divers kinds, which have produced many new kinds, and them not barren, as the general opinion is. We make a number of kinds of serpents, worms, flies, fishes of putrefaction, whereof some are advanced (in effect) to be perfect creatures, like beasts or birds, and have sexes, and do propagate. Neither do we this by chance, but we know beforehand of what matter and commixture, what kind of those creatures will arise.

"We have also particular pools where we make trials upon fishes, as we have said before of beasts and birds.

"We have also places for breed and generation of those kinds of worms and flies which are of special use; such as are with you your silkworms and bees.

"I will not hold you long with recounting of our brew-houses, bake-houses, and kitchens, where are made divers drinks, breads, and meats, rare and of special effects. Wines we have of grapes, and drinks of other juice, of fruits, of grains, and of roots, and of mixtures with honey, sugar, manna, and fruits dried and decocted; also of the tears or wounding of trees, and of the pulp of canes. And these drinks are of several ages, some to the age or last of forty years. We have drinks also brewed with several herbs, and roots, and spices; yea, with several fleshes, and white-meats; whereof some of the drinks are such as they are in effect meat and drink both, so that divers, especially in age, do desire to live with them with little or no meat or bread. And above all we strive to have drinks of extreme thin parts, to insinuate into the body, and yet without all biting, sharpness, or fretting; insomuch as some of them put upon the back of your hand, will with a little stay pass through to the palm, and yet taste mild to the mouth. We have also waters, which we ripen in that fashion, as they become nourishing, so that they are indeed excellent drinks, and many will use no other. Bread we have of several grains, roots, and kernels; yea, and some of flesh, and fish, dried; with divers kinds of leavings and seasonings; so that some do extremely move appetites, some do nourish so, as divers do live of them, without any other meat, who live very long. So for meats, we have some of them so beaten, and made tender, and mortified, yet without all corrupting, as a weak heat of the stomach will turn them into good chilus, as well as a strong heat would meat otherwise prepared. We have some meats also and bread, and drinks, which taken by men, enable them to fast long after; and some other, that used make the very flesh of men's bodies sensibly more hard and tough, and their strength far greater than otherwise it would be.

"We have dispensatories or shops of medicines; wherein you may easily think, if we have such variety of plants, and living creatures, more than you have in Europe (for we know what you have), the simples, drugs, and ingredients of medicines, must likewise be in so much the greater variety. We have them likewise of divers ages, and long fermentations. And for their preparations, we have not only all manner of exquisite distillations, and separations, and especially by gentle heats, and percolations through divers strainers, yea, and substances; but also exact forms of composition, whereby they incorporate almost as they were natural simples.

"We have also divers mechanical arts, which you have not; and stuffs made by them, as papers, linen, silks, tissues, dainty works of feathers of wonderful lustre, excellent dyes, and many others, and shops likewise as well for such as are not brought into vulgar use amongst us, as for those that are. For you must know, that of the things before recited, many of them are grown into use throughout the kingdom, but yet, if they did flow from our invention, we have of them also for patterns and principals.

"We have also furnaces of great diversities, and that keep great diversity of heats; fierce and quick, strong and constant, soft and mild, blown, quiet, dry, moist, and the like. But above all we have heats, in imitation of the sun's and heavenly bodies' heats, that pass divers inequalities, and as it were orbs, progresses, and returns whereby we produce admirable effects. Besides, we have heats of dungs, and of bellies and maws of living creatures and of their bloods and bodies, and of hays and herbs laid up moist, of lime unquenched, and such like. Instruments also which generate heat only by motion. And farther, places for strong insulations; and again, places under the earth, which by nature or art yield heat. These divers heats we use, as the nature of the operation which we intend requireth.

"We have also perspective-houses, where we make demonstrations of all lights and radiations, and of all colours; and out of things uncoloured and transparent, we can represent unto you all several colours, not in rainbows, as it is in gems and prisms, but of themselves single. We represent also all multiplications of light, which we carry to great distance, and make so sharp, as to discern small points and lines. Also all colourations of light: all delusions and deceits of the sight, in figures, magnitudes, motions, colours; all demonstrations of shadows. We find also divers means, yet unknown to you, of producing of light, originally from divers bodies. We procure means of seeing objects afar off, as in the heaven and remote places; and represent things near as afar off, and things afar off as near; making feigned distances. We have also helps for the sight far above spectacles and glasses in use; we have also glasses and means to see small and minute bodies, perfectly and distinctly; as the shapes and colours of small flies and worms, grains, and flaws in gems, which cannot otherwise be seen, observations in urine and blood not otherwise to be seen. We make artificial rainbows, halos, and circles about light. We represent also all manner of reflections, refractions, and multiplications of visual beams of objects.

"We have also precious stones, of all kinds, many of them of great beauty and to you unknown; crystals likewise, and glasses of divers kind; and amongst them some of metals vitrificated, and other materials, besides those of which you make glass. Also a number of fossils, and imperfect minerals, which you have not. Likewise loadstones of prodigious virtue: and other rare stones, both natural and artificial.

"We have also sound-houses, where we practise and demonstrate all sounds and their generation. We have harmony which you have not, of quarter-sounds and lesser slides of sounds. Divers instruments of music likewise to you unknown, some sweeter than any you have; with bells and rings that are dainty and sweet. We represent small sounds as great and deep, likewise great sounds, extenuate and sharp; we make divers tremblings and warblings of sounds, which in their original are entire. We represent and imitate all articulate sounds and letters, and the voices and notes of beasts and birds. We have certain helps, which set to the ear do further the hearing greatly; we have also divers strange and artificial echoes, reflecting the voice many times, and as it were tossing it; and some that give back the voice louder than it came, some shriller and some deeper; yea, some rendering the voice, differing in the letters or articulate sound from that they receive. We have all means to convey sounds in trunks and pipes, in strange lines and distances.

"We have also perfume-houses, wherewith we join also practices of taste. We multiply smells which may seem strange: we imitate smells, making all smells to breathe out of other mixtures than those that give them. We make divers imitations of taste likewise, so that they will deceive any man's taste. And in this house we contain also a confiture-house, where we make all sweetmeats, dry and moist, and divers pleasant wines, milks, broths, and salads, far in greater variety than you have.

"We have also engine-houses, where are prepared engines and instruments for all sorts of motions. There we imitate and practise to make swifter motions than any you have, either out of your muskets or any engine that you have; and to make them and multiply them more easily and with small force, by wheels and other means, and to make them stronger and more violent than yours are, exceeding your greatest cannons and basilisks. We represent also ordnance and instruments of war and engines of all kinds; and likewise new mixtures and compositions of gunpowder, wild-fires burning in water and unquenchable, also fire-works of all variety, both for pleasure and use. We imitate also flights of birds; we have some degrees of flying in the air. We have ships and boats for going under water and brooking of seas, also swimming-girdles and supporters. We have divers curious clocks and other like motions of return, and some perpetual motions. We imitate also motions of living creatures by images of men, beasts, birds, fishes, and serpents; we have also a great number of other various motions, strange for equality, fineness and subtilty.

"We have also a mathematical-house, where are represented all instruments, as well of geometry as astronomy, exquisitely made.

"We have also houses of deceits of the senses, where we represent all manner of feats of juggling, false apparitions, impostures and illusions, and their fallacies. And surely you will easily believe that we, that have so many things truly natural which induce admiration, could in a world of particulars deceive the senses if we would disguise those things, and labour to make them more miraculous. But we do hate all impostures and lies, insomuch as we have severely forbidden it to all our fellows, under pain of ignominy and fines, that they do not show any natural work or thing adorned or swelling, but only pure as it is, and without all affectation of strangeness.

"These are, my son, the riches of Salomon's House.

"For the several employments and offices of our fellows, we have twelve that sail into foreign countries under the names of other nations (for our own we conceal), who bring us the books and abstracts, and patterns of experiments of all other parts. These we call merchants of light.

"We have three that collect the experiments which are in all books. These we call deprepators.

"We have three that collect the experiments of all mechanical arts, and also of liberal sciences, and also of practices which are not brought into arts. These we call mystery-men.

"We have three that try new experiments.

"Such as themselves think good. These we call pioneers or miners.

"We have three that draw the experiments of the former four into titles and tables, to give the better light for the drawing of observations and axioms out of them. These we call compilers. We have three that bend themselves, looking into the experiments of their fellows, and cast about how to draw out of them things of use and practice for man's life and knowledge, as well for works as for plain demonstration of causes, means of natural divinations, and the easy and clear discovery of the virtues and parts of bodies. These we call dowry-men or benefactors.

"Then after divers meetings and consults of our whole number, to consider of the former labours and collections, we have three that take care out of them to direct new experiments, of a higher light, more penetrating into Nature than the former. These we call lamps.

"We have three others that do execute the experiment so directed, and report them. These we call inoculators.

"Lastly, we have three that raise the former discoveries by experiments into greater observations, axioms, and aphorisms. These we call interpreters of Nature.

"We have also, as you must think, novices and apprentices, that the succession of the former employed men do not fail; besides a great number of servants and attendants, men and women. And this we do also: we have consultations, which of the inventions and experiences which we have discovered shall be published, and which not: and take all an oath of secrecy for the concealing of those which we think fit to keep secret: though some of those we do reveal sometime to the state, and some not.

"For our ordinances and rites, we have two very long and fair galleries: in one of these we place patterns and samples of all manner of the more rare and excellent inventions: in the other we place the statues of all principal inventors. There we have the statue of your Columbus, that discovered the West Indies: also the inventor of ships: your Monk that was the inventor of ordnance and of gunpowder: the inventor of music: the inventor of letters: the inventor of printing: the inventor of observations of astronomy: the inventor of works in metal: the inventor of glass: the inventor of silk of the worm: the inventor of wine: the inventor of corn and bread: the inventor of sugars; and all these by more certain tradition than you have. Then we have divers inventors of our own, of excellent works; which since you have not seen, it were too long to make descriptions of them; and besides, in the right understanding of those descriptions you might easily err. For upon every invention of value we erect a statue to the inventor, and give him a liberal and honourable reward. These statues are some of brass, some of marble and touchstone, some of cedar and other special woods gilt and adorned; some of iron, some of silver, some of gold.

"We have certain hymns and services, which we say daily, of laud and thanks to God for His marvellous works. And forms of prayers, imploring His aid and blessing for the illumination of our labours; and turning them into good and holy uses.

"Lastly, we have circuits or visits, of divers principal cities of the kingdom; where as it cometh to pass we do publish such new profitable inventions as we think good. And we do also declare natural divinations of diseases, plagues, swarms of hurtful creatures, scarcity, tempest, earthquakes, great inundations, comets, temperature of the year, and divers other things; and we give counsel thereupon, what the people shall do for the prevention and remedy of them."

And when he had said this, he stood up; and I, as I had been taught, knelt down; and he laid his right hand upon my head, and said, "God bless thee, my son, and God bless this relation which I have made. I give thee leave to publish it, for the good of other nations; for we here are in God's bosom, a land unknown." And so he left me; having assigned a value of about two thousand ducats for a bounty to me and my fellows. For they give great largesses, where they come, upon all occasions.

THE REST WAS NOT PERFECTED.

CAMPANELLA'S CITY OF THE SUN.

The City of the Sun.

A Poetical Dialogue between a Grandmaster of the Knights Hospitallers and a Genoese Sea-captain, his guest.

G.M. Prithee, now, tell me what happened to you during that voyage?

Capt. I have already told you how I wandered over the whole earth. In the course of my journeying I came to Taprobane, and was compelled to go ashore at a place, where through fear of the inhabitants I remained in a wood. When I stepped out of this I found myself on a large plain immediately under the equator.

G.M. And what befell you here?

Capt. I came upon a large crowd of men and armed women, many of whom did not understand our language, and they conducted me forthwith to the City of the Sun.

G.M. Tell me after what plan this city is built and how it is governed?

Capt. The greater part of the city is built upon a high hill, which rises from an extensive plain, but several of its circles extend for some distance beyond the base of the hill, which is of such a size that the diameter of the city is upwards of two miles, so that its circumference becomes about seven. On account of the humped shape of the mountain, however, the diameter of the city is really more than if it were built on a plain.

It is divided into seven rings or huge circles named from the seven planets, and the way from one to the other of these is by four streets and through four gates, that look towards the four points of the compass. Furthermore, it is so built that if the first circle were stormed, it would of necessity entail a double amount of energy to storm the second; still more to storm the third; and in each succeeding case the strength and energy would have to be doubled; so that he who wishes to capture that city must, as it were, storm it seven times. For my own part, however, I think that not even the first wall could be occupied, so thick are the earthworks and so well fortified is it with breastworks, towers, guns and ditches.

When I had been taken through the northern gate (which is shut with an iron door so wrought that it can be raised and let down, and locked in easily and strongly, its projections running into the grooves of the thick posts by a marvellous device), I saw a level space seventy paces[1] wide between the first and second walls. From hence can be seen large palaces all joined to the wall of the second circuit, in such a manner as to appear all one palace. Arches run on a level with the middle height of the palaces, and are continued round the whole ring. There are galleries for promenading upon these arches, which are supported from beneath by thick and well-shaped columns, enclosing arcades like peristyles, or cloisters of an abbey.

[1] A pace was 1-9/25 yards, 1,000 paces making a mile.

But the palaces have no entrances from below, except on the inner or concave partition, from which one enters directly to the lower parts of the building. The higher parts, however, are reached by flights of marble steps, which lead to galleries for promenading on the inside similar to those on the outside. From these one enters the higher rooms, which are very beautiful, and have windows on the concave and convex partitions. These rooms are divided from one another by richly decorated walls. The convex or outer wall of the ring is about eight spans thick; the concave, three; the intermediate walls are one, or perhaps one and a half. Leaving this circle one gets to the second plain, which is nearly three paces narrower than the first. Then the first wall of the second ring is seen adorned above and below with similar galleries for walking, and there is on the inside of it another interior wall enclosing palaces. It has also similar peristyles supported by columns in the lower part, but above are excellent pictures, round the ways into the upper houses. And so on afterwards through similar spaces and double walls, enclosing palaces, and adorned with galleries for walking, extending along their outer side, and supported by columns, till the last circuit is reached, the way being still over a level plain.

But when the two gates, that is to say, those of the outmost and the inmost walls, have been passed, one mounts by means of steps so formed that an ascent is scarcely discernible, since it proceeds in a slanting direction, and the steps succeed one another at almost imperceptible heights. On the top of the hill is a rather spacious plain, and in the midst of this there rises a temple built with wondrous art.

G.M. Tell on, I pray you! Tell on! I am dying to hear more.

Capt. The temple is built in the form of a circle; it is not girt with walls, but stands upon thick columns, beautifully grouped. A very large dome, built with great care in the centre or pole, contains another small vault as it were rising out of it, and in this is a spiracle, which is right over the altar. There is but one altar in the middle of the temple, and this is hedged round by columns. The temple itself is on a space of more than three hundred and fifty paces. Without it, arches measuring about eight paces extend from the heads of the columns outwards, whence other columns rise about three paces from the thick, strong and erect wall. Between these and the former columns there are galleries for walking, with beautiful pavements, and in the recess of the wall, which is adorned with numerous large doors, there are immovable seats, placed as it were between the inside columns, supporting the temple. Portable chairs are not wanting, many and well adorned. Nothing is seen over the altar but a large globe, upon which the heavenly bodies are painted, and another globe upon which there is a representation of the earth. Furthermore, in the vault of the dome there can be discerned representations of all the stars of heaven from the first to the sixth magnitude, with their proper names and power to influence terrestrial things marked in three little verses for each. There are the poles and greater and lesser circles according to the right latitude of the place, but these are not perfect because there is no wall below. They seem, too, to be made in their relation to the globes on the altar. The pavement of the temple is bright with precious stones. Its seven golden lamps hang always burning, and these bear the names of the seven planets.

At the top of the building several small and beautiful cells surround the small dome, and behind the level space above the bands or arches of the exterior and interior columns there are many cells, both small and large, where the priests and religious officers dwell to the number of forty-nine.

A revolving flag projects from the smaller dome, and this shows in what quarter the wind is. The flag is marked with figures up to thirty-six, and the priests know what sort of year the different kinds of winds bring and what will be the changes of weather on land and sea. Furthermore, under the flag a book is always kept written with letters of gold.

G.M. I pray you, worthy hero, explain to me their whole system of government; for I am anxious to hear it.

Capt. The great ruler among them is a priest whom they call by the name Hoh, though we should call him Metaphysic. He is head over all, in temporal and spiritual matters, and all business and lawsuits are settled by him, as the supreme authority. Three princes of equal power—viz., Pon, Sin and Mor—assist him, and these in our tongue we should call Power, Wisdom and Love. To Power belongs the care of all matters relating to war and peace. He attends to the military arts, and, next to Hoh, he is ruler in every affair of a warlike nature. He governs the military magistrates and the soldiers, and has the management of the munitions, the fortifications, the storming of places, the implements of war, the armories, the smiths and workmen connected with matters of this sort.

But Wisdom is the ruler of the liberal arts, of mechanics, of all sciences with their magistrates and doctors, and of the discipline of the schools. As many doctors as there are, are under his control. There is one doctor who is called Astrologus; a second, Cosmographus; a third, Arithmeticus; a fourth, Geometra; a fifth, Historiographus; a sixth, Poeta; a seventh, Logicus; an eighth, Rhetor; a ninth, Grammaticus; a tenth, Medicus; an eleventh, Physiologus; a twelfth, Politicus; a thirteenth, Moralis. They have but one book, which they call Wisdom, and in it all the sciences are written with conciseness and marvellous fluency of expression. This they read to the people after the custom of the Pythagoreans. It is Wisdom who causes the exterior and interior, the higher and lower walls of the city to be adorned with the finest pictures, and to have all the sciences painted upon them in an admirable manner. On the walls of the temple and on the dome, which is let down when the priest gives an address, lest the sounds of his voice, being scattered, should fly away from his audience, there are pictures of stars in their different magnitudes, with the powers and motions of each, expressed separately in three little verses.

On the interior wall of the first circuit all the mathematical figures are conspicuously painted—figures more in number than Archimedes or Euclid discovered, marked symmetrically, and with the explanation of them neatly written and contained each in a little verse. There are definitions and propositions, &c. &c. On the exterior convex wall is first an immense drawing of the whole earth, given at one view. Following upon this, there are tablets setting forth for every separate country the customs both public and private, the laws, the origins and the power of the inhabitants; and the alphabets the different people use can be seen above that of the City of the Sun.

On the inside of the second circuit, that is to say of the second ring of buildings, paintings of all kinds of precious and common stones, of minerals and metals, are seen; and a little piece of the metal itself is also there with an apposite explanation in two small verses for each metal or stone. On the outside are marked all the seas, rivers, lakes and streams which are on the face of the earth; as are also the wines and the oils and the different liquids, with the sources from which the last are extracted, their qualities and strength. There are also vessels built into the wall above the arches, and these are full of liquids from one to three hundred years old, which cure all diseases. Hail and snow, storms and thunder, and whatever else takes place in the air, are represented with suitable figures and little verses. The inhabitants even have the art of representing in stone all the phenomena of the air, such as the wind, rain, thunder, the rainbow, &c.

On the interior of the third circuit all the different families of trees and herbs are depicted, and there is a live specimen of each plant in earthenware vessels placed upon the outer partition of the arches. With the specimens there are explanations as to where they were first found, what are their powers and natures, and resemblances to celestial things and to metals: to parts of the human body and to things in the sea, and also as to their uses in medicine, &c. On the exterior wall are all the races of fish, found in rivers, lakes and seas, and their habits and values, and ways of breeding, training and living, the purposes for which they exist in the world, and their uses to man. Further, their resemblances to celestial and terrestrial things, produced both by nature and art, are so given that I was astonished when I saw a fish which was like a bishop, one like a chain, another like a garment, a fourth like a nail, a fifth like a star, and others like images of those things existing among us, the relation in each case being completely manifest. There are sea-urchins to be seen, and the purple shell-fish and mussels; and whatever the watery world possesses worthy of being known is there fully shown in marvellous characters of painting and drawing.

On the fourth interior wall all the different kinds of birds are painted, with their natures, sizes, customs, colours, manner of living, &c.; and the only real phoenix is possessed by the inhabitants of this city. On the exterior are shown all the races of creeping animals, serpents, dragons and worms; the insects, the flies, gnats, beetles, &c., in their different states, strength, venoms and uses, and a great deal more than you or I can think of.

On the fifth interior they have all the larger animals of the earth, as many in number as would astonish you. We indeed know not the thousandth part of them, for on the exterior wall also a great many of immense size are also portrayed. To be sure, of horses alone, how great a number of breeds there is and how beautiful are the forms there cleverly displayed!

On the sixth interior are painted all the mechanical arts, with the several instruments for each and their manner of use among different nations. Alongside the dignity of such is placed, and their several inventors are named. But on the exterior all the inventors in science, in warfare, and in law are represented. There I saw Moses, Osiris, Jupiter, Mercury, Lycurgus, Pompilius, Pythagoras, Zamolxis, Solon, Charondas, Phoroneus, with very many others. They even have Mahomet, whom nevertheless they hate as a false and sordid legislator. In the most dignified position I saw a representation of Jesus Christ and of the twelve Apostles, whom they consider very worthy and hold to be great. Of the representations of men, I perceived Cæsar, Alexander, Pyrrhus and Hannibal in the highest place; and other very renowned heroes in peace and war, especially Roman heroes, were painted in lower positions, under the galleries. And when I asked with astonishment whence they had obtained our history, they told me that among them there was a knowledge of all languages, and that by perseverance they continually send explorers and ambassadors over the whole earth, who learn thoroughly the customs, forces, rule and histories of the nations, bad and good alike. These they apply all to their own republic, and with this they are well pleased. I learnt that cannon and typography were invented by the Chinese before we knew of them. There are magistrates, who announce the meaning of the pictures, and boys are accustomed to learn all the sciences, without toil and as if for pleasure, but in the way of history only until they are ten years old.

Love is foremost in attending to the charge of the race. He sees that men and women are so joined together, that they bring forth the best offspring. Indeed, they laugh at us who exhibit a studious care for our breed of horses and dogs, but neglect the breeding of human beings. Thus the education of the children is under his rule. So also is the medicine that is sold, the sowing and collecting of fruits of the earth and of trees, agriculture, pasturage, the preparations for the months, the cooking arrangements, and whatever has any reference to food, clothing, and the intercourse of the sexes. Love himself is ruler, but there are many male and female magistrates dedicated to these arts.

Metaphysic then with these three rulers manage all the above-named matters, and even by himself alone nothing is done; all business is discharged by the four together, but in whatever Metaphysic inclines to the rest are sure to agree.

G.M. Tell me, please, of the magistrates, their services and duties, of the education and mode of living, whether the government is a monarchy, a republic, or an aristocracy.

Capt. This race of men came there from India, flying from the sword of the Magi, a race of plunderers and tyrants who laid waste their country, and they determined to lead a philosophic life in fellowship with one another. Although the community of wives is not instituted among the other inhabitants of their province, among them it is in use after this manner. All things are common with them, and their dispensation is by the authority of the magistrates. Arts and honours and pleasures are common, and are held in such a manner that no one can appropriate anything to himself.

They say that all private property is acquired and improved for the reason that each one of us by himself has his own home and wife and children. From this self-love springs. For when we raise a son to riches and dignities, and leave an heir to much wealth, we become either ready to grasp at the property of the state, if in any case fear should be removed from the power which belongs to riches and rank; or avaricious, crafty, and hypocritical, if any one is of slender purse, little strength, and mean ancestry. But when we have taken away self-love, there remains only love for the state.

G.M. Under such circumstances no one will be willing to labour, while he expects others to work, on the fruit of whose labours he can live, as Aristotle argues against Plato.

Capt. I do not know how to deal with that argument, but I declare to you that they burn with so great a love for their fatherland, as I could scarcely have believed possible; and indeed with much more than the histories tell us belonged to the

Romans, who fell willingly for their country, inasmuch as they have to a greater extent surrendered their private property. I think truly that the friars and monks and clergy of our country, if they were not weakened by love for their kindred and friends, or by the ambition to rise to higher dignities, would be less fond of property, and more imbued with a spirit of charity towards all, as it was in the time of the Apostles, and is now in a great many cases.

G.M. St. Augustine may say that, but I say that among this race of men, friendship is worth nothing; since they have not the chance of conferring mutual benefits on one another.

Capt. Nay, indeed. For it is worth the trouble to see that no one can receive gifts from another. Whatever is necessary they have, they receive it from the community, and the magistrate takes care that no one receives more than he deserves. Yet nothing necessary is denied to any one. Friendship is recognized among them in war, in infirmity, in the art contests, by which means they aid one another mutually by teaching. Sometimes they improve themselves mutually with praises, with conversation, with actions and out of the things they need. All those of the same age call one another brothers. They call all over twenty-two years of age, fathers; those who are less than twenty-two are named sons. Moreover, the magistrates govern well, so that no one in the fraternity can do injury to another.

G.M. And how?

Capt. As many names of virtues as there are amongst us, so many magistrates there are among them. There is a magistrate who is named Magnanimity, another Fortitude, a third Chastity, a fourth Liberality, a fifth Criminal and Civil Justice, a sixth Comfort, a seventh Truth, an eighth Kindness, a tenth Gratitude, an eleventh Cheerfulness, a twelfth Exercise, a thirteenth Sobriety, &c. They are elected to duties of that kind, each one to that duty for excellence in which he is known from boyhood to be most suitable. Wherefore among them neither robbery nor clever murders, nor lewdness, incest, adultery, or other crimes of which we accuse one another, can be found. They accuse themselves of ingratitude and malignity when any one denies a lawful satisfaction to another, of indolence, of sadness, of anger, of scurrility, of slander, and of lying, which curseful thing they thoroughly hate. Accused persons undergoing punishment are deprived of the common table, and other honours, until the judge thinks that they agree with their correction.

G.M. Tell me the manner in which the magistrates are chosen.

Capt. You would not rightly understand this, unless you first learnt their manner of living. That you may know then, men and women wear the same kind of garment, suited for war. The women wear the toga below the knee, but the men above. And both sexes are instructed in all the arts together. When this has been done as a start, and before their third year, the boys learn the language and the alphabet on the walls by walking round them. They have four leaders, and four elders, the first to direct them, the second to teach them, and these are men approved beyond all others. After some time they exercise themselves with gymnastics, running, quoits, and other games, by means of which all their muscles are strengthened alike. Their feet are always bare, and so are their heads as far as the seventh ring. Afterwards they lead them to the offices of the trades, such as shoemaking, cooking, metal-working, carpentry, painting, &c. In order to find out the bent of the genius of each one, after their seventh year, when they have already gone through the mathematics on the walls, they take them to the readings of all the sciences; there are four lectures at each reading, and in the course of four hours the four in their order explain everything.

For some take physical exercise or busy themselves with public services or functions, others apply themselves to reading. Leaving these studies all are devoted to the more abstruse subjects, to mathematics, to medicine, and to other sciences. There is continual debate and studied argument amongst them, and after a time they become magistrates of those sciences or mechanical arts in which they are the most proficient; for every one follows the opinion of his leader and judge, and goes out to the plains to the works of the field, and for the purpose of becoming acquainted with the pasturage of the dumb animals. And they consider him the more noble and renowned who has dedicated himself to the study of the most arts and knows how to practise them wisely. Wherefore they laugh at us in that we consider our workmen ignoble, and hold those to be noble who have mastered no pursuit; but live in ease, and are so many slaves given over to their own pleasure and lasciviousness; and thus as it were from a school of vices so many idle and wicked fellows go forth for the ruin of the state.

The rest of the officials, however, are chosen by the four chiefs, Hoh, Pon, Sin and Mor, and by the teachers of that art over which they are fit to preside. And these teachers know well who is most suited for rule. Certain men are proposed by the magistrates in council, they themselves not seeking to become candidates, and he opposes who knows anything against those brought forward for election, or if not, speaks in favour of them. But no one attains to the dignity of Hoh except him who knows the histories of the nations, and their customs and sacrifices and laws, and their form of government, whether a republic or a monarchy. He must also know the names of the lawgivers and the inventors in science, and the laws and the history of the earth and the heavenly bodies. They think it also necessary that he should understand all the mechanical arts, the physical sciences, astrology and mathematics. (Nearly every two days they teach our mechanical art. They are not allowed to overwork themselves, but frequent practice and the paintings render learning easy to them. Not too much care is given to the cultivation of languages, as they have a goodly number of interpreters who are grammarians in the state.) But beyond everything else it is necessary that Hoh should understand metaphysics and theology; that he should know thoroughly the derivations, foundations and demonstrations of all the arts and sciences; the likeness and difference of things; necessity, fate, and the harmonies of the universe; power, wisdom, and the love of things and of God; the stages of life and its symbols; everything relating to the heavens, the earth and the sea;

and the ideas of God, as much as mortal man can know of Him. He must also be well read in the Prophets and in astrology. And thus they know long beforehand who will be Hoh. He is not chosen to so great a dignity unless he has attained his thirty-fifth year. And this office is perpetual, because it is not known who may be too wise for it or who too skilled in ruling.

G.M. Who indeed can be so wise? If even any one has a knowledge of the sciences it seems that he must be unskilled in ruling.

Capt. This very question I asked them and they replied thus: "We, indeed, are more certain that such a very learned man has the knowledge of governing, than you who place ignorant persons in authority, and consider them suitable merely because they have sprung from rulers or have been chosen by a powerful faction. But our Hoh, a man really the most capable to rule, is for all that never cruel nor wicked, nor a tyrant, inasmuch as he possesses so much wisdom. This, moreover, is not unknown to you, that the same argument cannot apply among you, when you consider that man the most learned who knows most of grammar, or logic, or of Aristotle or any other author. For such knowledge as this of yours much servile labour and memory work is required, so that a man is rendered unskilful; since he has contemplated nothing but the words of books and has given his mind with useless result to the consideration of the dead signs of things. Hence he knows not in what way God rules the universe, nor the ways and customs of Nature and the nations. Wherefore he is not equal to our Hoh. For that one cannot know so many arts and sciences thoroughly, who is not esteemed for skilled ingenuity, very apt at all things, and therefore at ruling especially. This also is plain to us that he who knows only one science, does not really know either that or the others, and he who is suited for only one science and has gathered his knowledge from books, is unlearned and unskilled. But this is not the case with intellects prompt and expert in every branch of knowledge and suitable for the consideration of natural objects, as it is necessary that our Hoh should be. Besides in our state the sciences are taught with a facility (as you have seen) by which more scholars are turned out by us in one year than by you in ten, or even fifteen. Make trial, I pray you, of these boys." In this matter I was struck with astonishment at their truthful discourse and at the trial of their boys, who did not understand my language well. Indeed it is necessary that three of them should be skilled in our tongue, three in Arabic, three in Polish, and three in each of the other languages, and no recreation is allowed them unless they become more learned. For that they go out to the plain for the sake of running about and hurling arrows and lances, and of firing harquebuses, and for the sake of hunting the wild animals and getting a knowledge of plants and stones, and agriculture and pasturage; sometimes the band of boys does one thing, sometimes another.

They do not consider it necessary that the three rulers assisting Hoh should know other than the arts having reference to their rule, and so they have only a historical knowledge of the arts which are common to all. But their own they know well, to which certainly one is dedicated more than another. Thus Power is the most learned in the equestrian art, in marshalling the army, in marking out of camps, in the manufacture of every kind of weapon and of warlike machines, in planning stratagems, and in every affair of a military nature. And for these reasons, they consider it necessary that these chiefs should have been philosophers, historians, politicians, and physicists. Concerning the other two triumvirs, understand remarks similar to those I have made about Power.

G.M. I really wish that you would recount all their public duties, and would distinguish between them, and also that you would tell clearly how they are all taught in common.

Capt. They have dwellings in common and dormitories, and couches and other necessaries. But at the end of every six months they are separated by the masters. Some shall sleep in this ring, some in another; some in the first apartment, and some in the second; and these apartments are marked by means of the alphabet on the lintel. There are occupations, mechanical and theoretical, common to both men and women, with this difference, that the occupations which require more hard work, and walking a long distance, are practised by men, such as ploughing, sowing, gathering the fruits, working at the threshing-floor, and perchance at the vintage. But it is customary to choose women for milking the cows, and for making cheese. In like manner, they go to the gardens near to the outskirts of the city both for collecting the plants and for cultivating them. In fact, all sedentary and stationary pursuits are practised by the women, such as weaving, spinning, sewing, cutting the hair, shaving, dispensing medicines, and making all kinds of garments. They are, however, excluded from working in wood and the manufacture of arms. If a woman is fit to paint, she is not prevented from doing so; nevertheless, music is given over to the women alone, because they please the more, and of a truth to boys also. But the women have not the practice of the drum and the horn.

And they prepare their feasts and arrange the tables in the following manner. It is the peculiar work of the boys and girls under twenty to wait at the tables. In every ring there are the suitable kitchens, barns, and stores of utensils for eating and drinking, and over every department an old man and an old woman preside. These two have at once the command of those who serve, and the power of chastising, or causing to be chastised, those who are negligent or disobedient; and they also examine and mark each one, both male and female, who excels in his or her duties.

All the young people wait upon the older ones who have passed the age of forty, and in the evening when they go to sleep the master and mistress command that those should be sent to work in the morning, upon whom in succession the duty falls, one or two to separate apartments. The young people, however, wait upon one another, and that alas! with some unwillingness. They have first and second tables, and on both sides there are seats. On one side sit the women, on the other the men; and as in the refectories of the monks, there is no noise. While they are eating a young man reads a book from a platform, intoning distinctly and sonorously, and often the magistrates question them upon the more important parts of the reading. And truly it is pleasant to observe in what manner these young people, so beautiful and clothed in garments so suitable, attend to them, and to see at the same time so many friends, brothers, sons, fathers and mothers all in their turn living together with so much honesty, propriety and love. So each one is given a napkin, a plate, fish, and a dish of food. It is the duty of the medical officers to tell the cooks what repasts shall be prepared on each day, and what food for the old, what for the young, and what for the sick. The magistrates receive the full-grown and fatter portion, and they from their share always distribute something to the boys at the table who have shown themselves more studious in the morning at the lectures and debates concerning wisdom and arms. And this is held to be one of the most distinguished honours. For six days they ordain to sing with music at table. Only a few, however, sing; or there is one voice accompanying the lute and one for each other instrument. And when all alike in service join their hands, nothing is found to be wanting. The old men placed at the head of the cooking business and of the refectories of the servants praise the cleanliness of the streets, the houses, the vessels, the garments, the workshops and the warehouses.

They wear white undergarments to which adheres a covering, which is at once coat and legging, without wrinkles. The borders of the fastenings are furnished with globular buttons, extended round and caught up here and there by chains. The coverings of the legs descend to the shoes and are continued even to the heels. Then they cover the feet with large socks, or as it were half-buskins fastened by buckles, over which they wear a half-boot, and besides, as I have already said, they are clothed with a toga. And so aptly fitting are the garments, that when the toga is destroyed, the different parts of the whole body are straight-way discerned, no part being concealed. They change their clothes for different ones four times in the year, that is when the sun enters respectively the constellations Aries, Cancer, Libra and Capricorn, and according to the circumstances and necessity as decided by the officer of health. The keepers of clothes for the different rings are wont to distribute them, and it is marvellous that they have at the same time as many garments as there is need for, some heavy and some slight, according to the weather. They all use white clothing, and this is washed in each month with lye or soap, as are also the workshops of the lower trades, the kitchens, the pantries, the barns, the store-houses, the armories, the refectories and the baths. Moreover, the clothes are washed at the pillars of the peristyles, and the water is brought down by means of canals which are continued as sewers. In every street of the different rings there are suitable fountains, which send forth their water by means of canals, the water being drawn up from nearly the bottom of the mountain by the sole movement of a cleverly contrived handle. There is water in fountains and in cisterns, whither the rain-water collected from the roofs of the houses is brought through pipes full of sand. They wash their bodies often, according as the doctor and master command. All the mechanical arts are practised under the peristyles, but the speculative are carried on above in the walking galleries and ramparts where are the more splendid paintings, but the more sacred ones are taught in the temple. In the halls and wings of the rings there are solar time-pieces and bells, and hands by which the hours and seasons are marked off.

G.M. Tell me about their children.

Capt. When their women have brought forth children, they suckle and rear them in temples set apart for all. They give milk for two years or more as the physician orders. After that time the weaned child is given into the charge of the mistresses, if it is a female, and to the masters, if it is a male. And then with other young children they are pleasantly instructed in the alphabet, and in the knowledge of the pictures, and in running, walking and wrestling; also in the historical drawings, and in languages; and they are adorned with a suitable garment of different colours. After their sixth year they are taught natural science, and then the mechanical sciences. The men who are weak in intellect are sent to farms, and when they have become more proficient some of them are received into the state. And those of the same age and born under the same constellation are especially like one another in strength and in appearance, and hence arises much lasting concord in the state, these men honouring one another with mutual love and help. Names are given to them by Metaphysicus, and that not by chance but designedly, and according to each one's peculiarity, as was the custom among the ancient Romans. Wherefore one is called Beautiful (*Pulcher*), another the Big-nosed (*Naso*), another the Fat-legged (*Cranipes*) another Crooked (*Torvus*) another Lean (*Macer*) and so on. But when they have become very skilled in their professions and done any great deed in war or in time of peace, a cognomen from art is given to them, such as Beautiful, the great painter (*Pulcher, Pictor Magnus*), the golden one (*Aureus*) the excellent one (*Excellens*) or the strong (*Strenuus*); or from their deeds, such as Naso the Brave (*Nason Fortis*) or the cunning, or the great, or very great conqueror; or from the enemy any one has overcome, Africanus, Asiaticus, Etruscus; or if any one has overcome Manfred or Tortelius, he is called Macer Manfred or Tortelius, and so on. All these cognomens are added by the higher magistrates, and very often with a crown suitable to the deed or art, and with the flourish of music. For gold and silver is reckoned of little value among them except as material for their vessels and ornaments, which are common to all.

G.M. Tell me, I pray you, is there no jealousy among them or disappointment to that one who has not been elected to a magistracy, or to any other dignity to which he aspires?

Capt. Certainly not. For no one wants either necessaries or luxuries. Moreover, the race is managed for the good of the commonwealth and not of private individuals, and the magistrates must be obeyed. They deny what we hold—viz., that it is natural to man to recognize his offspring and to educate them, and to use his wife and house and children as his own. For they say that children are bred for the preservation of the species and not for individual pleasure, as St. Thomas also asserts. Therefore the breeding of children has reference to the commonwealth and not to individuals, except in so far as they are constituents of the commonwealth. And since individuals for the most part bring forth children wrongly and educate them wrongly, they consider that they remove destruction from the state, and therefore, for this reason, with most sacred fear, they commit the education of the children, who as it were are the element of the republic, to the care of magistrates; for the safety of the community is not that of a few. And thus they distribute male and female breeders of the best natures according to philosophical rules. Plato thinks that this distribution ought to be made by lot, lest some men seeing that they are kept away from the beautiful women, should rise up with anger and hatred against the magistrates; and he thinks further that those who do not deserve cohabitation with the more beautiful women, should be deceived whilst the lots are being led out of the city by the magistrates, so that at all times the women who are suitable should fall to their lot, not those whom they desire. This shrewdness, however, is not necessary among the inhabitants of the City of the Sun. For with them deformity is unknown. When the women are exercised they get a clear complexion, and become strong of limb, tall and agile, and with them beauty consists in tallness and strength. Therefore, if any woman dyes her face, so that it may become beautiful, or uses high-heeled boots so that she may appear tall, or garments with trains to cover her wooden shoes, she is condemned to capital punishment. But if the women should even desire them, they have no facility for doing these things. For who indeed would give them this facility? Further, they assert that among us abuses of this kind arise from the leisure and sloth of women. By these means they lose their colour and have pale complexions, and become feeble and small. For this reason they are without proper complexions, use high sandals, and become beautiful not from strength, but from slothful tenderness. And thus they ruin their own tempers and natures, and consequently those of their offspring. Furthermore, if at any time a man is taken captive with ardent love for a certain woman, the two are allowed to converse and joke together, and to give one another garlands of flowers or leaves, and to make verses. But if the race is endangered, by no means is further union between them permitted. Moreover, the love born of eager desire is not known among them; only that born of friendship.

Domestic affairs and partnerships are of little account, because, excepting the sign of honour, each one receives what he is in need of. To the heroes and heroines of the republic, it is customary to give the pleasing gifts of honour, beautiful wreaths, sweet food or splendid clothes, while they are feasting. In the daytime all use white garments within the city, but at night or outside the city they use red garments either of wool or silk. They hate black as they do dung, and therefore they dislike the Japanese, who are fond of black. Pride they consider the most execrable vice, and one who acts proudly is chastised with the most ruthless correction. Wherefore no one thinks it lowering to wait at table or to work in the kitchen or fields. All work they call discipline, and thus they say that it is honourable to go on foot, to do any act of nature, to see with the eye, and to speak with the tongue; and when there is need, they distinguish philosophically between tears and spittle.

Every man who, when he is told off to work, does his duty, is considered very honourable. It is not the custom to keep slaves. For they are enough, and more than enough, for themselves. But with us, alas! it is not so. In Naples there exists seventy thousand souls, and out of these scarcely ten or fifteen thousand do any work, and they are always lean from overwork and are getting weaker every day. The rest become a prey to idleness, avarice, ill-health, lasciviousness, usury and other vices, and contaminate and corrupt very many families by holding them in servitude for their own use, by keeping them in poverty and slavishness, and by imparting to them their own vices. Therefore public slavery ruins them; useful works, in the field, in military service and in arts, except those which are debasing, are not cultivated, the few who do practise them doing so with much aversion. But in the City of the Sun, while duty and work is distributed among all, it only falls to each one to work for about four hours every day. The remaining hours are spent in learning joyously, in debating, in reading, in reciting, in writing, in walking, in exercising the mind and body, and with play. They allow no game which is played while sitting, neither the single die nor dice, nor chess, nor others like these. But they play with the ball, with the sack, with the hoop, with wrestling, with hurling at the stake. They say, moreover, that grinding poverty renders men worthless, cunning, sulky, thievish, insidious, vagabonds, liars, false witnesses, &c.; and that wealth makes them insolent, proud, ignorant, traitors, assumers of what they know not, deceivers, boasters, wanting in affection, slanderers, &c. But with them all the rich and poor together make up the community. They are rich because they want nothing, poor because they possess nothing; and consequently they are not slaves to circumstances, but circumstances serve them. And on this point they strongly recommend the religion of the Christians, and especially the life of the Apostles.

G.M. This seems excellent and sacred, but the community of women is a thing too difficult to attain. The holy Roman Clement says that wives ought to be common in accordance with the apostolic institution, and praises Plato and Socrates, who thus teach, but the Glossary interprets this community with regard to obedience. And Tertullian agrees with the Glossary, that the first Christians had everything in common except wives.

Capt. These things I know little of. But this I saw among the inhabitants of the City of the Sun that they did not make this exception. And they defend themselves by the opinion of Socrates, of Cato, of Plato, and of St. Clement but, as you say, they misunderstand the opinions of these thinkers. And the inhabitants of the solar city ascribe this to their want of education, since they are by no means learned in philosophy. Nevertheless, they send abroad to discover the customs of nations, and the best of these they always adopt. Practice makes the women suitable for war and other duties. Thus they agree with Plato, in whom I have read these same things. The reasoning of our Cajetan does not convince me, and least of all that of Aristotle. This thing, however, existing among them is excellent and worthy of imitation—viz., that no physical defect renders a man incapable of being serviceable except the decrepitude of old age, since even the deformed are useful for consultation. The lame serve as guards, watching with the eyes which they possess. The blind card wool with their hands, separating the down from the hairs, with which latter they stuff the couches and sofas; those who are without the use of eyes and hands give the use of their ears or their voice for the convenience of the state, and if one has only one sense, he uses it in the farms. And these cripples are well treated, and some become spies, telling the officers of the state what they have heard.

G.M. Tell me now, I pray you, of their military affairs. Then you may explain their arts, ways of life and sciences, and lastly their religion.

Capt. The triumvir, Power, has under him all the magistrates of arms, of artillery, of cavalry, of foot-soldiers, of architects, and of strategists, and the masters and many of the most excellent workmen obey the magistrates, the men of each art paying allegiance to their respective chiefs. Moreover, Power is at the head of all the professors of gymnastics, who teach military exercise, and who are prudent generals, advanced in age. By these the boys are trained after their twelfth year. Before this age, however, they have been accustomed to wrestling, running, throwing the weight and other minor exercises, under inferior masters. But at twelve they are taught how to strike at the enemy, at horses and elephants, to handle the spear, the sword, the arrow and the sling; to manage the horse; to advance and to retreat; to remain in order of battle; to help a comrade in arms; to anticipate the enemy by cunning; and to conquer.

The women also are taught these arts under their own magistrates and mistresses, so that they may be able if need be to render assistance to the males in battles near the city. They are taught to watch the fortifications lest at some time a hasty attack should suddenly be made. In this respect they praise the Spartans and Amazons. The women know well also how to let fly fiery balls, and how to make them from lead; how to throw stones from pinnacles and to go in the way of an attack. They are accustomed also to give up wine unmixed altogether, and that one is punished most severely who shows any fear.

The inhabitants of the City of the Sun do not fear death, because they all believe that the soul is immortal, and that when it has left the body it is associated with other spirits, wicked or good, according to the merits of this present life. Although they are partly followers of Bramah and Pythagoras, they do not believe in the transmigration of souls, except in some cases, by a distinct decree of God. They do not abstain from injuring an enemy of the republic and of religion, who is unworthy of pity. During the second month the army is reviewed, and every day there is practice of arms, either in the cavalry plain or within the walls. Nor are they ever without lectures on the science of war. They take care that the accounts of Moses, of Joshua, of David, of Judas Maccabeus, of Cæsar, of Alexander, of Scipio, of Hannibal, and other great soldiers should be read. And then each one gives his own opinion as to whether these generals acted well or ill, usefully or honourably, and then the teacher answers and says who are right.

G.M. With whom do they wage war, and for what reasons, since they are so prosperous?

Capt. Wars might never occur, nevertheless they are exercised in military tactics and in hunting, lest perchance they should become effeminate and unprepared for any emergency. Besides there are four kingdoms in the island, which are very envious of their prosperity, for this reason that the people desire to live after the manner of the inhabitants of the City of the Sun, and to be under their rule rather than that of their own kings. Wherefore the state often makes war upon these because, being neighbours, they are usurpers and live impiously, since they have not an object of worship and do not observe the religion of other nations or of the Brahmins. And other nations of India, to which formerly they were subject, rise up as it were in rebellion, as also do the Taprobanese, whom they wanted to join them at first. The warriors of the City of the Sun, however, are always the victors.

As soon as they suffered from insult or disgrace or plunder, or when their allies have been harassed, or a people have been oppressed by a tyrant of the state (for they are always the advocates of liberty), they go immediately to the council for deliberation. After they have knelt in the presence of God that He might inspire their consultation, they proceed to examine the merits of the business, and thus war is decided on. Immediately after a priest, whom they call Forensic, is sent away. He demands from the enemy the restitution of the plunder, asks that the allies should be freed from oppression, or that the tyrant should be deposed. If they deny these things war is declared by invoking the vengeance of God—the God of Sabaoth—for destruction of those who maintain an unjust cause. But if the enemy refuse to reply, the priest gives him the space of one hour for his answer, if he is a king, but three if it is a republic, so that they cannot escape giving a response. And in this manner is war undertaken against the insolent enemies of natural rights and of religion. When war has been declared, the deputy of Power performs everything, but Power, like the Roman dictator, plans and wills everything, so that hurtful tardiness may be avoided. And when anything of great moment arises he consults Hoh and Wisdom and Love.

Before this, however, the occasion of war and the justice of making an expedition is declared by a herald in the great council. All from twenty years and upwards are admitted to this council, and thus the necessaries are agreed upon. All kinds of weapons stand in the armories, and these they use often in sham fights. The exterior walls of each ring are full of guns prepared by their labours, and they have other engines for hurling which are called cannons, and which they take into battle upon mules and asses and carriages. When they have arrived in an open plain they enclose in the middle the provisions, engines of war, chariots, ladders and machines and all fight courageously. Then each one returns to the standards, and the enemy thinking that they are giving and preparing to flee, are deceived and relax their order: then the warriors of the City of the Sun, wheeling into wings and columns on each side, regain their breath and strength, and ordering the artillery to discharge their bullets they resume the fight against a disorganized host. And they observe many ruses of this kind. They overcome all mortals with their stratagems and engines. Their camp is fortified after the manner of the Romans. They pitch their tents and fortify with wall and ditch with wonderful quickness. The masters of works, of engines and hurling machines, stand ready, and the soldiers understand the use of the spade and the axe.

Five, eight, or ten leaders learned in the order of battle and in strategy consult together concerning the business of war, and command their bands after consultation. It is their wont to take out with them a body of boys, armed and on horses, so that they may learn to fight, just as the whelps of lions and wolves are accustomed to blood. And these in time of danger betake themselves to a place of safety, along with many armed women. After the battle the women and boys soothe and relieve the pain of the warriors, and wait upon them and encourage them with embraces and pleasant words. How wonderful a help is this! For the soldiers, in order that they may acquit themselves as sturdy men in the eyes of their wives and offspring, endure hardships, and so love makes them conquerors. He who in the fight first scales the enemy's walls receives after the battle a crown of grass, as a token of honour, and at the presentation the women and boys applaud loudly; that one who affords aid to an ally gets a civic crown of oak-leaves; he who kills a tyrant dedicates his arms in the temple and receives from Hoh the cognomen of his deed, and other warriors obtain other kinds of crowns. Every horse-soldier carries a spear and two strongly tempered pistols, narrow at the mouth, hanging from his saddle. And to get the barrels of their pistols narrow they pierce the metal which they intend to convert into arms. Further, every cavalry soldier has a sword and a dagger. But the rest, who form the light-armed troops, carry a metal cudgel. For if the foe cannot pierce their metal for pistols and cannot make swords, they attack him with clubs, shatter and overthrow him. Two chains of six spans length hang from the club, and at the end of these are iron balls, and when these aimed at the enemy they surround his neck and drag him to the ground; and in order that they may be able to use the club more easily, they do not hold the reins with their hands, but use them by means of the feet. If perchance the reins are interchanged above the trappings of the saddle, the ends are fastened to the stirrups with buckles and not to the feet. And the stirrups have an arrangement for swift movement of the bridle, so that they draw in or let out the rein with marvellous celerity. With the right foot they turn the horse to the left and with the left to the right. This secret, moreover, is not known to the Tartars. For, although they govern the reins with their feet, they are ignorant nevertheless of turning them and drawing them in and letting them out by means of the block of the stirrups. The light-armed cavalry with them are the first to engage in battle, then the men forming the phalanx with their spears, then the archers for whose services a great price is paid, and who are accustomed to fight in lines crossing one another as the threads of cloth, some rushing forward in their turn and others receding. They have a band of lancers strengthening the line of battle, but they make trial of the swords only at the end.

After the battle they celebrate the military triumphs after the manner of the Romans, and even in a more magnificent way. Prayers by the way of thank-offerings are made to God, and then the general presents himself in the temple, and the deeds, good and bad, are related by the poet or historian, who according to custom was with the expedition. And the greatest chief, Hoh, crowns the general with laurel and distributes little gifts and honours to all the valorous soldiers, who are for some days free from public duties. But this exemption from work is by no means pleasing to them, since they know not what it is to be at leisure, and so they help their companions. On the other hand, they who have been conquered through their own fault, or have lost the victory, are blamed; and they who were the first to take to flight are in no way worthy to escape death, unless when the whole army asks their lives, and each one takes upon himself a part of their punishment. But this indulgence is rarely granted, except when there are good reasons favouring it. But he who did not bear help to an ally or friend is beaten with rods. That one who did not obey orders is given to the beasts, in an enclosure, to be devoured, and a staff is put in his hand, and if he should conquer the lions and the bears that are there, which is almost impossible, he is received into favour again. The conquered states or those willingly delivered up to them, forthwith have all things in common, and receive a garrison and magistrates from the City of the Sun, and by degrees they are accustomed to the ways of the city, the mistress of all, to which they even send their sons to be taught without contributing anything for expense.

It would be too great trouble to tell you about the spies and their master, and about the guards and laws and ceremonies, both within and without the state, which you can of yourself imagine. Since from childhood they are chosen according to their inclination and the star under which they were born, therefore each one working according to his natural propensity does his duty well and pleasantly, because naturally. The same things I may say concerning strategy and the other functions.

There are guards in the city by day and by night, and they are placed at the four gates, and outside the walls of the seventh ring, above the breastworks and towers and inside mounds. These places are guarded in the day by women, in the night by men. And lest the guard should become weary of watching, and in case of a surprise, they change them every three hours, as is the custom with our soldiers. At sunset, when the drum and symphonia sound, the armed guards are distributed. Cavalry and infantry make use of hunting as the symbol of war, and practise games and hold festivities in the plains. Then the music strikes up, and freely they pardon the offences and faults of the enemy, and after the victories they are kind to them, if it has been decreed that they should destroy the walls of the enemy's city and take their lives. All these things are done on the same day as the victory, and afterwards they never cease to load the conquered with favours, for they say that there ought to be no fighting, except when the conquerors give up the conquered, not when they kill them. If there is a dispute among them concerning injury or any other matter (for they themselves scarcely ever contend except in matters of honour), the chief and his magistrates chastise the accused one secretly, if he has done harm in deeds after he has been first angry. If they wait until the time of the battle for the verbal decision, they must give vent to their anger against the enemy, and he who in battle shows the most daring deeds is considered to have defended the better and truer cause in the struggle, and the other yields, and they are punished justly. Nevertheless, they are not allowed to come to single combat, since right is maintained by the tribunal, and because the unjust cause is often apparent when the more just succumbs, and he who professes to be the better man shows this in public fight.

G.M. This is worth while, so that factions should not be cherished for the harm of the fatherland, and so that civil wars might not occur, for by means of these a tyrant often arises, as the examples of Rome and Athens show. Now, I pray you, tell me of their works and matter connected therewith.

Capt. I believe that you have already heard about their military affairs and about their agricultural and pastoral life, and in what way these are common to them, and how they honour with the first grade of nobility whoever is considered, to have a knowledge of these. They who are skilful in more arts than these they consider still nobler, and they set that one apart for teaching the art in which he is most skilful. The occupations which require the most labour, such as working in metals and building, are the most praiseworthy amongst them. No one declines to go to these occupations, for the reason that from the beginning their propensities are well known, and among them, on account of the distribution of labour, no one does work harmful to him, but only that which is necessary for him. The occupations entailing less labour belong to the women. All of them are expected to know how to swim, and for this reason ponds are dug outside the walls of the city and within them near to the fountains.

Commerce is of little use to them, but they know the value of money, and they count for the use of their ambassadors and explorers, so that with it they may have the means of living. They receive merchants into their states from the different countries of the world, and these buy the superfluous goods of the city. The people of the City of the Sun refuse to take money, but in importing they accept in exchange those things of which they are in need, and sometimes they buy with money; and the young people in the City of the Sun are much amused when they see that for a small price they receive so many things in exchange. The old men, however, do not laugh. They are unwilling that the state should be corrupted by the vicious customs of slaves and foreigners. Therefore they do business at the gates, and sell those whom they have taken in war or keep them for digging ditches and other hard work without the city, and for this reason they always send four bands of soldiers to take care of the fields, and with them there are the labourers. They go out of the four gates from which roads with walls on both sides of them lead to the sea, so that goods might easily be carried over them and foreigners might not meet with difficulty on their way.

To strangers they are kind and polite; they keep them for three days at the public expense; after they have first washed their feet, they show them their city and its customs, and they honour them with a seat at the council and public table, and there are men whose duty it is to take care of and guard the guests. But if strangers should wish to become citizens of their state, they try them first for a month on a farm, and for another month in the city, then they decide concerning them, and admit them with certain ceremonies and oaths.

Agriculture is much followed among them; there is not a span of earth without cultivation, and they observe the winds and propitious stars. With the exception of a few left in the city all go out armed, and with flags and drums and trumpets sounding, to the fields, for the purposes of ploughing, sowing, digging, hoeing, reaping, gathering fruit and grapes; and they set in order everything, and do their work in a very few hours and with much care. They use waggons fitted with sails which are borne along by the wind even when it is contrary, by the marvellous contrivance of wheels within wheels.

And when there is no wind a beast draws along a huge cart, which is a grand sight.

The guardians of the land move about in the meantime, armed and always in their proper turn. They do not use dung and filth for manuring the fields, thinking that the fruit contracts something of their rottenness, and when eaten gives a short and poor subsistence, as women who are beautiful with rouge and from want of exercise bring forth feeble offspring. Wherefore they do not as it were paint the earth, but dig it up well and use secret remedies, so that fruit is borne quickly and multiplies, and is not destroyed. They have a book for this work, which they call the Georgics. As much of the land as is necessary is cultivated, and the rest is used for the pasturage of cattle.

The excellent occupation of breeding and rearing horses, oxen, sheep, dogs and all kinds of domestic and tame animals, is in the highest esteem among them as it was in the time of Abraham. And the animals are led so to pair that they may be able to breed well.

Fine pictures of oxen, horses, sheep, and other animals are placed before them. They do not turn out horses with mares to feed, but at the proper time they bring them together in an enclosure of the stables in their fields. And this is done when they observe that the constellation Archer is in favourable conjunction with Mars and Jupiter. For the oxen they observe the Bull, for the sheep the Ram, and so on in accordance with art. Under the Pleiades they keep a drove of hens and ducks and geese, which are driven out by the women to feed near the city. The women only do this when it is a pleasure to them. There are also places enclosed, where they make cheese, butter, and milk-food. They also keep capons, fruit and other things, and for all these matters there is a book which they call the Bucolics. They have an abundance of all things, since every one likes to be industrious, their labours being slight and profitable. They are docile, and that one among them who is head of the rest in duties of this kind they call king. For they say that this is the proper name of the leaders, and it does not belong to ignorant persons. It is wonderful to see how men and women march together collectively, and always in obedience to the voice of the king. Nor do they regard him with loathing as we do, for they know that although he is greater than themselves, he is for all that their father and brother. They keep groves and woods for wild animals, and they often hunt.

The science of navigation is considered very dignified by them, and they possess rafts and triremes, which go over the waters without rowers or the force of the wind, but by a marvellous contrivance. And other vessels they have which are moved by the winds. They have a correct knowledge of the stars, and of the ebb and flow of the tide. They navigate for the sake of becoming acquainted with nations and different countries and things. They injure nobody, and they do not put up with injury, and they never go to battle unless when provoked. They assert that the whole earth will in time come to live in accordance with their customs, and consequently they always find out whether there be a nation whose manner of living is better and more approved than the rest. They admire the Christian institutions and look for a realisation of the apostolic life in vogue among themselves and in us. There are treaties between them and the Chinese, and many other nations, both insular and continental, such as Siam and Calicut, which they are only just able to explore. Furthermore, they have artificial fires, battles on sea and land, and many strategic secrets. Therefore they are nearly always victorious.

G.M. Now it would be very pleasant to learn with what foods and drinks they are nourished, and in what way and for how long they live.

Capt. Their food consists of flesh, butter, honey, cheese, garden herbs, and vegetables of various kinds. They were unwilling at first to slay animals, because it seemed cruel; but thinking afterwards that it was also cruel to destroy herbs which have a share of sensitive feeling, they saw that they would perish from hunger unless they did an unjustifiable action for the sake of justifiable ones, and so now they all eat meat. Nevertheless, they do not kill willingly useful animals, such as oxen and horses. They observe the difference between useful and harmful foods, and for this they employ the science of medicine. They always change their food. First they eat flesh, then fish, then afterwards they go back to flesh, and nature is never incommoded or weakened. The old people use the more digestible kind of food, and take three meals a day, eating only a little. But the general community eat twice, and the boys four times, that they might satisfy nature. The length of their lives is generally one hundred years, but often they reach two hundred.

As regards drinking, they are extremely moderate. Wine is never given to young people until they are ten years old, unless the state of their health demands it. After their tenth year they take it diluted with water, and so do the women, but the old men of fifty and upwards use little or no water. They eat the most healthy things, according to the time of the year.

They think nothing harmful which is brought forth by God, except when there has been abuse by taking too much. And therefore in the summer they feed on fruits, because they are moist and juicy and cool, and counteract the heat and dryness. In the winter they feed on dry articles, and in the autumn they eat grapes, since they are given by God to remove melancholy and sadness; and they also make use of scents to a great degree. In the morning, when they have all risen they comb their hair and wash their faces and hands with cold water. Then they chew thyme or rock parsley or fennel, or rub their hands with these plants. The old men make incense, and with their faces to the east repeat the short prayer which Jesus Christ taught us. After this they go to wait upon the old men, some go to the dance, and others to the duties of the state. Later on they meet at the early lectures, then in the temple, then for bodily exercise. Then for a little while they sit down to rest, and at length they go to dinner.

Among them there is never gout in the hands or feet, no catarrh, nor sciatica, nor grievous colics, nor flatulency, nor hard breathing. For these diseases are caused by indigestion and flatulency, and by frugality and exercise they remove every humour and spasm. Wherefore it is unseemly in the extreme to be seen vomiting or spitting, since they say that this is a sign either of little exercise or of ignoble sloth, or of drunkenness or gluttony. They suffer rather from swellings or from the dry spasm, which they relieve with plenty of good and juicy food. They heal fevers with pleasant baths and with milk-food, and with a pleasant habitation in the country and by gradual exercise. Unclean diseases cannot be prevalent with them because they often clean their bodies by bathing in wine, and soothe them with aromatic oil, and by the sweat of exercise they diffuse the poisonous vapour which corrupts the blood and the marrow. They do suffer a little from consumption, because they cannot perspire at the breast, but they never have asthma, for the humid nature of which a heavy man is required. They cure hot fevers with cold potations of water, but slight ones with sweet smells, with cheese-bread or sleep, with music or dancing. Tertiary fevers are cured by bleeding, by rhubarb or by a similar drawing remedy, or by water soaked in the roots of plants, with purgative and sharp-tasting qualities. But it is rarely that they take purgative medicines. Fevers occurring every fourth day are cured easily by suddenly startling the unprepared patients, and by means of herbs producing effects opposite to the humours of this fever. All these secrets they told me in opposition to their own wishes. They take more diligent pains to cure the lasting fevers, which they fear more, and they strive to counteract these by the observation of stars and of plants, and by prayers to God. Fevers recurring every fifth, sixth, eighth or more days, you never find whenever heavy humours are wanting.

They use baths, and moreover they have warm ones according to the Roman custom, and they make use also of olive oil. They have found out, too, a great many secret cures for the preservation of cleanliness and health. And in other ways they labour to cure the epilepsy, with which they are often troubled.

G.M. A sign this disease is of wonderful cleverness, for from it Hercules, Scotus, Socrates, Callimachus, and Mahomet have suffered.

Capt. They cure by means of prayers to heaven, by strengthening the head, by acids, by planned gymnastics, and with fat cheese-bread sprinkled with the flour of wheaten corn. They are very skilled in making dishes, and in them they put spice, honey, butter and many highly strengthening spices, and they temper their richness with acids, so that they never vomit. They do not drink ice-cold drinks nor artificial hot drinks, as the Chinese do; for they are not without aid against the humours of the body, on account of the help they get from the natural heat of the water; but they strengthen it with crushed garlic, with vinegar, with wild thyme, with mint, and with basil, in the summer or in time of special heaviness. They know also a secret for renovating life after about the seventieth year, and for ridding it of affliction, and this they do by a pleasing and indeed wonderful art.

G.M. Thus far you have said nothing concerning their sciences and magistrates.

Capt. Undoubtedly I have. But since you are so curious I will add more. Both when it is new moon and full moon they call a council after a sacrifice. To this all from twenty years upwards are admitted, and each one is asked separately to say what is wanting in the state, and which of the magistrates have discharged their duties rightly and which wrongly. Then after eight days all the magistrates assemble, to wit, Hoh first, and with him Power, Wisdom and Love. Each one of the three last has three magistrates under him, making in all thirteen, and they consider the affairs of the arts pertaining to each one of them; Power, of war; Wisdom, of the sciences; Love, of food, clothing, education and breeding. The masters of all the bands, who are captains of tens, of fifties, of hundreds, also assemble, the women first and then the men. They argue about those things which are for the welfare of the state, and they choose the magistrates from among those who have already been named in the great council. In this manner they assemble daily, Hoh and his three princes, and they correct, confirm and execute the matters passing to them, as decisions in the elections; other necessary questions they provide of themselves. They do not use lots unless when they are altogether doubtful how to decide. The eight magistrates under Hoh, Power, Wisdom and Love are changed according to the wish of the people, but the first four are never changed, unless they, taking counsel with themselves, give up the dignity of one to another, whom among them they know to be wiser, more renowned, and more nearly perfect. And then they are obedient and honourable, since they yield willingly to the wiser man and are taught by him. This, however, rarely happens. The principals of the sciences, except Metaphysics, who is Hoh himself, and is as it were the architect of all science, having rule over all, are attached to Wisdom. Hoh is ashamed to be ignorant of any possible thing. Under Wisdom therefore is Grammar, Logic, Physics, Medicine, Astrology, Astronomy, Geometry, Cosmography, Music, Perspective, Arithmetic, Poetry, Rhetoric, Painting, Sculpture. Under the triumvir Love are Breeding, Agriculture, Education, Medicine, Clothing, Pasturage, Coining.

G.M. What about their judges?

Capt. This is the point I was just thinking of explaining. Everyone is judged by the first master of his trade, and thus all the head artificers are judges. They punish with exile, with flogging, with blame, with deprivation of the common table, with exclusion from the church and from the company of women. When there is a case in which great injury has been done, it is punished with death, and they repay an eye with an eye, a nose for a nose, a tooth for a tooth, and so on, according to the law of retaliation. If the offence is wilful the council decides. When there is strife and it takes place undesignedly, the sentence is mitigated; nevertheless, not by the judge but by the triumvirate, from whom even it may be referred to Hoh, not on account of justice but of mercy, for Hoh is able to pardon. They have no prisons, except one tower for shutting up rebellious enemies, and there is no written statement of a case, which we commonly call a lawsuit. But the accusation and witnesses are produced in the presence of the judge and Power; the accused person makes his defence, and he is immediately acquitted or condemned by the judge; and if he appeals to the triumvirate, on the following day he is acquitted of condemned. On the third day he is dismissed through the mercy and clemency of Hoh, or receives the inviolable rigour of his sentence. An accused person is reconciled to his accuser and to his witnesses, as it were, with the medicine of his complaint, that is, with embracing and kissing. No one is killed or stoned unless by the hands of the people, the accuser and the witnesses beginning first. For they have no executioners and lictors, lest the state should sink into ruin. The choice of death is given to the rest of the people, who enclose the lifeless remains in little bags and burn them by the application of fire, while exhorters are present for the purpose of advising concerning a good death. Nevertheless, the whole nation laments and beseeches God that His anger may be appeased, being in grief that it should as it were have to cut off a rotten member of the state. Certain officers talk to and convince the accused man by means of arguments until he himself acquiesces in the sentence of death passed upon him, or else he does not die. But if a crime has been committed against the liberty of the republic, or against God, or against the supreme magistrates, there is immediate censure without pity. These only are punished with death. He who is about to die is compelled to state in the presence of the people and with religious scrupulousness the reasons for which he does not deserve death, and also the sins of the others who ought to die instead of him, and further the mistakes of the magistrates. If, moreover, it should seem right to the person thus asserting, he must say why the accused ones are deserving of less punishment than he. And if by his arguments he gains the victory he is sent into exile, and appeases the state by means of prayers and sacrifices and good life ensuing. They do not torture those named by the accused person, but they warn them. Sins of frailty and ignorance are punished only with blaming, and with compulsory continuation as learners under the law and discipline of those sciences or arts against which they have sinned. And all these things they have mutually among themselves, since they seem to be in very truth members of the same body, and one of another.

This further I would have you know, that if a transgressor, without waiting to be accused, goes of his own accord before a magistrate, accusing himself and seeking to make amends, that one is liberated from the punishment of a secret crime, and since he has not been accused of such a crime, his punishment is changed into another. They take special care that no one should invent slander, and if this should happen they meet the offence with the punishment of retaliation. Since they always walk about and work in crowds, five witnesses are required for the conviction of a transgressor. If the case is otherwise, after having threatened him, he is released after he has sworn an oath as the warrant of good conduct. Or if he is accused a second or third time, his increased punishment rests on the testimony of three or two witnesses. They have but few laws, and these short and plain, and written upon a flat table, and hanging to the doors of the temple, that is between the columns. And on single columns can be seen the essences of things described in the very terse style of Metaphysics—viz., the essences of God, of the angels, of the world, of the stars, of man, of fate, of virtue, all done with great wisdom. The definitions of all the virtues are also delineated here, and here is the tribunal, where the judges of all the virtues have their seat. The definition of a certain virtue is written under that column where the judges for the aforesaid virtue sit, and when a judge gives judgment he sits and speaks thus: O son, thou hast sinned against this sacred definition of beneficence, or of magnanimity, or of another virtue, as the case may be. And after discussion the judge legally condemns him to the punishment for the crime of which he is accused—viz., for injury for despondency, for pride, for ingratitude, for sloth, &c. But the sentences are certain and true correctives, savouring more of clemency than of actual punishment.

G.M. Now you ought to tell me about their priests, their sacrifices, their religion, and their belief.

Capt. The chief priest is Hoh, and it is the duty of all the superior magistrates to pardon sins. Therefore the whole state by secret confession, which we also use, tell their sins to the magistrates, who at once purge their souls and teach those that are inimical to the people. Then the sacred magistrates themselves confess their own sinfulness to the three supreme chiefs, and together they confess the faults of one another, though no special one is named, and they confess especially the heavier faults and those harmful to the state. At length the triumvirs confess their sinfulness to Hoh himself, who forthwith recognizes the kinds of sins that are harmful to the state, and succours with timely remedies. Then he offers sacrifices and prayers to God. And before this he confesses the sins of the whole people, in the presence of God, and publicly in the temple, above the altar, as often as it had been necessary that the fault should be corrected. Nevertheless, no transgressor is spoken of by his name. In this manner he absolves the people by advising them that they should beware of sins of the aforesaid kind. Afterwards he offers sacrifice to God, that He should pardon the state and absolve it of its sins, and to teach and defend it. Once in every year the chief priests of each separate subordinate state confess their sins in the presence of Hoh. Thus he is not ignorant of the wrong-doings of the provinces, and forthwith he removes them with all human and heavenly remedies.

Sacrifice is conducted after the following manner: Hoh asks the people which one among them wishes to give himself as a sacrifice to God for the sake of his fellows. He is then placed upon the fourth table, with ceremonies and the offering up of prayers: the table is hung up in a wonderful manner by means of four ropes passing through four cords attached to firm pulley-blocks in the small dome of the temple. This done they cry to the God of mercy, that He may accept the offering, not of a beast as among the heathen, but of a human being. Then Hoh orders the ropes to be drawn and the sacrifice is pulled up above to the centre of the small dome, and there it dedicates itself with the most fervent supplications. Food is given to it through a window by the priests, who live around the dome, but it is allowed a very little to eat, until it has atoned for the sins of the state. There with prayer and fasting he cries to the God of heaven that He might accept its willing offering. And after twenty or thirty days, the anger of God being appeased, the sacrifice becomes a priest, or sometimes, though rarely, returns below by means of the outer way for the priests. Ever after this man is treated with great benevolence and much honour, for the reason that he offered himself unto death for the sake of his country. But God does not require death. The priests above twenty-four years of age offer praises from their places in the top of the temple. This they do in the middle of the night, at noon, in the morning and in the evening, to wit, four times a day they sing their chants in the presence of God. It is also their work to observe the stars and to note with the astrolabe their motions and influences upon human things, and to find out their powers. Thus they know in what part of the earth any change has been or will be, and at what time it has taken place, and they send to find whether the matter be as they have it. They make a note of predictions, true and false, so that they may be able from experience to predict most correctly. The priests, moreover, determine the hours for breeding and the days for sowing, reaping, and gathering the vintage, and are as it were the ambassadors and intercessors and connection between God and man. And it is from among them mostly that Hoh is elected. They write very learned treatises and search into the sciences. Below they never descend, unless for their dinner and supper, so that the essence of their heads do not descend to the stomachs and liver. Only very seldom, and that as a cure for the ills of solitude, do they have converse with women. On certain days Hoh goes up to them and deliberates with them concerning the matters which he has lately investigated for the benefit of the state and all the nations of the world.

In the temple beneath one priest always stands near the altar praying for the people, and at the end of every hour another succeeds him, just as we are accustomed in solemn prayer to change every fourth hour. And this method of supplication they call perpetual prayer. After a meal they return thanks to God. Then they sing the deeds of the Christian, Jewish, and Gentile heroes, and of those of all other nations, and this is very delightful to them. Forsooth, no one is envious of another. They sing a hymn to Love, one to Wisdom, and one each to all the other virtues, and this they do under the direction of the ruler of each virtue. Each one takes the woman he loves most, and they dance for exercise with propriety and stateliness under the peristyles. The women wear their long hair all twisted together and collected into one knot on the crown of the head, but in rolling it they leave one curl. The men, however, have one curl only and the rest of their hair around the head is shaven off. Further, they wear a slight covering, and above this a round hat a little larger than the size of their head. In the fields they use caps, but at home each one wears a biretto white, red, or another colour according to his trade or occupation. Moreover, the magistrates use grander and more imposing-looking coverings for the head.

They hold great festivities when the sun enters the four cardinal points of the heavens, that is, when he enters Cancer, Libra, Capricorn, and Aries. On these occasions they have very learned, splendid, and as it were comic performances. They celebrate also every full and every new moon with a festival, as also they do the anniversaries of the founding of the city, and of the days when they have won victories or done any other great achievement. The celebrations take place with the music of female voices, with the noise of trumpets and drums, and the firing of salutations. The poets sing the praises of the most renowned leaders and the victories. Nevertheless, if any of them should deceive even by disparaging a foreign hero, he is punished. No one can exercise the function of a poet who invents that which is not true, and a license like this they think to be a pest of our world, for the reason that it puts a premium upon virtue and often assigns it to unworthy persons, either from fear or flattery, or ambition or avarice. For the praise of no one is a statue erected until after his death; but whilst he is alive, who has found out new arts and very useful secrets, or who has rendered great service to the state either at home or on the battle-field, his name is written in the book of heroes. They do not bury dead bodies, but burn them, so that a plague may not arise from them, and so that they may be converted into fire, a very noble and powerful thing, which has its coming from the sun and returns to it. And for the above reasons no chance is given for idolatry. The statues and pictures of the heroes, however, are there, and the splendid women set apart to become mothers often look at them. Prayers are made from the state to the four horizontal corners of the world. In the morning to the rising sun, then to the setting sun, then to the south, and lastly to the north; and in the contrary order in the evening, first to the setting sun, to the rising sun, to the north, and at length to the south. They repeat but one prayer, which asks for health of body and of mind, and happiness for themselves and all people, and they conclude it with the petition "As it seems best to God." The public prayer for all is long, and it is poured forth to heaven. For this reason the altar is round and is divided crosswise by ways at right angles to one another. By these ways Hoh enters after he has repeated the four prayers, and he prays looking up to heaven. And then a great mystery is seen by them. The priestly vestments are of a beauty and meaning like to those of Aaron. They resemble Nature and they surpass Art.

They divide the seasons according to the revolution of the sun, and not of the stars, and they observe yearly by how much time the one precedes the other. They hold that the sun approaches nearer and nearer, and therefore by ever-lessening circles reaches the tropics and the equator every year a little sooner. They measure months by the course of the moon, years by that of the sun. They praise Ptolemy, admire Copernicus, but place Aristarchus and Philolaus before him. They take great pains in endeavouring to understand the construction of the world, and whether or not it will perish, and at what time. They believe that the true oracle of Jesus Christ is by the signs in the sun, in the moon, and in the stars, which signs do not thus appear to many of us foolish ones. Therefore they wait for the renewing of the age, and perchance for its end. They say that it is very doubtful whether the world was made from nothing, or from the ruins of other worlds, or from chaos, but they certainly think that it was made, and did not exist from eternity. Therefore they disbelieve in Aristotle, whom they consider a logician and not a philosopher. From analogies, they can draw many arguments against the eternity of the world. The sun and the stars they, so to speak, regard as the living representatives and signs of God, as the temples and holy living altars, and they honour but do not worship them. Beyond all other things they venerate the sun, but they consider no created thing worthy the adoration of worship. This they give to God alone, and thus they serve Him, that they may not come into the power of a tyrant and fall into misery by undergoing punishment by creatures of revenge. They contemplate and know God under the image of the Sun, and they call it the sign of God, His face and living image, by means of which light, heat, life, and the making of all things good and bad proceeds. Therefore they have built an altar like to the Sun in shape, and the priests praise God in the sun and in the stars, as it were His altars, and in the heavens, His temple as it were; and they pray to good angels, who are, so to speak, the intercessors living in the stars, their strong abodes. For God long since set signs of their beauty in heaven, and of His glory in the Sun. They say there is but one heaven, and that the planets move and rise of themselves when they approach the sun or are in conjunction with it.

They assert two principles of the physics of things below, namely, that the Sun is the father, and the Earth the mother; the air is an impure part of the heavens; all fire is derived from the sun. The sea is the sweat of earth, or the fluid of earth combusted, and fused within its bowels; but is the bond of union between air and earth, as the blood is of the spirit and flesh of animals. The world is a great animal, and we live within it as worms live within us. Therefore we do not belong to the system of stars, sun, and earth, but to God only; for in respect to them which seek only to amplify themselves, we are born and live by chance; but in respect to God, whose instruments we are, we are formed by prescience and design, and for a high end. Therefore we are bound to no Father but God, and receive all things from Him. They hold as beyond question the immortality of souls, and that these associate with good angels after death, or with bad angels, according as they have likened themselves in this life to either. For all things seek their like. They differ little from us as to places of reward and punishment. They are in doubt whether there are other worlds beyond ours, and account it madness to say there is nothing. Nonentity is incompatible with the infinite entity of God. They lay down two principles of metaphysics, entity which is the highest God, and nothingness which is the defect of entity. Evil and sin come of the propensity to nothingness; the sin having its cause not efficient, but in deficiency. Deficiency is, they say, of power, wisdom or will. Sin they place in the last of these three, because he who knows and has the power to do good is bound also to have the will, for will arises out of them. They worship God in Trinity, saying God is the supreme Power, whence proceeds the highest Wisdom, which is the same with God, and from these comes Love, which is both Power and Wisdom; but they do not distinguish persons by name, as in our Christian law, which has not been revealed to them. This religion, when its abuses have been removed, will be the future mistress of the world, as great theologians teach and hope. Therefore Spain found the New World (though its first discoverer, Columbus, greatest of heroes, was a Genoese), that all nations should be gathered under one law. We know not what we do, but God knows, whose instruments we are. They sought new regions for lust of gold and riches, but God works to a higher end. The sun strives to burn up the earth, not to produce plants and men, but God guides the battle to great issues. His the praise, to Him the glory!

G.M. Oh, if you knew what our astrologers say of the coming age, and of our age, that has in it more history within a hundred years than all the world had in four thousand years before! Of the wonderful invention of printing and guns, and the use of the magnet, and how it all comes of Mercury, Mars, the Moon, and the Scorpion!

Capt. Ah, well! God gives all in His good time. They astrologize too much.

A FRAGMENT OF
JOSEPH HALL'S
MUNDUS ALTER ET IDEM
(*THE OTHER-AND SAME WORLD*)
TRANSLATED BY
Dr. WILLIAM KING.

INTRODUCTORY SKETCH.

Joseph Hall was born at Bristow Park, by Ashby-de-la-Zouch, in the year 1574, and educated at Emmanuel College, Cambridge. In 1597 he published three books, and in 1598 three more books, of Satires, "*Virgidemiarum,* Six Bookes." These satires, with others published about the same time by Marlowe and Marston, were burnt by order of Whitgift, Archbishop of Canterbury, who had no relish for that kind of writing. Nine years later, in the year 1607, at the age of thirty-two, Hall published the satire now to be described. He was a witty and an earnest man, who rose to honour in the Church, became successively Bishop of Exeter and of Norwich; as Bishop of Norwich was in controversy with John Milton on Church Discipline; suffered patiently imprisonment and persecution from the Puritans; and closed an honourable life of more than fourscore years in 1656. He has been called by some the Christian Seneca.

His early work, the "Mundus Alter et Idem," represents an ideal world divided into regions answering to man's chief weaknesses or vices. He gave with it a map of its Crapulia, Latronia, &c., fully peopled, with a neighbouring land in which there are no signs of settlement, *Terra Sancta, ignota etiam adhuc,* the Holy Land, even yet unknown.

Joseph Hall's new world is also figured as an Austral Continent. They are good travellers, he says, who tell what they have seen in known lands, but he is a better who not only travels but is himself the maker of the lands he travels through. He chose his day, and went aboard the good ship Phantasy, quitted harbour, sailed away, reached in two years the Fortunate Isles, and, leaving the shores of Africa behind him, came in sight of the black headland of Crapulia.

Here Introduction ends and Travel begins with the part partly translated by Dr. King: Crapulia, named from Crapula, is the Land of Inebriate Excess, and its two provinces, Pamphagonia and Yvronia, mean by their names the provinces of Omnivorous Gluttony and Drunkenness. Dr. King has translated six chapters, and begun the seventh, which is upon the wars of the Pamphagonians, to which they march forth armed with spits and two-pronged forks and heavy ribs of beef. In their free city, Ucalegon, built near the borders of Moronia, the citizens live happy as monks. They are so well shut in by high rocks that they can laugh at enemies, and through a hollow in the rocks with softest pace creeps the river Oysivius (the Idle). There is only one way up, their rocks for the inhabitants, and that is not by zigzag steps, but by a rope and basket. Birds wholly peculiar to the place supply food by being themselves eatable, and by the great multitude of their eggs, and by the loads of fish they bring into their nests to feed their young. The citizens make to themselves also beds of the soft feathers of these birds. This valley yields to the people of Ucalegon everything except what they don't care for. They are free, therefore, to sup, sleep, rise, dine, and lie down.

Husbandry, as among the old Egyptians, consists chiefly in feeding pigs, for the husbandmen wait on the rich. One, with a gentle touch, opens the richer man's eyes when he wakes; another fans him with a flapper while he eats; another puts bits into his mouth when it opens. There are two cities under Ucalegon, Livona and Roncara (Snort and Snore), which have like privileges, except that here the inhabitants are almost always asleep, and fatten wonderfully.

These are among the laws of Crapulia:—It is a crime to drink alone. Whoever has defrauded Nature by fasting four hours after sleep shall be compelled to sup. When the mouth is full it is enough to answer questions by holding out a finger. What cook soever shall treat food so that it cannot be eaten, shall be tied to a stake beside which is hung meat half raw or half burnt, and shall remain so tied until somebody comes who will eat that meat.

No coin of metal is current in Crapulia, but they make payment in kind. Thus two sparrows are one starling, two starlings are one fieldfare, two fieldfares one hen, two hens one goose, two geese one lamb, two lambs one kid, two kids one goat, two goats one cow, and so forth.

The next chapter is on the Religion of the Crapulians. They hate Jove because his thunder turns the wine sour and he spoils ripe fruit by raining on it. Their God is Time, who eats everything.

But I hasten, says the traveller, to the palace of the Grand Duke, whither I was happily led by my genius. The first Duke must have been as large as the man two of whose teeth were dug up at Cambridge, each as big as a man's head. On his tomb is an inscription. "I Omasius, Duke of Fagonia, Lord, Victor, Prince and God lie here. No man shall say I starved, shall pass by fasting, or salute me sober. Let him be my heir who can, my subject who will, my enemy who dares. Farewell and Fatten."

After a description of the Island of Hunger, the traveller passes from Pamphagonia to Yvronia, the other province of Crapulia.

These are among the laws of Yvronia:—A cup must be either full or empty. Whoever takes or returns a cup half empty shall be guilty of *lèse societé*. The sober man who hurts a drunkard, shall be cut off from wine for ever: if he kill a drunkard, he shall die by thirst. To walk from supper in a right line shall be criminal. He who adds water to wine shall be degraded to the table of the dogs.

Yvronia having been described in seven chapters, the traveller in this Other-and-Same World passes on to Viraginia, the land of the Viragoes. This is Gynia Nova, miswritten New Guinea. The chief of its many provinces is Linguadocia, in which Garrula is one of the famous cities. In Viraginia the traveller was at once made prisoner, but permitted to see the land after he had subscribed to certain articles, as, That in word or deed he would work no ill to the nobler sex; That he would never interpose a word when a woman was speaking; That wherever he might be he would concede domestic rule to the woman; That he would never deny to a wife any ornament of dress she looked at.

As to its form of government, the state seemed to be a democracy, in which all governed and none obeyed. They settled affairs at public meetings, in which all spoke and none listened; and they had a perpetual Parliament.

The men in Viraginia are subject to the women. When a wife leaves her house for any reason, she places the care of her husband under any other woman of the household until she returns. A husband who survives his wife, is married at once to his wife's maid, or goes into bondage to the nearest mother of a family, because it is not permitted that any man shall become master in his own house.

The women sit while the men serve, sleep when the men are roused to get up, scold them when they complain, and beat them. That day is worthy to be marked with a white stone to which men can say good-bye with a whole skin.

Contrary to the custom with us, the women in Viraginia cut their hair and let their nails grow. Some of them also practise with profit the gymnastic art, so that they can make beautiful use of teeth, nails, and heels. A nobler and more cleanly polished place is not to be seen than Viraginia, where everything is washed, cooked and cared for by the men, and there is nothing unbecoming but the garments of the men themselves.

The next land to be visited was Moronia, Foolsland, the vastest, the most uncultivated and the most populous of all these countries. To the east is Variana or Moronia Mobilis, to the north is Moronia Aspera, to the south Moronia Felix, and to the west Moronia Pia. The people are, nearly all of them, tall and fat, with palish hair, prominent lips, and very thick ears. In midwinter they go with their chests open, and the rest of the body lightly clothed, that the warmth may enter the more readily, and the cold go out of them; but in summer they put on thick overcoats and cloaks, and all the clothes they have, to shut out the heat. They shave their heads, either because they remember that they were born bald, or to allay the heat of the brain, or because the hair comes between the brain and heaven, and checks the freedom of the mind in going heavenward.

Provinces, towns and people of Moronia having been visited and fully described, the traveller through this Other-and-Same World then proceeds to describe Lavernia, the Land of Thieves and Cheats, who obtain great part of their plunder from Moronia. In this land the Larcinians require much attention. And at the end of all, adds Joseph Hall, "These men, these manners, these cities I have seen, have marvelled at, have laughed at, and at last, broken by the toils of so great a journey, have returned to my own land. Peregrinus, quondam Academicus."

Dr. William King was born in the year 1663, son of Ezekiel King, a gentleman of London. He was educated at Westminster School and Christ Church, Oxford. He early inherited a fair estate, took his Master of Arts degree in 1688, and began his career as writer with a refutation of attacks upon Wiclif in the "History of Heresy," by M. Varillas. He then chose law for a profession, in 1692 graduated as LL.D., and was admitted an Advocate at Doctor's Commons. He kept a light heart and a lighter purse than beseemed one of his fraternity, publishing playful satires, at times showing an earnest mind under his mirth. In or soon after the year 1702 Dr. King went to Ireland as judge of the High Court of Admiralty, sole Commissioner of the Prizes, Vicar-General to the Lord Primate, and Keeper of the Records in Birmingham's Tower, in which office he was succeeded in 1708 by Joseph Addison. Dr. King, who had not increased his credit for a love of work, returned to London about that time, and following his own way of mirth began publishing "Useful Transactions in Philosophy and other sorts of learning." In 1709 he published the best of his playful poems, "The Art of Cookery, in imitation of Horace's Art of Poetry; with some letters to Dr. Lister and others, occasioned principally by the Title of a Book published by the Doctor, being the works of Apicius Cœlius concerning the Soups and Sauces of the Ancients." When he came across Joseph Hall's satire, he found it so much to his mind that he began to translate as follows:—

CRAPULIA.

CHAPTER I.

The Situation of the Country.

Crapulia is a very fair and large territory, which on the north is bounded with the Æthiopic Ocean, on the east with Laconia and Viraginia, on the south by Moronia Felix, and westward with the Tryphonian Fens. It lies in that part of the universe where is bred the monstrous bird called Ruc, that for its prey will bear off an elephant in its talons; and is described by the modern geographers.

The soil is too fruitful, and the heavens too serene; so that I have looked upon them with a silent envy, not without pity, when I considered they were blessings so little deserved by the inhabitants. It lies in seventy-four degrees of longitude, and sixty degrees of latitude, and eleven degrees distant from the Cape of Good Hope; and lies, as it were, opposite to the whole coast of Africa. It is commonly divided into two provinces, Pamphagonia and Ivronia, the former of which is of the same length and breadth as Great Britain (which I hope will not be taken as any reflection), the other is equal to the High and Low Dutch Lands. Both obey the same prince, are governed by the same laws, and differ very little in their habit or their manners.

CHAPTER II.

phagonia; or, Glutton's Paradise.

Pamphagonia is of a triangular figure, like that of ancient Egypt, or the Greek letter delta, Δ. It is mountainous, inclosed with very high hills; its soil is of the richest, so that birds which come thither to feed, if they tarry but three months, grow so very fat and weighty, that they cannot fly back again over the mountains, but suffer themselves to be taken up in the hand, and are as delicious as the ortolan or the beccaficos of the Italians. And it is no wonder to them who know that geese in Scotland are generated from leaves fallen into the water, and believe the testimony of one of our ambassadors, that in the north-east parts of the world lambs grow upon stalks like cabbages and eat up the grass all around about them, to find the same sort of provisions in this country. Besides, the fish upon that coast are in such plenty, and so voracious (whether they conform themselves to the genius of the place and people, or presage to themselves the honour of so magnificent a sepulchre as was given to Nero's turbot), that, as soon as the hook is cast in, they press to it as the ghosts in Lucian did to Charon's boat, and cling to the iron as miners do to a rope that is let down when the light of their candle forbodes some malignant exhalation.

The sea-ports, with which this country abounds more than any other, are of no other use than to receive and take in such things as are edible, which they have for their superfluous wool and hides: nor may the inhabitants export anything that has the least relation to the palate. You see nothing there but fruit-trees. They hate plains, limes, and willows, as being idle and barren, and yielding nothing useful but their shade. There are hops, pears, plums, and apples, in the hedge-rows, as there is in all Ivronia; from whence the Lombards, and some counties in the west of England, have learned their improvements. In ancient times, Frugonia, or the Land of Frugality, took in this country as one of its provinces; and histories tell us, that, in Saturn's time, the Frugonian princes gave laws to all this part of the world, and had their palace there; and that their country was called Fagonia, from the simplicity of their diet, which consisted only in beech-mast. But that yoke has been long ago shaken off; their manners are wholly changed, and, from the universality of their food, they have obtained, in their own country language, the title of Pamphagones.

CHAPTER III.
The First Province of Pamphagonia.

Friviandy, or Tight-bittia (that we may take the provinces in their order), were it not for a temperament peculiar to the place, is rather of the hottest to produce those who are properly called good trencher-men. Its utmost point, which other geographers call the Promontory of the Terra Australis, is of the same latitude as the most southerly parts of Castile, and is about forty-two degrees distant from the equator. The inhabitants have curled hair and dusky complexions, and regard more the delicacy than the largeness and number of their dishes. In this very promontory, which we shall call the black one from its colour (for it is a very smoky region, partly from the frequent vapours of the place, partly from its vicinity to the Terra del Fogo, which, by the common consent of geographers, lies on the right hand of it, but rather nearer than they have placed it), is the city Lucina, whose buildings are lofty, but apt to be smoky and offensive to the smell; from whence a colony went, perhaps, as far as the Indies, where it remains to this day by the name of Cochin-China.

Here is the famous temple of the great deity Omasius Gorgut, or Gorbelly. It is a vast pile, and contains a thousand hearths, and as many altars, which are constantly employed in the Rucal Festivals. In the midst is a high pyramid, as lofty as the hand of man can erect it, little inferior to those of Memphis. It is called the Cheminean Tower. This, rising high, gives the signal of war to the adjoining countries: for, as we by beacons lighted upon a high hill discover the danger of an approaching enemy, so these, on the contrary, do the same by letting their smoke cease and their fires go out: for, when the perpetual vapour ceases to roll forth in thick and dark clouds of smoke, it is a token that the Hambrians are drawing nearer, than whom there can be no enemy more terrible to this nation. There are several smaller towns, that lie under the dominion of this supreme city. Charbona is the largest village, and, what is seldom seen elsewhere, lies all under ground. Upon its barren soil arises another, though of less note, called Favillia. After these lies Tenaille, a narrow town, and Batillû, a broad one, both considerable. On the left are some subservient petty hamlets, as Assadora, Marmitta, Culliera, as useful for the reception of strangers, amongst which, that of Marmitta is watered by the river Livenza; which, as is said of a fountain in the Peak of Derby, boils over twice in four-and-twenty hours.

CHAPTER IV.

The Second Province of Pamphagonia.

Next to this is the Golosinian district, the most pleasant part of Pamphagonia, covered with dates, almonds, figs, olives, pomegranates, oranges, citrons, and pistaches; through which run the smoothest of streams, called the Oglium. Here is the beautiful city of Marzapane, with noble turrets glittering with gold, but lying too open to the enemy. Over it hang the Zucker hills, out of whose bowels they draw something that is hard, white, and sparkling, but sweet as that moisture which the ancients gathered out of the reeds which grew in Arabia and the Indies. You shall find few people here, who are grown up, but what have lost their teeth, and have stinking breaths. Near to this is the little city Seplasium, which admits of no tradesmen but perfumers. It is a town of great commerce with the people of Viraginia, especially the Locanians, who use to change their looking-glass with them for oils and pastils. The agreeableness of the place, and the bounty of the heavens, is favourable to their art; for the whole track of land, at certain seasons, is covered with aromatic comfits, that fall like hail-stones: which Anathumiasis I take to be essentially the same as that aerial honey which we often find upon our oaks, especially in the spring, and that it differs only in thickness; for whereas that honey is sprinkled in drops, the little globules are hardened by the intense cold of the middle region, and rebound in falling.

CHAPTER V.
Of the Third Province of Pamphagonia.

In the fifty-fifth degree, we come into the plains of Lecania, and so into the very heart of Pamphagonia, where the chief city we meet with is Cibinium, which is washed with the acid streams of the river Assagion. In the forum, or market-place, is the tomb (as I conjecture by the footsteps of some letters now remaining) of Apicius, that famous Roman, not very beautiful, but antique. It is engraved upon the shell of a sea-crab; and it might happen, notwithstanding what Seneca says, that this famous epicure, after having sought for larger shell-fish than the coast of Gallia could supply him with, and then going in vain to Africa to make a farther inquiry, might hear some rumour concerning this coast, steer his course thither, and there die of a surfeit. But this I leave to the critics. Here I shall only mention the most fertile fields of Lardana and Ossulia. The delicious situation of Mortadella, the pleasantest of places, had wonderfully delighted me, had it not been for the salt-works which often approach too near it. There is an offensive stinking town called Formagium, alias Butterboxia, and Mantica, a boggy place near the confines of Ivronia.

I hasten to the metropolis of the whole region, which, whether you respect the uniformity of the building, the manners of the people, or their way of living, their rules for behaviour, their law and justice, will show as much as if I were to descend to particulars.

CHAPTER VI.

Of the Metropolis of Pamphagonia, and the Customs of the Inhabitants.

There are but very few villages in this country, as well as in some others; from whence a traveller may conjecture, that the country towns are devoured by the cities, which are not so many in number as they are large and populous; of which the mother and governess is called Artocreopolis. The report goes, that in ancient times there were two famous cities, Artopolis and Creatium, which had many and long contests about the superiority: for so it happens to places, as well as men, that increase in power; insomuch as the two most flourishing Universities in the world (to both of which I bear the relation of a son, though I am more peculiarly obliged to one of them for my education), notwithstanding they are sisters, could not abstain from so ungrateful a contention.

Artopolis boasted of its antiquity, and that it had flourished in the Saturnian age, when it had as yet no rival. Creatium set forth its own splendour, pleasantness, and power. At last, a council being called, Creatium got the preference by the universal votes of the assembly; for such is the iniquity of the times, that though the head be covered with grey hairs, yet nothing is allowed to the reverence of antiquity, when encountered by a proud and upstart novelty. The other city is now so far neglected, that the ruins or footsteps of its magnificence are scarce remaining, any more than of Verulam, as is most elegantly set forth by our noble poet Spenser in his verses on that subject; the latter usurping the name of the other, as well as the other has now the double title of Artocreopolis. The city is more extensive than beautiful: it is fortified with a large and deep ditch of running water, which washes almost all the streets, wherein are a thousand several ponds for fish; upon which swim ducks, geese, swans, and all sorts of water-fowl, which has been wisely imitated by the people of Augsburg. This ditch is called Gruessa. There are two walls, whose materials were furnished by the flesh-market; for they are made of bones, the larger serving for the foundations, the lesser for the superstructure, whilst the smallest fill up what is wanting in the middle; being all cemented with the whites of eggs, by a wonderful artifice. The houses are not very beautiful, nor built high after the manner of other cities; so that there is no need of an Augustus to restrain the buildings to the height of seventy feet, as was done at Rome; nor is there room for a Seneca or Juvenal to complain of the multitude of their stairs and number of their stories.

They have no regard for staircases; for indeed none of the citizens care for them, partly from the trouble of getting up them (especially when, as they often do, they have drunk heartily) as much as for the danger of getting down again. Their houses are all covered with large blade-bones, very neatly joined together. There are no free citizens admitted, but such whose employment has more immediately some relation to the table. Husbandmen, smiths, millers, and butchers, live in their colonies, who, when they have a belly of an unwieldy bulk, are promoted to be burgesses; to which degree none were anciently admitted but cooks, bakers, victuallers, and the gravest senators, who are chosen here, as in other places, not for their prudence, riches, or length of beard; but for their measure, which they must come up to yearly if they will pretend to bear any office in the public. As any one grows in dimensions, he rises in honour; so that I have seen some who, from the meanest and most contemptible village, have, for their merits, been promoted to a more famous town, and at last obtained the senatorial dignity in this most celebrated city: and yet, when by some disease (as it often happens), or by age, they have grown leaner than they are allowed to be by the statutes, have lost their honour, together with the bulk of their carcass. Their streets were paved with polished marble; which seemed strange amongst a people so incurious, both because the workmanship was troublesome, and there might be danger in its being slippery. But the true reason of it was, that they might not be forced to lift their feet higher than ordinary by the inequality of the pavement, and likewise that the chairs of the senators might the more easily be pushed forward; for they never go on foot, or on horseback, nor even in a coach, to the exchange, or their public feasts, because of their weight; but they are moved about in great easy elbow-chairs, with four wheels to them, and continue sitting so fixed, in the same posture, snoring and flabbering till they are wheeled home again.

At the four gates of the city, whose form is circular, there sit in their turns as many senators, who are called Buscadores. These carefully examine all who come in and go out, those that go out, lest they should presume by chance to do it fasting, which they can easily judge of by the extent of their bellies, and the matter being proved, they are fined in a double supper: those that come in, to see what they bring with them upon their return; for they must neither depart with empty stomachs, nor come back with empty hands. Every month, according to the laws, which they unwillingly transgress, there are stated feasts, at which all the senators are obliged to be present, that after dinner (for no person can give his vote before he has dined) they may deliberate concerning the public affairs. The name of their common-hall is Pythanoscome. Every one knows his own seat, and his conveniences and a couch to repose upon when the heat of their wine and seasoned dainties incline them to it. Their greatest delicacies are served up at the first course; for they think it foolish not to eat the best things with the greatest appetite: nor do they cut their boars, sheep, goats, and lambs into joints or quarters, as commonly we do, but convey them whole to table, by the help of machines, as I remember to have read in Petronius Arbiter. They are fineable who rise before they have set six hours; for then the edge of their stomach is blunted. They eat and drink so leisurely, for the same reason as the famous Epicure of old wished that his neck were as long as a crane's. They measure the seasonable time for their departure after this method: they have a door to their town-house, which is wide enough for the largest man to enter when he is fasting: through this the guests pass; and when any one would depart, if he stops in this passage, he is trusted to go out at another door; but if it be as easy as if he were fasting, the master of the ceremonies makes him tarry till he comes to be of a statutable magnitute: after which example, Willfrid's needle in Belvior Castle was a pleasant trial of Roman Catholic sanctity. They have gardens of many acres extent, but not like those of Adonis or Alcinoüs; for nothing delightful is to be expected in them, neither order, nor regularity of walk, nor grass-plots, nor variety of flowers in the borders: but you will find all planted with cabbages, turnips, garlick, and musk-melons, which were carried hence to Italy, and are in quantity sufficient to feast an hundred Pythagoreans.

There is a public college, or hospital, whither they are sent who have got the dropsy, gout, or asthma, by their eating and drinking; and there they are nourished at the public expense. As for such as have lost their teeth by their luxury, or broken them by eating too greedily or incautiously, they are provided for in the island of Sorbonia. All the richer sort have several servants, in the nature of vassals, to cultivate their gardens, and be employed in inferior offices, who have their liberty when they can arrive at such a bulkiness. If any of the grandees of the country die of a surfeit, he is given, as being all made up of the most exquisite dainties, to be eaten up by his servants; and this they do that nothing should be lost that is so delicate. The men are thick and fat to a miracle; nor will any one salute another whose chin does not come to the midst of his breast, and his paunch falls to his knees. The women are not unlike them, and in shape resemble the Italians, and have breasts like the Hottentots. They go almost naked, having no regard to their garments. The magistrates and persons of better figure have gowns made of the skins of such beasts as they have eaten at one meal. All wear a knife, with a large spoon, hanging upon their right arm. Before their breasts they wear a smooth skin, instead of a napkin, to receive what falls out of their mouths, and to wipe them upon occasion; which whether it be more black or greasy, is hard to determine.

They are of a very slow apprehension, and no way fit for any science; but yet understand such arts as they have occasion for. Their schools are public-houses, where they are educated in the sciences of eating, drinking, and carving; over which, one Archisilenius, an exquisite Epicure, was then provost, who, instead of grammar, read some fragments of Apicius. Instead of a library, there is a public repository of drinking-vessels, in which cups of all orders and sizes are disposed into certain classes. Cups and dishes are instead of books. The younger scholars have less, the elder have greater; one has a quart, the other a pottle, the other a gallon: this has a hen, that a goose, a third a lamb or a porker: nor have they any liberty, or recess, till the whole is finished; and if by a seven years' stuffing they are no proficients in fatness, are presently banished into the Fancetic Islands; nor are they suffered long to stay there idle and without improvement. Hither likewise are sent all physicians who prescribe a course of diet to any person. When any one is sick, without recourse to Æsculapius, they make him eat radish, and drink warm water; which, according to Celsus, will purge and vomit him. Venison is that which they most delight in; but they never take it in hunting, but by nets and gins. They look upon the swine as the most profitable and best of all animals; whether it is for the likeness of its manners, as being good for nothing but the table, or else from its growing fat on the sudden with the worst of nutriment. It may not seem credible, yet parsimony appears in the midst of their profuseness: but then it is very ill placed, for it is in crumbs, bones, and crusts. They do not so much as keep any dogs, cats, hawks, or anything that eats flesh. If any person suffer meat to stink, he is impaled; but venison and rabbits are to have the *haut-gout*: and then their cheese is kept till it is overrun with little animals, which they devour with mustard and sugar. This is an odd sort of custom, derived from the Dutch.

The country abounds with rivers, which ebb and flow according to their digestion, and generally overflow at the beginning of January, and towards the end of February, and do mischief to the neighbouring country.

CHAPTER VII.
Of the Wars of the Pamphagonians.

The Pamphagones have perpetual wars with the Hambrians, or the Fancetic Islands, and the Frugonians.

Cætera desunt.

THE END.

www.ingramcontent.com/pod-product-compliance
Lightning Source LLC
LaVergne TN
LVHW050622100826
845148LV00011B/1686

* 9 7 8 1 7 7 0 8 3 3 1 3 5 *